The Scattering
A History of the London Irish Centre, 1954-2004

First published 2004
by the London Irish Centre, 50-52 Camden Square, London, NW1 9XB

ISBN 0 948667 99 0

The Illustrations

The following have kindly given permission for the reproduction of illustrations.
The figures refer to page numbers.

Arlington House: *24*
Ettwein Bridges, architects: *29, 242*
Bob Buchanan: *10*
Doris Daly: *159*
Brian Harvey: *200*
Geoff Holland: *231*
Greater London Authority: *236*
Keith Roberts Associates: *97, 116, 124, 132, 138, 139*
London Borough of Brent, P.J. Fahey Collection: *27, 32, 37, 46, 47, 48, 53*
London Borough of Camden, Local Studies and Archives Centre: *11, 14, 16*
London Irish Centre Archive: *frontispiece, 18, 56, 60, 62, 64, 65, 76, 79, 85, 90, 95, 107, 112, 123, 126, 130, 133, 136, 140, 144, 149, 151, 152, 155, 167, 168, 173, 183, 185, 202, 216, 225. 241*
Irish Post: 192 (both pictures)
Tom McCabe: *78, 81, 94, 99, 102, 106, 162*
Mel McNally: *178, 197, 214 (right), 228, 233*
Claude Malone: *147*
Sally Mulready: *105*
Joanne O'Brien: *122, 143, 163, 170, 198, 232, cover*
John Richardson: *15, 69*
Bridie Shaw: *214 (left)*
Terry Smith Archives: *22*
Westminster Diocesan Archives: *39*

Produced by Historical Publications Ltd
32 Ellington Street, London N7 8PL
(Tel: 020 7607 1628)
Cover design by Stephen Marsh
Reproduction by Square Group, London SE1
Printed by Edelvives, Zaragoza, Spain

The Scattering

A History of the
London Irish Centre, 1954-2004

Gerry Harrison

THE LONDON IRISH CENTRE

Dancing at the London Irish Centre, 1985.

Contents

Acknowledgements

During my research for this book I found a page from the *Irish Times*, dated 31 March 1967, in a cupboard at the London Irish Centre. It appeared to be from a business supplement of the newspaper. I wondered why it had been placed among a pile of other dusty, yellowing and torn papers, until I turned over and noticed the following, written by an erratic fountain pen in a margin:

> *In the Irish Centre where we met*
> *From Wexford, Tipp, Tyrone,*
> *We thank the saints that yet*
> *There is nothing like our own.*
> *So come fill up another cup –*
> *Yer man, you call that tay?*
> *And with every sup let's say*
> *Here Camden Square and the two priests there*
> *They're kings in every way.*

This literary doodle, perhaps motivated by a meeting at the Centre, is unsigned. No doubt it was created by someone who, over the years, has contributed to an Irish way of life in London, and the consequent development of the Centre.

I blame Jon Parry for this book. As Bursar of the Working Men's College (for Men and Women) in Crowndale Road, Camden Town, he taught, as a Welshman, an Irish Studies examination course. With my Armagh and Tyrone parenthood and everyone else on the course from the south, I was also by far the oldest of the entrants, and it is to Jon's credit that we all did so well. Jon will be the first to notice that this book is not an academic work of the sort that he made us study. This is intentional. The history and demography of Irish emigration to Britain in all its forms, periods and locations has already been extremely well researched and recorded. The bibliographies are extensive. This book, by contrast, is aimed at the general reader interested in discovering the part played by the London Irish Centre in this story.

For the opportunity and privilege of recording it I have first to thank Father Jerry Kivlehan, OMI, Director of the London Irish Centre, for his trust which led to a commission. I must also thank his staff, in particular Paul Murphy, who has supported this project. Although the Heritage Lottery Fund has funded the research for this book, and the accompanying exhibition, its publication is indebted to two extremely generous benefactors, John Griffin and John McCarthy.

Immensely useful as a primary source has been the previous work of Brian Harvey, which has kept me on the right track. I thank him also for his thoughtful editorial input. Jane Borges also assisted in the earlier stages.

For her practical help, I am very grateful to Jacqui Crimmins who typed all the transcripts of interviews without complaint, and to Tony Murray who carried out a preliminary excavation through the files and archives at the centre. Tony Murray is in charge of the Smurfit Archive at the Irish Studies Centre at the London Metropolitan University, where these files and archives will be professionally catalogued and placed in secure storage for future researchers. I should also like to thank Andy Duff, who saved me from one or two computer catastrophes; my publisher, John Richardson who has kindly displayed the patience of a lifetime when I have broken all the deadlines possible; and my wife, Ellie, for her forbearance.

I am most fortunate to have interviewed the following priests who have worked at the London Irish Centre. In alphabetical as opposed to any other order, they are Fr Jim Butler OMI, Paul Byrne OMI, Fr Patsy Carolan OMI, Fr Jerry Kivlehan OMI, Fr Tom McCabe OMI whose advice has always been valued, Fr Frank Ryan OMI whose own writings have been extremely helpful, Fr Tom Scully OMI, Fr Paddy Sheridan OMI and Monsignor Owen Sweeney. Other priests who have assisted include Fr Richard Haslam OMI and Fr Michael Hughes OMI. The letters OMI signify the Oblates of Mary Immaculate, the order which took over the directorship of the Centre and Irish Centre Housing. I have also been in fruitful correspondence with Claude Malone.

This book includes anonymous voices, but also many that are identifiable. I have used footnotes to give the names of those who have been good enough to give me the benefit of their knowledge of what, in the writing, has turned out to be quite a complex story. It could not have been compiled without their willingness to speak.

In alphabetical order they are Mary Allen, David Ashton-Hill, Bill Aulsberry, Tony Beatty, Angie Birtill, Bob Buchanan, Peggy Campbell, Cyril Cannon, Tom Connor, Frank Costello, John Cowley, Peggy Crowley, Doris Daly, Florrie Darcy, Joe Davis, Carol Delaney, Fr Ian Dickie, Noel Dinan, Ned Fogarty, Kate Foley, Satnam Gill, Maureen and Tommy Greaves, Kevin Haddick Flynn, Maeve Heath, Ron Heffernan, Brigid Hegarty, Patricia Herbert, Professor Mary Hickman, John Higgins, Paul Hill, Geoff Holland, Dave Horan, Tess Hutchinson, Patrick Keady, Paddy Keegan who has given a great deal of his time to correct my errors, Mary Kenny, Hugh Lake, Steve Lucas, Christopher O'Brien, Joe McGarry, Sr Joan Moriarty, Ray Morrish, Sally Mulready, Jim Myers, Sr Anne-Marie O'Boyle, Christopher O'Brien, Brendan O'Connor, Mossie O'Riordan, Pegeen O'Sullivan, Rev Bob Paul, John Quinn, Keith Roberts, Andy Rogers, Beverley Charles Rowe,Irene Ryan, Bridie Shaw, Lord Jock Stallard, June Swan, Seamus Taylor, John Twomey, Keith and Valerie Venness and Antonia Watson.

I must also mention the valuable research of the Camden History Society, which is so ably supported by the Camden Council officer team at its Local Studies and Archives Centre in Holborn.

The statistical records of the London Irish Centre are neither complete, consistent nor continuous. Their methods, categories and classifications have varied over the years. By way of a warning therefore, readers should be cautious about the statistical data, which I have kept to a minimum in order to make this book less technical and more accessible.

It has also been extremely difficult to verify some information. Some records can be incomplete and difficult to check, and individual memories can be selective or mistaken. Although I have tried to tell an accurate story, I accept responsibility for any errors in the text.

Except where I have quoted the word, for reasons of simplicity of language I have used 'emigrant' throughout, rather than immigrant or migrant. Of course it depends on whether you are coming or going.

Finally, the London Irish Centre thanks the Heritage Lottery Fund for its generosity. As the Irishman says, "Half the lies are not the truth".

Gerry Harrison, Kentish Town, London NW5, June 2004

CHAPTER ONE

A tale of two suitcases

A telling but often misquoted remark of the writer, art critic, jazz singer and all-round *bon viveur* George Melly says it all. *"Camden Town is as far from Euston Station as an Irishman with two suitcases can walk on a rainy night"*, he once stated in an interview.[1] Although he did not add this information, many of these Irishmen were perhaps on their way to the London Irish Centre, its address printed on a damp card held in their hands.

George Melly was from Liverpool. His name suggests an Irish origin so he may have known what he was talking about. He also lived in Gloucester Crescent, on the western side of Camden Town. On the eastern side, a few hundred yards away, is the Irish Centre.

A glance at the building now gives little indication of the people who have passed through its doors, or of their lives that have been so changed by the decision to make the journey to London. The history of the Centre and the experience of these people are now hidden among its archives and records. It is told in regular annual reports, but far more vividly in dusty files. Thousands of cards of casework exist, individual human stories stacked away in remote corners of this surprising warren of a building that has survived years of internal alterations. There seems no sense of order. That they had been almost forgotten is understandable, because serving the often pressing needs of ordinary people, day in and day out, means that the keeping of particular records, or even keeping them in one place, is not an immediate priority.

For fifty years the London Irish Centre, on the corner of Murray Street and Camden Square, has been rooted in its work with the poor or disadvantaged who have arrived at its door, or have been referred to its address from other agencies in Ireland or England. Its motivation was at first to provide a religious service. This was to ensure that decent Catholic men and women, who were away from home, townland and parish, remained attached to their faith. Its staff has been a mixture of clerics and professional workers, broadened by the contribution of ordinary volunteers, without whom the building would have ceased to function.

The overriding aim of the Centre was and still is never to refuse anyone who needs help or assistance. As Fr Jerry Kivlehan, who was assigned to the Centre in 1994 from St Teresa's parish in Liverpool and has remained in post until 2004, says, *"We have an open door policy, so that anyone that needs to has access to our services. And as I understand it, that's quite unique. We don't ask questions. It's a customer-focussed service. We endeavour to provide whatever they want, and I think we do that well"*.[2]

Those arriving at Euston in the mid-1950s who had nowhere else to go except

The corner of Murray Street, Stratford Villas and Camden Square in the early 1950s. This shows the building that would become the London Irish Centre, without its extensions.

to the address on the card, which had been given to them by the Legion of Mary[3] at the docks back home, when they boarded the *Princess Maude* or the *Hibernia*, the *Cambria*, or the *Munster*, or when they descended many hours later onto the bewildering and smoky platforms of Euston or Paddington Station, the route to the Centre was a bus or underground ride. Or a walk – with the suitcase or two, and sometimes with nothing – through Somers Town to Agar Grove. Sister Joan Moriarty, who was a welfare worker at the Centre from 1974 to 1984, tells an amusing anecdote. *"A client came in one day to the Irish Centre and he had four suitcases. I said how could he come all this way from Euston with four suitcases? Oh no, he said, I walked. I said how did you walk? He then demonstrated this. He said he took two suitcases and he walked a hundred yards, and then he put them down. He then went back for the other two and he brought them up. And he did that all the way from Euston to Camden Town".*[4]

Over the years the arrivals at the centre, and the client base which its welfare service serves, have gradually changed. In the 1950s they were of an Irish origin, but in recent years the building is used by a much wider ethnic mix. It was not unusual in the 1980s for the Greek community to hire the building for wedding receptions, and nowadays there is often a Bengali or Somali function in its McNamara Hall.

The great majority of Irish emigrants were young. At one time possibly homeless, sometimes destitute and often unemployed, they sought new footholds in a

Airport or another underground tunnel was to be dug in London, the impact was felt in Camden Square.

As Irish people consolidated in particular neighbourhoods, they were joined by others from home, most looking for a new opportunity in the big city but some escaping from problems, preferring the anonymity of a London environment to the gossip in a village in rural Ireland. In many cases they also brought with them degrees of loneliness, "takin' the boat" as individuals rather than in family groups, which led to their social lives centred on pubs or dance-halls.

The need to identify with each other was strong. There are still pubs with Irish county loyalties. Gangs of workmen on building sites were often recruited through agents with a link back home. Irish county associations developed, which strengthened these local ties.

For some, the lack of material success in their new, English environments became a cause of personal shame. The failure to escape from a hand-to-mouth existence as a labourer or a domestic servant meant a loss of self-esteem, which led to a rejection of any direct contact with the family at home. The good work in recent years of the Aisling Project, based at the London Irish Centre, has helped to reverse this by encouraging Irishmen and women to return for short breaks. This journey can be very difficult for someone who no longer has any ties. Once perhaps it was too easy to set off to Britain, but years later very difficult to return, even for a holiday. To return to live in Ireland is sometimes a journey too far.

A lack of family support often led to high incidences of illness and problems of mental health. This was exacerbated by poor housing. Until fairly recently the condition of the emigrant Irish in Britain, relative to other ethnic minorities, has

Arrivals at Euston Station in 1947.

new country. Now they include people who may already be in temporary housing, but often suffering difficulties associated with drink or drugs.

Prominent now are the survivors of those earlier Irish generations. Fifty years on, many have returned to the Centre for support. The Camden Elderly Irish Network and the London Irish Elders' Forum are based here. The plight of Irish elders in London still requires attention.

The early waves of Irish emigration in the 1940s and 1950s brought people desperate for work, often from rural origins. From the 1970s onwards they tended to come from more urban backgrounds, escaping a bleak future in their cities and towns. These waves rose and fell with the relative expansions or contractions of the British or Irish economies. When a major factory shut down in Limerick or there was a strike in Dublin, or when a new terminal was being built at Heathrow largely been ignored. There are many reasons for this, but their alleged 'invisibility' has been one. *"This exclusion of the Irish whenever issues of differential ethnic access to scarce resources is discussed is a dominant theme of every Irish welfare and advice agency in this country. Every agency records, either in its annual reports or in special research reports, the monumental task it faces in trying to persuade funding authorities of specific Irish needs in service provision and of the necessity of earmarking resources accordingly".*[5] Under the auspices of the Commission for Racial Equality, this keynote report articulated for the first time and at high level the disproportionate lack of resources for Irish emigrants. It was followed soon after by another equally challenging report, which pointed out that in housing, the Irish, certainly in London, were receiving far less in terms of local authority and Housing Corporation support than other Black and Minority Ethnic Housing Associations.[6]

On the whole, St Pancras Borough, later to become a part of Camden Council, has been relatively generous to the London Irish Centre in terms of grant-aid and social services support. However, in terms of support for its housing service, and that of other Irish Housing Associations, this has not always been so obvious.

In the last fifty years, gratitude has been expressed to the Irish for their contribution to the reconstruction of Britain after the devastation of World War II, yet during that time there have been periods in which intense anti-Irish racism has been shown, typified in the 'No Blacks, No Irish, No Dogs' signs which hung in landladies' front windows often alongside a 'Vacancies' sign. As Greg, who was later housed by the London Irish Centre has said, *"They were alright – a bit prejudiced you know. You'd look for a room and they'd say 'Oh, that room was taken yesterday', something like*

that. I'd say, 'Why didn't you take down the notice then?' The reply was 'Don't you speak to me like that, this is England'. 'Go stuff yourself', I'd say'".[7] He speaks with all the pride of the Corkman that he is.

More recently, the Troubles in Northern Ireland, and in particular the IRA mainland bombing campaign which led to the Prevention of Terrorism Act, 1974, persuaded many Irishmen and women, from whatever part of the island they came, to keep their heads down and their mouths shut. The Irish in Britain became known as 'a suspect community'. They felt criminalised. With this Act arrived an opportunity to harass ordinary and innocent Irish people. It meant that they were under continual scrutiny, particularly by searches at airports and docks. Fr Jerry Kivlehan was once questioned at Speke Airport, near Liverpool. He was asked by a policeman for his address, which was the presbytery at St Teresa's church. Having offered it, he was then accused of giving a wrong answer to a further question as to his religion. The police officer was convinced that only a Presbyterian would live in a presbytery. This was almost an arrestable offence.

Times have changed. It is now fashionable to identify with, rather than condemn, the Irish, to enjoy their *craic* and culture to the hilt, and to benefit from the economic success of the 'Celtic Tiger'. In Britain there are two weekly Irish newspapers, Irish events are advertised without embarrassment or shame, pubs with an Irish-ish theme have proliferated and St Patrick's Day Parades are proudly held once again in many British cities.

Agar Town

The route for George Melly's man with two suitcases leads from Euston Station through a district known as Somers Town.

Back in 1756, the Euston Road was the

first by-pass in the world, and was then appropriately called 'The New Road from Paddington to Islington'. It now carries 60,000 vehicles a day past three mainline stations – Euston, St Pancras and King's Cross – but was first conceived primarily as a route for graziers, drovers and others who were taking their flocks and herds to Smithfield market. It also had a military purpose, which was to enable marching troops to reach the Essex coast without passing through the cities of London and Westminster.[8] There were acres of fields to the north of it, which the landowner, Lord Somers, regarded as a landscape fertile for potential development.

Further north still, these fields led towards a cluster of homesteads that were to be named after the first Earl of Camden, Charles Pratt, who took his title from his residence, Camden Place, on Chislehurst Common in Kent. By 1791 he was also Lord of Cantelowes Manor and, as an entrepreneur Camden was keen to encourage the exploitation of his estate. To the east of Somers Town, behind what is now St Pancras Station, and perhaps in a more direct line to walk towards Camden Square, was a private estate which became known as Agar Town. Much of it lay in the area which now contains Camley Street, Elm Village and the Agar Grove Estate.

This was part of the prebendal manor of St Pancras, also attached to St Paul's Cathedral, and was leased to a lawyer, William Agar in 1810. It was described in 1854 thus: *"This tract of land was granted on a lease to a gentleman connected with the law, Mr Agar, after whom the district was named. At that time his large residence near Pratt Street was in the fields, and no houses had been built on the estate. Indeed, so retired was this place that within the last fifteen or sixteen years nightingales have been heard near a clump of trees at short distance from Mr Agar's house. The land* (after his death)

was soon let out into small strips, on leases for thirty years. No systematic plan of drainage was laid out: in fact the houses were planted down very much in the manner as the wooden huts and tents at the gold diggings: each man suited his means or fancy in the erection of an edifice on the land which for a few years was, on certain conditions, his own".[9]

At that time there was a huge demand for such small plots. In order to accommodate a burgeoning population, development around London's boundaries was necessary and short leases were of course extremely profitable.

An unprecedented surge of immigration had taken place in the 19th century as a result of the ravages of Ireland's famine. Although this had reached its peak in 1847, potato blight had been breaking out sporadically beforehand and was to continue until 1851.[10] For many years before and afterwards, the flood of cheap labour into London may have encouraged it but certainly coincided with the rapid spread of the city.

London clay was a plentiful commodity. More and more brickfields were soon covered with streets and buildings, among which the early provision of a public house was regarded as an attraction. *"On the pastures lately set out for building you may see a double line of trenches, with excavation either side, and a tavern of imposing elevation standing quite complete, awaiting the approaching row of houses".*[11] Railway lines to and from the north of England burst through these developments, north-west through Regent's Park or Gospel Oak, centrally between what is now Kentish Town, Camden Road and Agar Grove and under Camden Square, and north-eastwards through the area then known as Maiden Lane. In this part of London the tracks were often routed through cuttings and tunnels.

Paradise Row in Agar Town in 1853.

Another link, the Regent's Canal, which was built largely by 'navigators' from Ireland from 1814 to 1816, was finally opened to waterborne traffic after a series of legal disputes contested by William Agar at the places where it passed through his estate to what is now Camden Town. In 1820, nearby Chalk Farm was a major transhipment point, an area of wharves and warehouses connecting Limehouse Basin with Paddington Basin, and London with Birmingham.

In March 1851 Agar's estate was described in an article, which was published by Charles Dickens, as 'A Suburban Connemara', with an Irish population implied by the title. Within the text however there are few references to the Irish, except the intriguing *"the inhabitants themselves exhibit a genuine Irish apathy"*. The author indicates the names of filthy, mud-bound hovels as Tralee, Roscommon or Shamrock Cottage, and towards the end he summarises the place as *"a perfect reproduction of one of the worst towns of Ireland"*. In his last paragraph he appeals to his readers, *"These poor people cannot help themselves; toiling early and late, the struggle to provide for the ever-renewing wants of the day exacts all their time and energies. Who will help them?"*[12]

Conditions in Agar Town are now the subject of debate. There are contrary views as to whether it was a place of Irish squalor or of relatively decent homes. Its alternative name, 'Ague Town', typifies the first view.

A recent study by historian Steven Denford refutes this picture. He maintains that only a few Irish were living in Agar Town at that time, *"Looking at the 1851 census for Agar Town as a whole, at a time when the area was attracting attention as a notorious slum, one is struck by how ordinary it appears. Those who were born in Ireland are very much the exception".* His researches, based on analysis of the census, minutes of the St Pancras Vestry and Poor Law and health records, revealed that the accepted image of Agar Town as a filthy, insanitary shanty-town was inaccurate. In fact Denford sums up that *"Agar Town was not the hell hole of contemporary description. A poor district, no doubt, but most of its inhabitants appear to have been in employment and relatively few had recourse to poor relief".*[13]

As if to destroy the evidence, by 1867 Agar's estate was purchased, and the entire district was cleared by the arrival of the Midland Railway Company, which had received Parliamentary powers to make way for its route into, and sidings for, St Pancras Station. As compensation perhaps for the spiritual needs of the local population, the railway company built St Thomas' Church in Wrotham Road in 1863 to the north of this area. Designed by Samuel Teulon, who later designed the magnificent St Stephen's, Haverstock Hill, it was demolished a century later.

With the coming of the railway, the inhabitants of Agar Town were evicted or encouraged to move away. It is said that 32,000 people were displaced.[14] Whatever the numbers of Irish people living in Agar Town, it is assumed that many had previously arrived from the notorious rookeries or tenement areas of St Giles, the location of William Hogarth's engraving *Gin Lane*, which had been demolished by the building of New Oxford Street.

During this period of northward expansion, during which emigrants were landing in Britain in their thousands, patterns of their habitation in London became more concentrated. If not with two suitcases, Irish people and their few belongings found homes in a number of new districts. In this part of London, clusters developed in parts of what is now Camden Town, spreading north and east to Kentish Town, Kilburn and Cricklewood, and also eastwards into Islington.

Camden New Town

The area around Camden Square, an open space of two acres, was conceived as 'Camden New Town' and laid out from the 1840s by John Jeffreys Pratt, 2nd Earl of Camden and 1st Marquis, and son of the original Charles Pratt who had already sold the building leases on a wholesale basis to avoid piecemeal development. This area was described by John Norden, the Elizabethan topographer in the 1600s as an "utterly forsaken" place.[15] As if to deny this reputation, Camden New Town was designed as a spacious, residential neighbourhood with an imposing Gothic church, St Paul's, after the City cathedral with which it was connected, built within a central square. The parish of Camden New Town St Paul was created in 1852.

St Paul's Church, Camden Square, c.1905.

The excavation of cuttings for the new Midland Railway near King's Cross, 1867.

However, Pratt's grand scheme was soon undermined by railway lines. First there was the East & West India Docks & Birmingham Junction Railway through Camden Road station in 1850, and then the Midland Railway Company in 1867 out of the new St Pancras Station.

Nevertheless, the development of Camden New Town was completed in 1871 under the 2nd Marquis, George Charles Pratt. A busy man, he was both an MP and a Lord of the Admiralty. As if to enhance its exclusivity, Camden Square was gated at both ends of Murray Street. Straw was put down to muffle the sound of horse-drawn traffic on the cobbles when there was a funeral.[16] But by 1868, key-holding residents of the square were reluctant to use the central enclosure, because *"rowdy youths gained access by scaling the railings, and their 'vulgar language and rude demeanour' alarmed respectable householders, fearful of this threat to the morals of their offspring. The Enclo-sure rules forbade 'boisterous or dangerous games ...such as cricket, football, rounders, hockey, skipping with long ropes, trundling iron hoops, and shooting bows and arrows..."[17]* Local members of today's Camden Square Neighbourhood Association, who are so alarmed at some of the goings-on in their neighbourhood, now described in awkward contemporary jargon as "anti-social behaviour", may possibly agree that little has changed over the last 150 years.

Although the gothic St Paul's church was damaged during World War II and subsequently demolished in 1956, most of the houses around Camden Square have survived both World Wars and the depredations of the railway.[18]

A resident, Beverley Charles Rowe, has painstakingly researched the people who lived in them during the 19th century, but there is no record for no. 52 Camden Square, the home of the London Irish Centre, until 1854 when a Thomas Flemming, a surgeon, resided at this address.[19] It must have been one of the later buildings. Over succeeding years this substantial brick and rendered house was occupied by various doctors, physicians and surgeons and their families, not to mention the lodgers and the cook, the nurse and the parlour-maid. It is safe to assume that their clinics or surgeries might have also taken place on the premises.

From this research it is clear that then very few Irish indeed lived in these salubrious parts. It was too grand for even the middle-class Irish who were beginning to settle in London during the late 19th century. In 1867 William Butler Yeats opted for Primrose Hill, while twenty years later, George Bernard Shaw, who was an elected member of the St Pancras Vestry, preferred Fitzroy Square.

Like many parts of London, Camden New Town was adversely affected by the social changes that surrounded it. Apart from St Pancras, the bustling railway station of Kings Cross was closer still, bringing with it some welcome business but also other problems. Bombs had fallen here during World War II and damaged the area. Some of the spacious family houses, with room for lodgers if not staff, became rooming-houses once the landlords had moved away and sold their properties. Poorer families, who were sometimes severely exploited, replaced the original inhabitants. This mix of populations lingered in some streets even until the early 1960s, by the time that a London Irish Centre here had become an achievement for certain priests.

The northbound tunnel portals of the railway into and out of St Pancras begin just after Murray Mews, with the railway line remaining underground until it clears Camden Road. Above it, there was no building permitted because the weight was considered dangerous. From 1866 to 1897, certain houses above these tunnels were demolished when the railway was widened in 1898. The loads that these tunnels might withstand were later to become a major complication in the centre's expansion, and an expensive obstacle that very nearly destroyed its viability.

Before then, the land between nos. 44 and 48 Camden Square, where the houses had been demolished, remained a yard on which at one time a local resident called Wally Glover kept his old Rolls Royce. At the time that no. 52 Camden Square was acquired, this open space was also an orchard of apple and pear trees, and with beds of soft fruit such as strawberries. Local boys used to climb over the walls to help themselves. Alongside was a builder's yard, owned by Albert William Ridout. At one end, by Murray Mews, the rattle of trains echoed from below and sulphurous smoke from their funnels emerged frequently from an abyss. This reduced the value of housing in the immediate area. Just to the south, no. 49 Camden Square was the house owned by Wally Glover and reportedly "full of rats". No. 50 was divided into rooms and flats, one of which was rented by the formidable Mrs Gwendolyn Bailey.

Around the corner, Murray Street was a thriving local shopping community. One end was dominated by the Murray Arms public house, which was the local drinking place before a number of bars were opened over the years within the London Irish Centre. This shopping parade has seen better times. In the early 1950s its traders included Mr Cook, who sold electrical goods and whose son Don Cook was a political activist in St Pancras. There was also Mrs Jones and Dai Jones at the dairy, Mrs Rose with her greengrocer's shop, Charlie Bell the cobbler, and Mr Dennis, the newsagent. Davison's off-licence here was for a time run by Mrs George who, with her two sons, was also the licensee

The London Irish Centre before the architectural detail was restored to the façade of the building in 1975.

for the Murray Arms. She kept what is called 'a strict house', in which swearing was forbidden. However, she encouraged the playing of the pub piano. On the opposite side of the road was a café, and a sweetshop.[20] The attraction of certain supermarkets in Camden Town has since pulled customers away from Murray Street, allowing architects and others to move their offices into what were once retail premises.

Just prior to its acquisition by the Irish Priests' Committee for their Centre, no. 52 Camden Square, on the corner of Murray Street, had been leased for a brief period to the Methodist Church. Known as Henry Carter House, it was in 1952 a home for 'young ex-offenders' and then for a year it became an 'unmarried mother and baby home' for the West London Mission.[21] On sunny days the girls sat on the steps, minding their prams in the front garden.[22]

From the 1960s Camden Square and its neighbouring streets, originally conceived as the select New Town but somewhat crestfallen since the arrival of the railways, commenced a revival towards its current middle-class status. Nevertheless there were still a number of houses poorly converted into flats or bed-sitters jostling among those of the professionals. Some of the less well maintained properties were compulsorily purchased by Camden Council in the 1970s, and are now owned either by the council or by Housing Associations. In a post-war flourish, the previous St Pancras Council also built estates on nearby bomb-sites, one of which, St Pancras Way estate, was formally opened in 1948 by Aneurin Bevan, Minister of Health and architect of the National Health Service.[23] These have increased the diversity of local inhabitants, and have helped to make the area more cosmopolitan.

Although once again an affluent neighbourhood, there are still visible traces of the times when more impoverished inhabitants, including the Irish, lived around Camden Square. At its heart, the London Irish Centre still remains within walking distance of Euston for any man with his two suitcases, although he may have to contend these days with far greater volumes of traffic.

However the Irish now remain more conspicuous in nearby Camden Town where, it has been said, "the rough lie down..."

[1] As told to Jeremy Bugler in 1968.
[2] Interview Fr Jerry Kivlehan, June 2004.
[3] The Legion of Mary was founded in Dublin in 1921 by Frank Duff, in order to provide a lay service to support the clergy.
[4] Interview Sister Joan Moriarty, March 2004.
[5] From the introduction of *Discrimination and the Irish Community in Britain*, by Dr Mary Hickman and Dr Bronwen Walter, published by the Commission for Racial Equality, 1997.
[6] *Still beyond the Pale*, by Helen Cope, published by the Irish Housing Forum, 2001.
[7] From *Our Histories, our Futures*, published by Irish Centre Housing, 1999.
[8] 'London's first northern by-pass' by Catherine Durant, published in *Camden History Review*, Vol. 15
[9] *London Shadows: A Glance at the Homes of Thousands*, by George Godwin, 1854. Reprinted by Garland, 1985.
[10] *A Death-Dealing Famine*, by Christine Kinealy, Pluto Press 1997.
[11] *The Builder*, 25 February 1854.
[12] 'A Suburban Connemara', by W M Thomas, an article published in *Household Words*, published by Charles Dickens in 1851.
[13] *Agar Town: The Life and Death of a Victorian Slum*, by Steven L J Denford, published by Camden History Society, 1995.
[14] *The Streets of St Pancras, Somers Town and the Railway Lands*, published by the Camden History Society, 2002.
[15] *The Fields Beneath*, by Gillian Tindall, first published by Maurice Tmeple Smith 1977.
[16] Interview David Ashton-Hill, April 2004.
[17] From the Camden Square Gardens minute books, included in *The Streets of Camden Town*, published by the Camden History Society, 2003.
[18] *The Streets of Camden Town*, Camden History Society 2003.
[19] *Who lived in Camden Square in the 19th century?* by Beverley Charles Rowe, 2003.
[20] Interview Irene Ryan, March 2004.
[21] *Methodist Church, West London Mission, 1887-1987*, published by the West London Mission.
[22] Interview Irene Ryan, March 2004.
[23] From *A History of Camden*, by John Richardson, published by Historical Publications in association with the London Borough of Camden, 1999.

CHAPTER TWO

Where "the rough lie down"

It has been said that whereas Hyde Park was famous for the 'pride' and Cricklewood was enjoyed for the 'ride', or the entertainment to be found in its large public houses that resembled palaces. In Cricklewood's dance-halls such as the National and the Galtymore circling mirrors showered coloured lights down on the swaying crowd below. But in Camden Town it was 'where the rough lie down'. The rough did indeed lie down in Camden Town's Arlington House, the largest men's hostel in Europe.

Camden Town was perhaps a hub, and from here an Irish diaspora or 'the scattering' occurred. The attraction of Camden Town for emigrants, with or without their suitcases, existed long before the post-war surge of emigration.

Although he did not walk there from Euston station, or even with a card in his hand to direct him to Camden Square, the story of Dennis is typical. It begins in Ireland in the 1930s. He was from rural Kerry, where his father insisted that he continue at school. However, Dennis was beaten by the teachers so refused to remain there. He made his way to London, *"I was the greenest man ever to come out of Ireland, I tell you. I was never in a toilet, never in a bus, never in a train"*. He arrived in London in 1935, while still in his late teens. In those days Euston Station had no roof above the arrivals platform, and in front of the station was the imposing Euston Arch, which was demolished in 1961. He had no idea how to look for a job, so outside the station he asked people in the street. *"I met a policeman and asked him where I'd find a job"*. *"Go to Patrick Street"*, said the policeman, but Dennis did not then realise that this was a gibe. *"He had an answer for me, because he thought I was taking the piss"*. In Oxford Street he met an Englishman who suggested that he try the hotels. *"I got a job as a kitchen porter, washing the hotplates, but I flooded them once. The manageress sacked me the next morning"*.

Dennis later left London, travelling around the country in a variety of jobs including in a Butlin's Holiday Camp in Somerset, where he was paid *"a pound a week, full board and ten cigarettes a day"*. By 1939 he was working for a large construction company based in Manchester, building air raid shelters and airfields. He was given three months' detention in 1944 for ignoring his call-up papers, because a Mayo man had persuaded him to go haymaking with him in Yorkshire. The Military Police discovered Dennis, but once he was in uniform and on the parade ground he found it difficult to keep in step.

After a spell in Ireland in 1954 he returned to London permanently. *"I was too fond of the drink, d'oul' bottle"*. He also returned to the construction industry. *"The big firms were the best, but I finished up with the subbies. I ended up with a subbie from Dollis Hill, he's now a multi-millionaire, a dead loss. They were exploiting their countrymen. He didn't stamp my cards. I was three years with him in an oul' dirty filthy job. When I finished with him I went to the Citizens' Advice Bureau enquiring after my redundancy pay, but the subbie said, 'He can take me to court if he likes'. I wouldn't get a lot of satisfaction taking a millionaire to court".* Dennis was one of many thousands in the heyday of post-war reconstruction who suffered from this form of exploitation at work, known as 'the lump'.

He lived throughout this time in London in digs, and remembers that various landladies also gained at his expense. He was charged good money for a bed and often given food *"hardly fit for humans. Full board and a bed. Starve the lodger and get rich quick, that's what they used to do".* In his last bedsit before moving into Irish Centre Housing's An Caislean, which provides accommodation for retired and elderly men, his television set was stolen. A neighbour told him that it was his landlord who was responsible. Dennis was not surprised. *"The landlord had twenty houses between Cricklewood and Harlesden. He later sold the lot and went back to Castlebar".*[1] It was time for Dennis to reconsider.

He had heard of the London Irish Centre from friends, and made contact, searching for secure housing but explaining that he also had a problem with drink. He was lucky to be housed immediately. He says that at An Caislean the food and accommodation is the best he has ever enjoyed. He even gets out *"for a few pints nearly every day",* and is now able to travel over to his brother in Ireland. During his long life, he has fully participated in the culture, the patterns of living and the whole Irish environment of north London.

Dennis was one of tens of thousands who had arrived in London, with little more than a willingness to work. This was largely found in the construction industry or in factories such as Gallaher's 'Black Cat' cigarette factory in Mornington Crescent near Camden Town, and Smith's, the clock manufacturer in Cricklewood, or in the West End hotel or bar trade. For women there were also jobs as domestic servants or in department stores, hotels and the developing health service. Clerical work was then rarely offered. However, as their knowledge accumulated and their understanding of where the opportunities lay increased, many Irish emigrants were able to reach positions of greater responsibility. There are now successful Irish business people whose skills and capabilities at that time were recognised and which projected them into entrepreneurial or managerial positions.

On the Buildings

The construction industry could be a very demanding, unsympathetic field of work. With some similarity to the tradition of old Irish hiring fares, men who wanted building jobs had to turn up from 6.00 am at the pick ups in streets such as Kilburn High Road, Cricklewood Broadway, Holloway Road and Camden High Street. Further afield, Hammersmith or the Elephant and Castle were other locations. In the 1950s London's smog had not been eliminated, and on winter mornings it was dark and there was often rain. The men standing around waiting for the 'pickups', often in their hundreds, were known as 'skins'.

Joe McGarry describes where the major contractors had their particular stands in Camden High Street. On the eastern side, in Kentish Town Road, was Lowery's, who preferred to employ Connemara men, and south of them was RSK, known casually as 'road side killers'. RSK owned Thames Trader lorries, and if it was raining its men

An early morning pick-up in Camden Town.

sheltered in the back under a tarpaulin canopy. The Mayo company, McNicholas, was to be found further south. John Murphy and Co. collected his men from near Peter's Café in Camden Road. Here his notorious agent, nicknamed 'Elephant John', would pull in fifty men at a time in a hired coach. This was a period when no one asked for names, because so many worked under the lump, in which real names were kept secret. Kerryman John Murphy's brother, Joseph, another builder, was down the road.

The Murphy brothers were big local employers with major yards in Kentish Town and Camden Town, while RSK, which specialised in electrical installations, had a yard nearby in Gospel Oak. This firm did not pay as well as the Murphy brothers, but was understood to be more considerate. Other firms included Press and O. C. Summers.

If Summers *"had a pull on"*, it meant that the company had a big cable run to install. The more men tugging a 30,000-volt cable from the drum, the easier would be the task. Casuals were usually hired for this. If they were needed for two or three days they became 'regular casuals'.[2]

Beyond these firms were the larger contractors such as Wimpey, McAlpine, Laing, Mowlem and Tarmac. On his deathbed, 'Concrete' Bob McAlpine is reputed to have said, *"If the men wish to honour my death, allow them two minutes' silence. But keep the big Mixer going, and keep Paddy behind it."*[3]

The shuffling groups of men sometimes emerged from cafés. In Camden Town there was Lee's, a Greek establishment in Inverness Street, where hot buttered toast was piled up as an attraction in the window, ready for the 'charge' from Arlington House, and also Peter's Café in Camden Road.

Those who wanted to work in London would assemble in their allotted pitches at about 7.00 am. Those who did not mind work further afield had gathered well before, at 6.00 am or earlier. They would be swept away in vans, coaches and trucks to sites such as the bleak Isle of Grain in Kent, to the new Terminal Three of Heathrow Airport or to the coast of Essex to work on the North Sea Gas pipeline. *"The word was 'You want a shift?'"* The first thing the 'ganger man' or agent would look at was the working boots. *"He looked at you like a horse. The only thing he didn't inspect was your teeth. Your boots were your CV."* If the boots were damp and, better still, had a smear of concrete on them, there was a greater chance of a job because it was obvious that the wearer had been working the previous day.

The streets were often too cold for a chat, and they needed to be on their way. Christopher O'Brien describes the terse conversation that he would have had with an agent. *"I'd ask, 'Any work to be done?' He answered 'What kind of work?' 'Any kind of hard work'. The quick response was 'You jump in the back of that van then'."*[4] Work was hard, and in all weathers. If the conditions were too impossible to work under, there was no pay. Later, 'wet money' was introduced, which offered a fraction of what could be earned when the weather was drier. Occasionally there were skins who would have second thoughts, scared of the thought of a hard physical day's work after a sleepless night in the 'skipper' of a derelict building with only alcohol for company, and would in panic jump out at the first set of red lights, too sick from the drink.

The pick-up vehicles were usually driven by sub-contractors or subbies, paying their labourers by cash in hand at the end of a day. Depending on the subbie, payment usually meant a one pound deduction at 8.00 am, which was spent on cigarettes, matches and a bacon sandwich, but for some a 'wet breakfast' of a bottle of cider

from one of the Asian shops then appearing in London. At the end of the day the balance of six, seven or eight pounds was handed out. Sometimes payment was by cheque, and if the skin was mistrustful of banks and paperwork he could cash them in particular pubs.

In those pre-decimal days, one pound could buy eight pints. Often the landlord would make the skin wait until there was money in the till, which meant that he drank his wages while waiting for the till allegedly to be filled. The truth was that the till was usually already full, but waiting for this information often meant closing time, and most of the day's wages had by then been swallowed.

Many subbies hired labourers who signed with false names, so that they could not be traced by the Inland Revenue. 'Paddy McGinty' or even 'Eamonn Andrews' worked in many different locations each day. Others used the cards of friends who had returned to Ireland. There were also those subbies who deducted Income Tax and National Insurance but never passed it on to the authorities. Working on the lump, as this was called, was recognised as being extremely risky, particularly when there were accidents or injuries on sites in those days of slim safety standards. If an accident happened, there was no compensation or even the prospect of medical help. The only guarantee was the sack. There was also the prospect that the Revenue might catch up, but on the other hand the money, at upwards of five pounds a day, was relatively good. It was enough to buy a drink, but rarely enough to find secure accommodation.

A deposit was usually required for digs, and sometimes a week's rent in advance so, for some, sleeping rough was the only option. It was also fairly common, whether it was in bomb damaged houses, round the back of Euston Station or in the old

Bedford Theatre in Camden Town, a few doors from the Brighton pub. In its last years before demolition in 1969, this former 'Palace of Varieties' was left open at night. Its doors had been forced, and the dress circle and upper gallery were filled with dossers. The higher the accommodation, the less likely the police were to find them.

For decades, men lived on the margins of normal life in this manner, while they built a London for those who were more fortunate.

Freddie Boland, Ireland's Ambassador in London, had notified the Taoiseach Eamonn De Valera as early as 1951 of the appalling conditions in which large numbers of Irish emigrants were living. He had mentioned the clergy's interest in *"keeping the Irish together in individual houses, as opposed to taking digs in English households"*. The Catholic Church even feared that English households might dilute the practice of their faith, just as unsupported emigration might allow others to take advantage of the lack of choice when it came to housing. Ambassador Boland added that in Southwark, south London, the local Canon approved of having as many as one hundred and fifty Irish people living together in three smallish houses because it was *"accommodation run by a man of good (Catholic) character"*.[5] Perhaps the ambassador was not to know that it was a parish priest in Southwark, Fr Ambrose Woods, who had already appealed in vain to the Irish government for support for Irish emigrants and, having been rejected, became the driving force behind the setting up of an Irish Centre.

In the Digs

Before the opening of the Centre, which had its own hostels, there was a desperate lack of affordable and adequate accommodation across London, particularly

The entrance to Arlington House, Camden Town.

north of the Thames. This was something an Irish Centre was intended to address.

Men working on the lump, subsisting on cash on a day-to-day basis, could not afford to choose. Women emigrants, who were in the majority, were perhaps more fortunate. Those working in hotels or hospitals often had accommodation provided. Otherwise there were the hostels, some of which were run by the Salvation Army or the YMCA. George Orwell said that these *"stink of prison or charity"*.[6]

For men, Arlington House just off Camden High Street once had beds for 1,200 residents. Opened in 1905, this was the last of a chain of hostels built by the Victorian philanthropist Lord Rowton, who was once Disraeli's private secretary. He wanted to provide clean and decent accommodation for working men, who had before been forced to stay in filthy and disease-ridden common lodging houses. George Orwell paid a shilling a night for a room with the use of a bathroom.

Over the years, many thousands have been housed here, some who are unremembered with no name and no known family, and are buried in paupers' graves in north London. Others became celebrated, including a pre-war resident from Inniskeen in Co. Monaghan, Patrick Kavanagh. The son of a small farmer and cobbler, he came to London, like so many before and after him, to escape poverty at home. He wrote about his Rowton (Arlington) House experience in *The Green Fool*, an autobiography published in 1938. *"Many Irish boys made Rowton House, Camden Town, first stop from Mayo. The soft voices of Mayo and Galway sounding in that gaunt impersonal place fell like warm rain on the arid patches of my imagination. These boys were true peasants. They walked with an awkward gait and were shy. To me they looked up as to a learned man and asked me questions I couldn't answer."*[7] After his book was greeted with critical acclaim, Paddy Kavanagh settled in Dublin as a poet, writer and journalist.

None of them now would recognise the far superior conditions that exist within the building, its total accommodation successively reduced after its rooms and facilities had been extended. Arlington House now houses about 400 residents, and is managed by the Housing Association, Novas Ouvertures.

Catherine Anne Sullivan, who was a welfare and advice worker at the London Irish Centre, which with its own hostels might have affected her comments with the view of a rival, wrote this (verbatim) description in 1963: *"Arlington House is the working mans hotel and there are 5 of these in London each run by a private company, but Arlington Rd. is the biggest. It takes 1068 men a night, 800 of whom are regulars. 35% of the men staying there are Irish. There are 5 different types of accommodation. The cheapest is 4/- a night and consists of a bed and chair in a separate cubicle. The sheets are only changed once a week no matter how many people sleep in them, unless they are terribly dirty. Canteen service is available and the cheapest breakfast is 2/6d, although breakfast is free on a Sunday. There are 30 rooms at £2-10-0 a week which are very nice. They are carpeted, have a chest of drawers, hot and cold running water and 2 lights. There is a waiting list for these rooms. Next there are 84 rooms at £2-0-0 a week, they also have hot and cold water. Then come 30 rooms at 35/6 a week and 680 rooms at 28/-, no hot or cold water, or chest of drawers etc. just the bare essentials. Breakfast is served from 6 a.m. to 10 a.m., lunch from 12 a.m. to 2 p.m. and tea from 4.30 p.m. to 8.30 p.m. There are 2 television lounges, billiard room and reading room, washing facilities, which are three flights down from the cubicles, and a baggage room and lockers."*[8]

There was a procedure for callers seeking accommodation which developed among advice workers in the London Irish Centre. Although separate hostels managed by the Centre for men and women were available, and increasing in their number and the number of bed spaces over the fifty years, they were often full. When this was the case, the next step was to recommend lodging houses with approved landladies. Initially, these landladies were scrutinised for the cleanliness and efficiency of their premises, and also for their adherence to the Catholic faith, but later on there was little time for this. However, the older callers might be directed to the landladies first, rather than the hostels. As Sr Joan Moriarty says, *"Guys in pubs could live in. Landladies were more selective. I think the older people coming over, people who had fallen on hard times in their 40s and 50s. Older people might not be used to hostels, so you sent them to the landladies that you had lined up at that time. They would be more comfortable. They weren't used to big dining-rooms and loud music, they needed a different kind of environment."*[9] Another option, local authority Housing Departments, were always under pressure from the numbers of people seeking roofs over their heads, and Irish emigrants had to be prepared for a wait, like everyone else.

Landladies accepted referrals from agencies such as the London Irish Centre or from the local priest, but also invited contact from a card in the newsagent's window. The 'No Irish' signs were dispensed with when there was money to be earned, particularly when the lodging houses became owned by previous arrivals from Ireland, those who had managed to establish themselves with enough money to acquire a property but who needed the additional income.

In some cases, the treatment of their lodgers by some Irish landlords and landladies was often so bad that they were described as people "who had abandoned their own". It could mean arriving back at night, in clothes that were wet through, and with nowhere to dry them. Or there might be five separate mattresses in one room on bare floorboards and a cold washbasin. In order to make extra income, bed spaces were sometimes doubled up to accommodate both day and night-shift workers from the factory. Other landlords did not allow their lodgers to enter the kitchen, and instead they had to rely on the electricity meter in their room to boil a kettle or use the café down the road. When the shilling was pushed through the slot, it would be remarkable if a shilling's worth of electricity was then available. This experience was a shock to young people, whose only memory, in spite of hardships at home, may have been the care of their mothers.

Some landladies, however, were famous for their hospitality, which might have included a comfortable bed and home-cooking, and where there would always be a kettle and conversation on the go in the kitchen. Occasionally the reputation of particular decent digs would travel back home, and there would be a flow of lodgers to that address from one village.

One characteristic of all digs was the rules. These stated the time lodgers had to be in at night, or that no visitors were permitted, or what day they could use the bath and please clean the bathroom after use, or the insistence that lights be turned off when not needed. It is no wonder that the lodgers tried to find something more permanent if they could. Sometimes there was an encouragement if not a rule that lodgers attended Sunday Mass. After a late Saturday night, men would be woken up to find that that their only good shirt had been washed and ironed. The nearest church was not hard to find, although there might be all sorts of distractions along the way.

At the Altar

There are now eleven Roman Catholic churches in the London Borough of Camden,[10] although there are others which could be described as high Anglican, a religious position which has been a feature of the Diocese of London. This is a small reduction from the number at the turn of the century.

The Church of the Sacred Heart of Jesus is perhaps the most spectacular surviving example of the power and influence of local Catholicism. In Quex Road, Kilburn, in the heart of the Irish community, this magnificent church has ministered to its congregation with clergy appointed from

The renewal of baptismal vows at the close of the Men's Mission, Church of the Sacred Heart of Jesus, Quex Road, Kilburn.

a Congregation known as the Oblates, a particular order of priests. In 1967 this order was to assume the running of the London Irish Centre.

The Catholic Churches of Camden and adjoining boroughs, whether a part of the Diocese of Westminster or ministered by a separate order of priests, offered a comforting environment to those whose working and home lives might have been suffering from the stress of establishing more than just an existence for themselves in England. Some assisted their parishioners with money. In the 1950s, after a heavy fall of snow, Father John Dore of the Sacred Heart paid a number of men to clear the streets. Their jobs had been cancelled because of the bad weather, and for some reason the council was not prepared to clear the snow itself.

After Sunday Mass, if the time was right,

there was the visit to the pub for a pint or two before a meal. Although now in north London many of the original Irish pubs have new identities, then the pub was a focus of social life. Often with a family room, it became a community of its own, sometimes based on individual Irish county connections. If there were no family rooms, children had to be content to stand outside with a bag of crisps.

Families were welcomed to the Catholic social clubs, run by the parish church, where darts, card games and bingo, accompanied by tea and cakes, passed the time. If someone was sick or needed to return to Ireland for a funeral, it was in these clubs, rather than the pub, that they might be able to borrow the money for the fare. There were some clubs with a bar, but others were dry, a welcome change for those who wished to avoid alcohol and the company it keeps. These were a particularly useful place to make contacts. Men and women often met their future spouses there, and booked the parish church for their wedding. Clubs also offered an opportunity for some priests to enjoy the company of some of the flock and hear the gossip about others. There has always been an ambivalence in the priesthood about these clubs, but they were also a place to recruit members of the Legion of Mary, who would assist in the parish but also go down to the stations early in the morning to meet people off the boat trains.

On the Town

Landladies often did not make their guests welcome until they came back to sleep, so the pub was an obvious place in which to spend the evenings, but they were largely a male domain. Camden had more than its share, and it is said that the first instance of traditional Irish music played in a pub in England was in the former Brighton in Camden High Street. It was a unique institution. Here an Irishman could meet old friends, receive news from home, locate contacts, find lodgings and be given 'the start'. For those who did not drink there were attractions such as the Coffee Stall, which was parked in Bonny Street, near Camden Road station.

There were tea dances in some places during the afternoons, but a weekend evening event usually meant a visit to a dance-hall. Women would go in their new taffeta frocks, and enjoy the dances for the company, even if the men there did not interest them. Often a group of twenty or more nurses from a hostel managed by one of the big hospitals a bus ride away would venture out, dancing together because of the shortage of men who might turn up when the pubs closed. If the men did, they stood or sat bashfully at one side

and the women at the other, except for the courageous few. These might have had to 'tank up' at the London Irish Centre or in another bar to reach that level of courage, and then these dance-halls blossomed into 'ballrooms of romance'.

Showbands from Ireland, which began to emerge in the late 1950s, toured these venues. It was said that you'd always meet a friend from back home in the 'Galty'. The Galtymore is the last surviving Irish dance-hall in north London, but soon to become a part of a hotel complex. The Estate, the Blarney, the Round Tower and the Garryowen in Hammersmith have all now disappeared. The Gresham, with its huge blow-up photographs of Dublin's O'Connell Street behind a stage which turned on a central spindle so the main act could set up its instruments and equipment behind the scenes while the first act warmed up the audience, is now a supermarket in the Holloway Road.

One venue which has survived, but with very different music, is the Forum in Kentish Town. Another is the Buffalo, but now in Camden High Street, which has retained the same family as its management, although after a period as the Carousel, it is now called the Electric Ballroom. With its original entrance at 180 Kentish Town Road, through an iron gate opposite what is now the car park of Sainsbury's, the Buffalo ballroom was first opened in the mid-1930s as a social centre for Irish emigrants. It was called the Buffalo because apparently that was its shape from the air, and was then managed by a man called Ginger Maloney. With a reputation for being a rough house, full of "different tribes of fighting Irishmen", the police were constantly called in and, after one fight too many, it was closed down.

Bill Fuller, a contractor and amateur wrestler from Co. Kerry, was, ironically, the man who saved it. During the London blitz he had assembled a workforce of 2,000 men to deal with bomb damage with such effect that it was said, *"What Hitler did not knock down, Bill Fuller did."*[11] He saw a future after the War in providing an entertainment for the people he knew in Camden Town. *"The Buffalo had been closed down by the police, who had put a big lock on the gate,"* says Fuller, who still owns the premises today, *"so I went to see Inspector Harris in Holmes Road, and he was a hard man to bargain with, but I said 'I'll make a deal with you: if you're ever called in to sort out a fight here, I'll put the lock back on the gate.'"* Bill Fuller re-opened the Buffalo, and since then has retained the iron gate in Kentish Town Road as a souvenir, but relocated its entrance to Camden High Street.

It was popular because of its music. *"In those early days, I always had good Irish music"*, says Fuller. *"It was mainly old-time waltzes, reels and jigs – and, after a while, the quick step came in. At first, I used to make up my own bands: I had a blind pianist called Billy and another lad called Tommy, who was half-Irish and half-Italian, who played the accordion."* Showbands also performed there. The Clipper Carlton, from Strabane in Northern Ireland, is generally credited as being the first, but Bill Fuller gives that honour to another. *"It was Mick Delahunty who had the first showband. He was like Joe Loss and he was a great showman, probably one of the best ever."*

"I remember seeing the Royal Showband at the Buffalo, says Vince Power, who came to London as a teenager in the early '60s and would later build a music empire of his own with the Mean Fiddler organisation. *"The only reason I remember that show is because they came from Waterford, which is where I'm from. But I used to go to the Buffalo quite often – I saw lots of bands there, such as The Miami Showband and Big Tom."*[12]

The iron gate entrance to the former Buffalo dance hall in Kentish Town Road.

On the door the bouncers insisted on ties, which could be rented on the spot for a shilling, and would refuse admittance for men whose "trousers were too narrow". Already tanked up, they'd have a mouthful of peppermints to hide the smell. In the street there were often lined up as many as six 'paddy wagons', a word of American origin and which obviously expressed a view about the Irish. An even more contemptuous view was implied in the forty-foot long cattle-truck that was sometimes parked outside, waiting to be filled with men swept from the street up a wooden ramp and into its body.

The police expected fights at the Buffalo, and they were rarely wrong. Alcohol was often smuggled in. Men on different sides in family feuds back home resumed the same sides if they met once again. The 'fighting men of Connemara' were notorious, as were the 'Tunnel Tigers', whose lives had been wrecked by working deep beneath London's streets without proper breathing apparatus. *"They were belting each other. Stools and tables were flying. People escaped by hiding in the toilets."*[13] Many fights were about women, but some escalated from an argument about the relative merits of GAA teams back home and became heightened by alcohol and the atmosphere.

It is said that an Irishman reveals himself by his walk, a jerky swaying motion known as the 'gouch' or 'gimp', or in Belfast as the 'gander'. This has been described "as if you're walking up a hill, hands in pockets, head swinging from side to side", a particular sign of a man from the country. The wide trousers and cowboy boots worn by some complemented this gait. The police could soon spot it, and whether or not they thought this walk signified drunkenness the paddy wagons were filled with harmless men from outside the dance-halls. Nor did the police discriminate. Even the Coffee Stall had its quota of arrests. One busy Magistrates' Court was next to the Police Station in King's Cross Road, and five shilling fines were regularly ordered for being drunk and disorderly. Or the charge might have been for insulting behaviour, for which there was usually a conditional discharge. Either way, it meant a court appearance, but far more damaging was the loss of a day's wages.[14]

Long before the Troubles returned to northern Ireland in the 1960s there had developed the apocryphal bargain, "If we give ye back the six counties, then can we have Camden Town?" A now almost outdated joke, perhaps, but it registers the notion of Camden Town as a traditional destination for the Irish emigrant. The Irish presence here, now diminished, gave it a distinctiveness.

It interesting that there is a debate at present between those who hanker after the 'character' of Camden Town of the past and those who look forward to a transformed town centre as a major shopping district dominated by sleek national retail chains. This debate has been brought into focus by recent redevelopment proposals at Camden Town Underground Station.

For the London Irish Centre, trying to establish itself in its premises up the road, the Irish presence here was a point of contact, a reference for its work. Throughout its fifty years it has reacted to this presence and tried to connect with it, in terms of welfare advice, accommodation, employment and also social activities, to ensure that the lives of Irish people here, and in the wider diaspora of Irish communities in Greater London, were as well or better considered here than at home.

[1]   *Our Histories, our Futures*, Colm Power for the Irish Centre Housing, 1999.
[2]   Information from Joe McGarry, May 2004.
[3]   *The Men who built Britain*, Ultan Cowley, Wolfhound Press, 2001.
[4]   Interview Christopher O'Brien, May 2004.
[5]   From *De Valera: long fellow, long shadow*, by Tim Pat Coogan, published by Hutchinson, 1993.
[6]   *Down and Out in Paris and London*, George Orwell, Penguin Books, 1940.
[7]   *The Green Fool*, Patrick Kavanagh, published by Penguin Books, 1984.
[8]   LIC Welfare Advice Service, July 1963.
[9]   Interview Sr Joan Moriarty, March 2004.
[10]   Information from *Neighbours, a Directory of Faith Communities in Camden*, published by Camden Council, 2002.
[11]   *The Men who built Britain, ibid*.
[12]   *The Rock'n'Roll Guide to Camden*, Ann Scanlon, published by Tristia. Reproduced by kind permission of 'Keep it Camden'.
[13]   Interview Christopher O'Brien, May 2004.
[14]   Interview Ned Fogarty, April 2004.

CHAPTER THREE

The continuous arrival of destitute people

Father Tom McNamara

Once a building for the Irish Centre had been acquired, the first priest to take charge was 'Father Mac', as he became known. Appointed by Westminster Archdiocese, Fr Tom McNamara looked upon the job of senior chaplain[1] here as similar as that of his former parish nearby in Holloway, but with an additional challenge: the focus on emigrants.

The building was something of an experiment. What could it offer to those emigrants who were then arriving in England, ill-prepared and in increasing numbers? In spite of the well-known cry heard at that time from pulpits across Ireland, "Mothers, save your daughters from pagan England", its needs would not be parochial, but would be imposed by the more fundamental demands of accommodation and employment, and it was important for Tom McNamara and his volunteer staff to meet these head-on. Their spiritual needs might have to wait.

Some would say that the life-blood of Ireland was draining away to Britain, and years before the establishment of the Centre this was worrying the authorities, in particular the clergy.

The surge in emigration, and the potential loss of numbers for Irish parishes, had been noted with alarm by the Catholic Church in Ireland. As early as 1942 the Archbishop of Dublin, John Charles McQuaid, had already set up a bureau for emigrants. Located at 18 Westland Row, near Pearse Station in Dublin where trains left for the port of Dun Laoghaire, it reported: *"A system of liaison with the clergy and Catholic societies in Ireland and Britain was gradually built up in order to ensure that the bureau would establish contact with as many as possible of our emigrants and keep in touch with their welfare abroad."*[2] By 1946 the bureau recorded that it had assisted 16,000 people in just over two years by meeting them on arrival in Dublin from elsewhere in the country, arranging overnight hostel accommodation and, before they set off, advising them on Catholic Associations abroad. Often prior enquiries were also made on their behalf regarding 'suitable' employment, from a religious point of view.

At the end of the Second World War, after the euphoria of victory had subsided, Londoners woke up to a devastated city. Collapsed buildings and dangerous structures ruined the streetscape. The infrastructure was in serious need of repair. Basic services were stretched if not absent. A new and socially reforming government elected in 1945 saw that it had a huge task ahead. But if austerity and rationing were still the order of the day, there was also a promise of renewal. The government also recognised that to rebuild Britain would require men and women prepared to roll up their sleeves. The Irish in particular, often escaping unemployment at home, were welcomed into Britain.

Fr Tom McNamara outside the entrance to the London Irish Centre with some new arrivals for the hostel.

Over the centuries, Irish emigrants had often been subjected to racist and insulting attacks by the host British community, so there was some caution about their arrival during wartime. Churchill's relationship with the Irish Taoiseach, De Valera, was not strengthened by the return to Ireland just before the War of the ports which the 1922 Treaty had previously allowed Britain to use. However, there was a UK permit office in Dublin, which directed applicants to specific areas as a condition of their admission to Britain. On arrival they were required to register with the police and report any changes of address. They were assigned to working on farms, aerodrome construction, demolition of bombed buildings and on the production line in munitions factories.

With controls on emigration lifting after the War, the Irish government expressed its concern at the loss of large numbers of men and women. England was regarded as 'the thirty-third state'. In later years there was more than a suspicion that particular Irish governments tacitly encouraged emigration for political and economic reasons. It helped keep unemployment figures down, it exported the needy, and valuable remittances would be sent home. At the end of the war, however, the government even considered banning emigration, but that would have been a denial of human rights. It finally dropped its full restrictions on women seeking work abroad in July 1946 and on men on 1 January 1948. But thousands, who had enlisted in the British armed forces or had come to specific wartime work in factories or hospitals, were already in Britain, demobbed or laid off and looking for future employment. They did not seem too keen to return to the 'auld sod'.

Saving Souls

By 1947, Fr Ambrose Woods, a parish priest who had been involved in youth welfare work, had experienced at first hand the bewildered arrival of Irish men and women into his parish in bomb-damaged Southwark, and knew only too well of the dangers that awaited them in a strange city. He had earlier approached the Irish government for help in setting up a hostel but had been refused. In a speech which he delivered a few years later, he described these dangers in the fairly lurid language of that time: *"We must not think of the vast body of Irish emigrants as all alike. They differ from each other according to their age groups, standard and type of education, intelligence, the environment in which they grew up ... In many instances the seeds of lapse from faith or morals are present before they leave their own Parish in Ireland."*

The condition of young people was a concern then, as it is now. *"One aspect of the problem merits special attention. I can only call it 'the murder of the Irish Innocents'. There are Irish fathers and mothers who send, or allow to go, to England their immature and uninformed children. At an age when their growing minds and bodies are still wide open to influences and experiences of any sort, and to ideas which will stay with them for life, they are sacrificed to Mammon. They are sent into the great cities and towns of England, into works and factories where the atmosphere is often materialistic, pagan and sometimes frankly immoral."*

On the other hand, towards the end of the same speech he praises the newly established London Irish Centre, in which he played such a formative part, as an instrument of reaction against any slide into sin. *"The new Irish Centre in London, the Legion of Mary and other organisations are working hard to keep our exiles good and decent. The Irish Centre is very concerned to arrange some practical method of liaison whereby parents and priests at home can direct those who are determined to come to England towards the various organisations working for their welfare. The Irish Centre is not a rescue organisation for down-and-outs. Its committee is composed of all the leading Irish organisations in London. Its aim is to introduce the Irish working boy and girl to all that is best in the Irish, or Catholic, life of London."*[3]

Since then, this aim of the London Irish Centre has scarcely changed, although the religious emphasis has diminished. Practical advice and help, often to the extremes of generosity, would be always offered, and sometimes accompanied with a Christian blessing when requested.

Five years before this speech, in 1948, a number of individual priests and lay people had been working together towards a plan, "a concrete scheme", to alleviate the problems of emigrants. When Ambrose Woods wrote to a Fr Carroll on 29 February to invite him to a meeting in Offley Road, near the Oval in south London, on 3 March, he said *"Many people write to the papers about the Irish in England. It is felt that if anything special is to be done, we ourselves, Irish priests, are in the best position to do it. A concrete scheme has been suggested to deal, in part, with the problems of our people in London."*[4]

The Leap Year date may have been a good omen, because the meeting was a success. A letter followed it to Cardinal Bernard Griffin, the Archbishop of Westminster, in which Ambrose Woods wrote, *"That in addition to the ordinary ministrations of priests in their parishes very much more could be done, and that special needs were apparent, and that these required a special approach."*[5] Cardinal Griffin responded, inviting Woods and Fr Michael Carey to meet him on 16 March.

The Plan was now advancing rapidly.

Further contacts and alliances among priests were made. Draft memos were sent, in which the situation of 'Irish workers in London' was analysed under such headings as Class, Facilities (religious, cultural, recreational, social); the Need; proposals such as The Centre (advice bureau, temporary hostel accommodation, large hall, meeting rooms, canteen, library and chapel); the organisation of this under trustees, management and staff, at which it was evident that The Centre was to be managed by the clergy; and finally cost and upkeep, where the difficulties were made clear.

Marked confidential, the Plan itself opened with a plea for *"A spiritual campaign in Ireland, to pray for the ending of emigration at present scale* (sic), *and for the salvation of exiles."* It also remarked on the *"complete lack of a Catholic or homely atmosphere"* among emigrant communities, but also warned of the *"undesirable"* nature of *"specifically Irish social workers"* with interests in the Connolly Clubs and communism, which were regarded as subversive.[6]

The Connolly Clubs, which later became known as the Connolly Association, had been founded in 1938 in Doughty Street, in the London Borough of St Pancras. Many of those attending had either been members of the London Branch of the Republican Congress or the League against Imperialism. After the War, the Association was accused, from pulpits in Ireland and by TDs in the Dail, of being a communist front. It did, of course, contain communists, but it also included members of the Labour Party and those with no party affiliation.[7]

As a result of pressure from Ambrose Woods and others, a conference of between fifty and sixty priests, principally from the three London area dioceses of Westminster, Southwark and Brentwood, was held in Westminster Cathedral Hall on 23 March 1948, in order to consider how this growing problem should be addressed. The hire of the hall was one nominal guinea. Chaired by Fr Michael Carey, the Irish Priests' Committee, as it became known, drew up a prospectus for what they were looking for in terms of a house of welcome for emigrants near to Euston or to Paddington Station. In the form of a wish-list, it also described the various elements desired, including a welfare or advice bureau, temporary hostel accommodation, a large hall, a canteen and lounge. Surprisingly, a chapel was not included at that time. After a day of deliberations, a resolution moved by the Very Revd Canon Joseph Reardon of St Patrick's, Soho, was passed unanimously. In the form of a letter to Cardinal Griffin it said *"We, the assembled Irish priests of London, approve of the scheme which has been proposed to help our people, and are convinced that one of the main results of the scheme should be to integrate Irish people into the Catholic life of the ordinary parish. We believe it is essential to have priests working at an (Irish) centre, and respectively beg Your Eminence in collaboration with the other Bishops to appoint priests to this work as soon as possible."*[8]

An Irish Bureau

One of the priests attending the event was a Corkman called Tom McNamara.

The decisions of the conference, including a formal approach to the Irish government for money and help, were also conveyed to Cardinal Griffin, Bishop Cyril Cowderoy of Southwark and Bishop Andrew Beck of Brentwood. Shortly afterwards, Cardinal Griffin replied that, *"With the Hierarchy's approval I agree to the setting up of an Irish Bureau here in north London...."*[9] The bishops also agreed to commit their influence to assisting the project, nominating priests from their dioceses, and were themselves willing to act as patrons.

Cardinal Griffin forwarded news of the project to the Archbishop of Armagh, Primate of All Ireland, John Francis D'Alton. To help it on its way, Archbishop D'Alton responded with a cheque for £500. Meanwhile, Ambrose Woods submitted to a number of significant bishops in the Catholic Hierarchy of Ireland a Memorandum and Proposals, which included the welcome news of Cardinal Griffin's support. The Plan was discussed at Maynooth in June, and the replies received by Ambrose Woods were all supportive.

With limitless energy, Woods commenced the search for a suitable property, considering and then rejecting an enormous war-time bomb damaged repair workers' hostel at 50 Onslow Square, in Fulham. In 1947 this had accommodated over 2,000 Irish labourers, who paid thirty shillings a week for bed, breakfast and an evening meal. Rationing was of course still enforced, and there were complaints that the food provided was not sufficient for an Irishman who needed his strength to rebuild London. Other potential premises in the areas of Earls Court, Bayswater, Edgware Road and Shepherds Bush were also considered. It seemed that a base near Paddington Station, where the trains arrived from Fishguard in Wales, across the Irish Sea from Rosslare, was the first objective rather than one near Euston.

In April 1950 a delegation in search of funds and briefed with the facts visited Dublin to meet John Costello, the Taoiseach, whose coalition government had been elected in 1948. This government had been reported as denying that any previous request for funds had been received. Prudently, the delegation, which included Ambrose Woods, Tom McNamara and William O'Brien, first sought the blessing of the Archbishop of Dublin, John McQuaid. Clutching a letter of support from Cardinal Bernard Griffin, it was cordially received at ministerial level and then by the Taoiseach at his offices.

The immediate response was favourable, but they were to wait for three years before learning that their journey had been in vain. As Ambrose Woods later noted in 1952, *"Help may never come from Dublin!"*[10] Some of the reasons could have been predicted. Apart from what may have been an excuse that no request had previously been received, John Costello showed his surprise that there were, in fact, so many Irishmen and women arriving in London. This in itself was remarkable. He also felt that there would be a difficulty in allocating funds because there was no budget for this, although it could perhaps come from the Department of Social Affairs. Another difficulty, he asserted, *"... would be to avoid giving the impression that the government favoured emigration."*[11]

This did not deter the Irish Priests' Committee. An executive was formed in 1953 to take the project forward. Its officers included four priests, with Michael Carey as Chairman, Tom McNamara and Bernard Manning as Joint Treasurers and Ambrose Woods as Secretary. They were joined by four lay people who were regarded as having the appropriate skills: Lawrie Arnold as Legal Adviser, who had held a legal position with the Water Board, Jack Steacey, a retired director of Monsanto Chemicals, James Conway, a builder who was the owner of the Emerald Dance Hall in Hammersmith, and James McGill. A building contractor, Stephen Hussey, was co-opted in November 1954. All shared a pledge to convert an appropriate building, when they found one.

Tom McNamara, whose home had been in Newtownshandrum, Co. Cork, had ar-rived in London as a student in the late 1930s, and had been ordained as a priest in 1940. He was immediately afterwards appointed as the Catholic chaplain at the RAF base at Hendon, Middlesex. No doubt it was the experience of dealing with large numbers of men and women under wartime conditions, and away from home, which developed in him a commitment to assist them. Hendon was followed by spells as a parish priest in Burnt Oak and Tollington Park in Holloway. A stocky man, he also had a strong interest in sport as the Chairman of the London County Board GAA, and Vice-President of the GAA for Britain.

While at Tollington Park, and with the support of his parish priest, Fr George Groves, McNamara had acquired two condemned houses at no. 2 Turle Road N4, as a temporary hostel for thirty men. The Diocese of Westminster had intended to build a Catholic school on this land, which also included the houses, but this was taking time. Eventually the school of Christ the King was erected here. In the meantime the houses were refurbished as a hostel. This was formally opened by Cardinal Griffin, accompanied by the Irish Ambassador, Dr Freddie Boland, on 18 November 1953, and operated as a hostel for older men until 1970.

Volunteers from the Legion of Mary, who regularly met emigrants off the boat trains at Paddington and Euston, now had somewhere they could send them.

Tom McNamara shared an awareness with the others of the dangers that young Irish people could face in a city like London. A year later he acquired, for the price of £6,500, nos. 29 and 31 Hornsey Lane Gardens, two connecting houses, and set about converting them into a hostel for forty girls and women. As a result of the rec-ommendation of Cardinal Griffin, the diocese had donated a loan to complete

The women's hostel, later known as the Marian Hostel, Hornsey Lane Gardens.

the purchase. It was modernised for £5,000, and again re-modernised in 1972 for a further £10,000. In two years, two hostels had been opened, meeting an important objective of the Irish Priests' Committee.

An extremely influential figure in the development of the Centre, and some would say a safe anchor when the seas around it became stormy, was Paddy Keegan, an accountant. From Ardagh in Co. Longford, he first met members of the committee in 1953. The treasurer, Bernard Manning, who was also from Ardagh, invited him to Brentwood to inspect the accounts. Keegan saw that they could be improved, and rewrote them. This later came to the notice of Jack Steacey, who asked him to take over. Paddy Keegan's

commitment to the centre, whether as a volunteer or as a paid accountant, continues to this day.

On the executive committee, Ambrose Woods' proposal that a centre be set up forthwith was unanimously approved, and a powerful case for funding was made. A meeting to announce the news followed at the Irish Club, in Eaton Square, SW3, at which £15.16s was collected at the door. An appeals committee was also formed, which drew up lists of potential lay and clerical supporters. A separate appeal specifically to acquire a property was launched, with Mr J. Ansboro, manager of the National Bank at 180, Strand, in central London, ready to offer financial backing. This bank was later to become the Bank of Ireland, and closely involved with the Centre. In March 1954 an account was set up here in the name of the Irish Centre Fund. All progress was reported to the three bishops who had now become patrons, those of Westminster, Southwark and Brentwood.

A letter from the Bishop of Southwark, Cyril Cowderoy, advised Ambrose Woods, "... most strongly (underlined) not to make any appeal to people in Ireland. My own impression at the moment is that it is considered in Ireland that the Irish emigrants, when they get here, are earning far more than those in a relative social position over there, and they imagine that these Irish lads and girls in London and elsewhere are relatively well-off and resent the idea that the poorer people in Ireland, either directly or indirectly, should provide them with a centre." A few days later Archbishop Griffin repeated this advice, but also enclosed a cheque for £1,000 towards the project. On 24 March 1954, Tom McNamara wrote to Woods, "Have you got the cheque or is it a promise?"[12] It was not a promise, and £1,017 11s was paid into the account at the National Bank. By the executive meeting on 3 November the amount had grown to £1,088 12s. 9d.

This amount was formally presented in January 1955 at a meeting in Westminster Hall to which Woods had invited Bishops Cowderoy and Beck. A leaflet, the merits or otherwise of which were the subject of an internal dogfight at the executive meeting, was finally agreed to be circulated in order to seek public donations for the Centre.[13] One could say that after a Leap Year Day start nine years before, the London Irish Centre was very definitely on its way and with money in the bank.

A Mission for Emigrants

While the concept of an Irish Centre in London had now become established, in Dublin the Hierarchy decided to put its considerable influence also behind a coordinated mission to assist Irish emigrants in England and Wales. On 7 February 1955 the provincials of Irish religious orders were invited to the Archbishop's House in Dublin and asked for their full cooperation by Archbishop John McQuaid.

The Oblates of Mary Immaculate, or Oblates as they are more familiarly known, were among those represented. The order was later to become vital in the development and expansion of the Centre. It had a reputation in teaching and reformatories and had worked with emigrant communities in England since the 1860s.

A record of the meeting states that the provincials were "Unanimous in expressing their understanding of the enterprise and their complete willingness to assist the bishops." The next step was to obtain the approval of Cardinal Bernard Griffin in Westminster, and through him the Hierarchy of England and Wales, so that the mission could operate in Britain. At their subsequent meeting in London the ultimate objective was described as "The integration of our people into the Catholic life of the parishes in which they live, but in the meantime that they lead a good life, go to mass, stem the leakage of the Irish from the church, stir up their faith, win back the lapsed, strengthen the wavering and encourage the good to be apostolic."[14] The emphasis was on religious observance, but some priests working at the front-line believed that for them welfare and other advice was an even greater priority. This divergence was to manifest itself in later years in the record of some directors of the Centre.

Various ideas had been proposed at the Dublin meeting. These included proposals to have all British employment agencies in Ireland licensed, for representatives to meet all Irish boat trains on their arrival in the English cities and lists to be kept of all lodging houses recommended by parish priests. The Irish newspapers were asked not to publish advertisements for lodging houses without consulting the Catholic Social Welfare Bureau as to their suitability. Special missions to assess the scale of the problem were dispatched to Britain, after which priests from the orders were loaned to welfare work in British towns and cities. Soundings had been taken among emigrant communities, and the work of Tom McNamara and others was already known.

The initiative to retain the faith was consolidated when the Irish Hierarchy established the Irish Commission on Emigration and Other Population Problems, which explored the nature and extent of emigration in the 1950s. This body later developed into the Irish Episcopal Commission for Emigrants[15] which has continued until the present day. One of its tasks is to co-ordinate the work of the Irish Chaplaincy, which was established in 1957.

The Commission discussed further ideas, which included a series of co-ordinated articles in the provincial Irish press on the potential dangers inherent in emigration and how the Commission would serve emigrants. There was even talk of the Commission itself publishing a special weekly newspaper, but this was not progressed once the finances were properly considered. Another idea was to designate the first Sunday in October each year as a day of prayer for emigrants.

Taking it further, Cardinal Bernard Griffin devoted his Pastoral Letter on Trinity Sunday, 10 July 1955, to the plight of the Irish in Britain. This 'Pastoral Letter of the Irish Hierarchy on the Spiritual Welfare of our Immigrants', reiterated some of the proposals of the Irish Hier-

---

PASTORAL LETTER FOR TRINITY SUNDAY 1955

BERNARD GRIFFIN, *CARDINAL PRIEST OF THE HOLY ROMAN CHURCH OF THE TITLE OF SAINT ANDREW AND SAINT GREGORY ON THE COELIAN HILL, BY THE GRACE OF GOD AND THE FAVOUR OF THE APOSTOLIC SEE ARCHBISHOP OF WESTMINSTER AND METROPOLITAN, TO THE CLERGY AND FAITHFUL OF THE DIOCESE, HEALTH AND BENEDICTION IN THE LORD.*

DEARLY BELOVED BRETHREN AND DEAR CHILDREN IN JESUS CHRIST:

INCREASING publicity has recently been given to the large numbers of Irish men and women crossing to this country. Immigration on so vast a scale has very great implications so far as the Catholic community is concerned. Its importance may be seen from the fact that in the ten years since the war the Catholic population of England and Wales has increased by over three-quarters of

The Pastoral Letter of Cardinal Bernard Griffin, 10 July 1955.

archy conference, but spelt them out for every parishioner in the Westminster diocese. In particular it stated, *"It is imperative that these new immigrants should be fired with the same zeal as inspired so many of those who came to this country in former years. They must be true sons of St Patrick, missionaries, apostles, carrying the torch of faith into their new surroundings. Yet it would be idle to pretend that the present situation is not fraught with difficulties and dangers. These exist to be overcome. It is the joint responsibility of the Catholics of our two countries to ensure that this mass movement of population be turned to the benefit of the Church. We cannot at this stage afford to lose ourselves in the argument about the wisdom of emigration from Ireland. We have to face up to the fact that Catholic boys and girls, most of them in their teens, are crossing the Irish Sea in ever-increasing numbers. It is not sufficient that we should think in terms of saving their faith. We must take every step to ensure that they prove a credit to their native land and are fully integrated within the Catholic community in this country."*[16]

Fr Joe Taaffe had been ministering to Irish workers in power plant construction at Blaenau Ffestiniog in the 1940s. Out of the Irish Chaplaincy also emerged a more formal camp chaplains scheme and in 1957 Archbishop John McQuaid called for priests to work with Irish labourers on large construction projects such as steel-works, power stations, airports and the M1 motorway. At its peak, the M1 contract employed 4,700 Irishmen. Two chaplains, Fr Joseph Nolan from Kerry and Fr Patrick McPartland from Armagh were appointed to look after their spiritual welfare.[17] Another who was appointed to this work was Fr Owen Sweeney, the priest at the huge steelworks site at Llanwern in Wales, who was later to follow Tom McNamara as senior chaplain into the Centre.

Still more specialised were those working with the Irish staff at bus companies or at the hotels of London's West End or Bayswater. Apart from being paid extremely poorly, hotel staff tended to be transitory with some able to obtain accommodation on the premises. Fr Michael Cleary, from the parish of Saints Anselm and Cecilia in Holborn Kingsway, was allowed by hotel managements to venture into the kitchens to extend the work of the Chaplaincy. The pattern was much the same: the priest would befriend the Irish man or woman, help them with their social or welfare problems, and also say Mass for them before their shifts commenced or afterwards. Fr Cleary, who would later

enjoy singing at the ballad sessions at the centre, even made a record album as the 'Singing Priest'.

Later, hospital chaplains were also assigned. It was estimated in 1976 that 23,500 Irish nurses were working in British hospitals, with 800 young women travelling to England each year to train. The message, however, was *"Many are still badly prepared"*. To reverse this, it was observed that *"The standard of religious practice is high, but there is cause for concern. Seminars for intending nurses should be held in each diocese."* This report adds some cautionary words, such as *"A directly religious programme could prove counter-productive, as a chaplain one needs to be careful lest one gives the impression of being exclusively for the Irish, and a chaplain must also consider the patients as well as the nurses."*[18]

Places to gather

In parallel with religious efforts to bring Irish people together, moves were taken by Irish people in Britain involved in the professions and the trade unions. In addition to the political Connolly Association, other more social associations were formed and premises were organised. In central London there was an increasing desire that they needed somewhere that they could call their own. This was partially met when the Irish Club finally opened its doors in Eaton Square in Belgravia, but this was a very different sort of place from that envisaged by the Irish Priests' Committee.

The Irish Club succeeded a number of different Irish clubs and societies in London, from the Irish Literary Society, which had been founded in 1891, through to the Gaelic League and the Four Provinces Club. They each appealed to different social or cultural interests, but they all shared a desire that Irish people in London should support each other in what was some-times a hostile environment.

The wartime home of Queen Wilhemina of the Netherlands, and in 1949 the former town-house of the Guinness family, 82 Eaton Square was regarded as an ideal location for a residential and social Irish Club. A 21-year lease of the property was negotiated with the Duke of Westmin-ster's estate, and very soon afterwards it provided a welcome mostly to middle-class Irish emigrants of first and second generation who had been meeting else-where since 1947. Apart from business and professional people, its membership covered a wide mix, including those from the theatrical and literary professions such as Siobhan McKenna, Cyril Cusack and Brendan Behan, but also officers from the Irish Guards, the 'Micks', who were sta-tioned nearby at Chelsea Barracks. There were others whose connections with Ire-land were perhaps slender, but who en-joyed the conviviality. George Bernard Shaw, perhaps the most celebrated Irish-man then living in England, was invited to join. His typically acerbic reply from his home in Hertfordshire was,"*I can imagine nothing less desirable than an Irish Club. Irish people in England should avoid each other like the plague. If they flock together like geese they might as well never have left Ireland. They don't admire, nor even like each other.*"[19] However, many ig-nored his advice, and the Irish Club was to enjoy an eventful history until its clo-sure in 2002.

Some of the 1950s' membership took an interest in the scheme to develop a separate Irish Centre, and invited the Irish Priests' Committee to meet on their premises. A concert in aid of funds, run on the lines of the Club's popular At Home series, was held in the ballroom on 6 December 1953 with an extraordinary array of different performers. Although the two institutions differed profoundly, one providing comfortable residential accommodation and the other intended to provide hostel accommodation to the unemployed, the Irish Club lent its formal support to the project. Key figures, such as Michael Casey and Dominic Donnelly, its Treasurer, were soon participating on the committee. Others, such as Stephen Hussey, were only too willing to use the hospitality of Eaton Square to encourage support for what would later become the London Irish Centre in Camden Square.

Despite small but significant attempts at dealing with some of the problems that faced Irish emigrants in London, the need for more accommodation and an accom-panying welfare service remained acute. As this increased, so did the demand for a proper administration, and the estab-lishing of a permanent headquarters. The Irish Priests' Committee began to envis-age a more functional building which would include a bureau where welfare advice could be requested and offered, and which would be able to "keep a reg-ister of decent lodgings for men and women", a hall which could be used as a social centre for meetings and recrea-tional purposes, with perhaps a games room, library and canteen attached, and additional hostel accommodation.

This progress was noted. The *Irish In-dependent* later reported that, "*His Emi-nence Cardinal Griffin, who is patron of the foundation, maintains a lively interest in its progress. Minutes of all committee meetings and a regular report from the chaplain find their way to the Archbishop's House, West-minster.*"[20]

The Premises found
The drive was now on for premises, and the focus of the search was on north London. Everyone joined in this task. In March 1954 Tom McNamara wrote to

Ambrose Woods to say he'd found *"a very valuable property"*, a former factory building in York Way, near Kings Cross. *"It might not look much to the undiscerning eye but possibilities are endless with the present building and space to one side to add to present building, 8800 square feet"*(sic).[21] It seems that even then there were those who believed expansion was important. The freehold was a relatively expensive £16,500, but it was not pursued.

Stephen Hussey was a partner of Hussey Brothers of Bayswater, a firm of contractors which specialised in renovating bomb-damaged premises. In due course the search was successful. His firm came across a suitable building in leafy Camden Square, NW1. No. 52 Camden Square was purchased on 5 August 1955 for £3,887 10s. Its proximity to the three railway terminals of Kings Cross, St Pancras and Euston was thought to be particularly convenient. Euston, of course, is the station at which arrived the boat trains from Holyhead, Liverpool and Greenock.

Cardinal Bernard Griffin offered a loan of £5,000 towards the building's conversion to a hostel and welfare centre, which was later repaid. Having been a Methodist home for mothers and babies, it was thought that any conversion of the building could be relatively inexpensive. With the voluntary labour of local Irishmen, and funded by a trickle of contributions, this house was gradually renovated to provide hostel accommodation upstairs for up to thirty men.

It was decided that the two hostels already in existence should be administered alongside the new one at 52 Camden Square. Its local parish offered Tollington Park to the Centre, and another group of volunteers helped to put it into a more serviceable condition as a hostel for older men. The girls' hostel in Hornsey Lane Gardens, which had been purchased by the Diocese of Westminster the year before, was also to be handed to the Centre for administration.

With unusually good fortune the building next door, no. 51 Camden Square, suddenly came on the market. This house, which consisted of self-contained flats occupied by sitting tenants, was quickly purchased for £2,740. It was not as suitable as the original building, but its proximity was considered as an opportunity not to be missed. Together, these two buildings could provide accommodation for forty people, but at first they opened with space for ten young Irishmen. The gardens at the rear meant that there was also room for expansion. In order to develop this, further and continuing appeals for funds were made. The pressing search for financial stability was to become a feature of the history of the London Irish Centre.

Some decanting of the sitting tenants from no. 51 Camden Square was necessary, so an available property at 1 North Villas, a few hundred yards away on the far corner of the Square, was purchased on 6 February 1956, into which they could move after it had been repaired and redecorated. This was also convenient as a home for some of the staff now working at the Centre. The building was later sold to Camden Council in September 1974.

Cardinal Griffin had already approved Tom McNamara's popular appointment as resident chaplain and co-ordinator of the incipient Irish Centre in 1955. His informality and amiable manner were to stand him in good stead when he took on the new assignment.

He immediately committed himself to assist the newly-arrived Irish emigrant. Unlike later directors who were appointed from the Oblates, he had to manage without additional staff from the church. However he did have a team of volunteers, both on his administrative committee and as workers at the Centre.

An excerpt from a welfare committee report of that time demonstrated the need that they were already having to meet: *"The most distressing aspect of social work at the Centre is the continuous arrival of destitute people of all ages. They may be young, running away from parents, society or the police. They may be middle-aged or elderly with problems of drink, gambling, illness, stability or improvidence. For generations the pattern is repeated.*

They arrive with only the clothes they were wearing, no money, no contacts, no plans, with a chequered work pattern and no references. They arrive in depression, having slept out for a few nights and appearing unwashed and very unkempt and certainly in no condition to appear before a prospective employer. They are also likely to arrive at weekends, late at night or in the early hours of the morning, when all the usual channels of assistance are closed. When this occurs their immediate needs are met and the long-term solutions are referred to the social workers."[22]

Others had more of a sense of purpose. One who arrived at the door in April 1955 was John, age 18 from Galway, and without a job, accommodation or money. As he has since said, *"At that stage you don't think about things like that. You'd see the guys coming home from England with stacks of money".* The Holyhead train had arrived at Euston at 7.30 am. John placed his case in the left luggage and hoped that he would find a job by 9.00 am. Without any ideas but with plenty of determination he walked vaguely in the direction of Camden Town and found himself outside Gallaher's Black Cat factory in Mornington Crescent. He retraced his steps southwards and at Marylebone Road he spotted an advertisement for staff at BHS Retailing. The store had opened at 9.00 am and John went in

to see the manager. A man in the queue said to him that he would not get a job without an address, and suggested that John tried the hostel where he was himself staying, in Turle Road.

John met Tom McNamara who noticed that he had made *"no arrangements at all",* and was offered a bed. He now had an address. After arithmetic and aptitude tests he obtained the job. However, payment was two weeks in arrears, and he would not have survived had not Tom McNamara given him two weeks' credit, and also lent him money until pay-day. John is now an extremely successful businessman.*"The fifties and sixties were great",* he has since said, *"There were jobs galore and the North (of Ireland) was not yet a problem."*[23]

The Camden Square buildings were opened formally on 27 September 1955 by Cardinal D'Alton, Archbishop of Armagh and blessed by Cardinal Bernard Griffin, sixth Archbishop of Westminster. The premises, with moulded shamrocks on either side of the Murray Street door and the crests of each Irish province above it, were named as the Blessed Oliver Plunkett House, after the Irish scholar, patriot and martyr. Oliver Plunkett, Archbishop of Armagh centuries before, had been savagely mutilated and hanged at Tyburn in London on 1 July 1681, having been implicated in the mendacious 'Popish Plot' of Titus Oates. John remembers the opening ceremony in Murray Street.*"It was a tremendous occasion. You could see the tears in people's eyes. The pride and the hope. They had never been given anything like this before."*[24] People queued in the street to kiss the ring of the Archbishop.

Inside the entrance, there is now a brass plaque to commemorate the event. With the words inscribed 'To the Glory of God and in Honour of the Blessed Oliver Plunkett' and remembering what it signifies, it is perhaps surprising that it does not have greater prominence within the building.

The aim of the new Centre was reiterated, to *"promote the social, recreational and spiritual welfare of Irish people in London"*. This had been clarified into three objectives:

"1. To form a social service bureau to give advice on various problems and to keep a register of decent lodgings for men and women.

2. To provide a hall for social and recreational functions.

3. To provide temporary hostel accommodation."[25]

It is interesting that there was not a religious dimension among them.

By the end of its first year, the Camden Square hostel, with beds for forty young men, had accommodated 479 men and placed 400 more at work.[26] Another 120 could be accommodated at the Tollington Park hostel for older men, and at the Hornsey Lane Gardens address for girls and women.

At the first AGM on 13 December 1955, the constitution which had been presented to Cardinal Griffin the previous June was amended, and a new executive was elected. It consisted of familiar priests such as Ambrose Woods, Tom McNamara as resident chaplain and Bernard Manning as honorary treasurer. There were also some less familiar ones at that time such as Rev. Monsignor Derek Worlock, a private secretary to Cardinal Griffin. Ten years later he was appointed to the title of Bishop of Portsmouth and eleven years after that as the Catholic Archbishop of Liverpool, where he worked closely with David Sheppard, the Anglican Bishop, in bringing attention to the problems facing that city. Together they wrote, *Better Together: Christian Partnership in a Hurt City*. They were known as 'Fish and Chips'.

The executive also included familiar lay people such as Jack Steacey as secretary, James Conway, Stephen Hussey as vice chair, Lawrie Arnold, Dr Edward (Ned) Carey, Tadgh Feehan from the Embassy, J. Ansboro and Sr B. H. Kenny. They were empowered *"to carry on and control the business and work of the council"*. Eight objectives were agreed, among them *"to aid and benefit Irish workers recently arrived in Great Britain or working in Britain ... by providing hostels, respectable lodgings, employment, spiritual and moral welfare, a social club ... and for this end co-operating with other charitable and welfare bodies..."*[27]

There were of course some Irish people who were not as disadvantaged as those who needed help from the Centre. Many were becoming successfully established in trades or in business. What they did miss was the opportunity to come together socially. The Irish Club, with its address in Eaton Square, was perhaps not the place for them, a view they may have shared with George Bernard Shaw.

Every Whit-Monday there was an Irish Festival at Mitcham Stadium in south London. It was of course based around GAA events, but there were other attractions such as step-dancing. Paddy Keegan remembers that volunteers organised the day, and one year he had to mark out the pitch, walking around behind a contraption that drew a white line. In due course the festival moved north to Wembley Stadium, where it became strictly a GAA event. It is an indication of the numbers that attended in the 1950s that they could fill Wembley Stadium.

The Counties participate

A nucleus of Irishmen and women had also been organising the annual St Patrick's Day parade, which from the late 1950s walked from Horse Guards to Westminster Cathedral for a 12 noon Mass on the

Sunday morning closest to 17 March. Although this event gained little publicity at the time, it was well attended. Marching under their county banners, this was an opportunity for new arrivals in England to meet each other with a sense of pride and maintain connections with home. The St Patrick's Day Parade Committee, as this small group later became known, held annual fund-raising dinners at the Gresham Ballroom in the Holloway Road, one of which was televised by RTE for the Eamonn Andrews Show.

By now, groups from individual counties were coming together for social and other purposes. One of the earliest was the Corkman's Association, which was born in Paddy Whitty's pub, the Lord High Admiral, in Victoria on St Patrick's Day in 1953. A founder member was of course Tom McNamara. Another group was from Clare, with John Vaughan, Joe Hanratty and Joe McCarthy, who started an association of Claremen from among their friends in Cricklewood and Kilburn. It is perhaps remarkable that the early county associations were so easily able to attract such figures as a later Ambassador, Hugh McCann, the then Minister for Foreign Affairs, Dr Patrick Hillery, a Clareman himself, and senior members of the clergy to their dinners.

In 1954, members of these groups and a few others held a meeting in a pub in Camden Town, possibly at the Dublin Castle, to set up a more nationally based Irish Counties Association. They included Pat Hegarty from Glencolumbcille in Donegal, Jim Fox from Leitrim, Gerry O'Flynn from Galway, Owen O'Neill from Kilkenny and James Conway from Cavan. In parallel with the aims of the Irish Centre they were keen to provide the beginnings of a social organisation where new migrants could feel at home, and also develop a welfare advice service including

a fund to which they contributed. This was to assist people in hardship, and the initiative had been supported by Dr Freddie Boland, the Irish Ambassador.[28] Pat Hegarty organised the creation of a welfare fund, which was launched at a reception in Camden Town at which £120, a considerable sum then, was raised.

On 7 February 1956, the executive committee was superseded by a council. The Cardinal Archbishop of Westminster and the Bishops of Southwark and Brentwood remained as episcopal patrons, and the four trustees appointed by them remained as part of the constitution. What was new was that the council included eighty different Irish societies, including county associations, companies such as Aer Lingus, local associations and cultural groups such as the GAA. Although in practice the number diminished, this became an extremely unwieldy structure. However, representing the Irish people of London, the council owned the freehold of the buildings in Camden Square and Murray Street.

This meeting also created the position of president, which was offered to Frank Pakenham, 7th Earl of Longford, who had been educated at Eton and Oxford. With his aristocratic ancestry in Ireland, an intellect that qualified him as a university don and with a respected political experience, he seemed ideal as someone who would be able to negotiate on behalf of the Centre. Elizabeth, Lady Longford, whom he had met at university, had persuaded him to renounce the Conservative Party, of which he was then a member, in favour of socialism and to convert to Roman Catholicism from the Irish Protestant ascendancy into which he had been born. Lord Longford was an inspired choice, but a cynic might suggest that he had been offered the position of president more because he was also the chairman

Members of the organising committee of the London Irish Centre. Front row, l-r: Fr Tom McNamara (Director), Monsignor Derek Worlock (later Bishop of Liverpool), Dominic Donnelly (chairman), Frank Pakenham (later Lord Longford, president), Michael Casey (secretary) and Tadgh Feehan (Irish Embassy). The back row includes Paddy Keegan (second left), Dr Matt Cranitch and John Vaughan (first and second right).

of the National Bank, which had been so helpful during the early fundraising period under the guidance of Mr J. Ansboro, manager of its branch in the Strand, than for his presentational ability.

Lord Longford's chairing skills were notoriously brisk. He was reported by Desmond Fisher as having conducted the second AGM, in 1956, held at the Irish Club, *"... with his usual efficiency. I think that the speed with which he dispatched the business rather disconcerted some of the committee members who expected leisurely speeches."*[29] Jack Steacey, a Tipperary man, was now the chairman. He worked hard, five days a week at the Centre, although

it was thought that he was also working for a papal decoration. It was to become a practice that the senior chaplain or director of the Centre became treasurer of the administrative committee, presumably because he knew better than most what the potential and actual expenses were and whether there was anything to meet them. When Jack Steacey retired, Tom McNamara took on the position of treasurer. Their relationship had never been cordial. On 11 July 1956 the Centre became a registered charity. The AGM also announced around £30,000 expenditure on additions and extensions to the building, including a chapel.

Royal Albert Hall Concert, March 1965.

During this time Tom McNamara, who said Mass three times on a Sunday and once on weekdays, and also heard confessions, was to be noticed acting more like a Clerk of Works. The alterations to the Centre were often done by volunteers, or men from the hostels, while they were looking for paid employment, and they needed supervision.

One of the principal methods the Centre used to raise income was through its St Patrick's concert each year at the Royal Albert Hall. Inventive methods of increasing this income dominated committee agendas. Because at least £2,000 was required each year just to hire the venue, a decision was made to insert Banker's Order forms into the tickets. Other practical ideas for fund-raising were considered, such as making appeals to lists of possible donors, the drafting of letters, and arrangements for distributing the appeals. A second letter would follow if the first apparently caused no reaction. The results were disappointing. By 7 July 1956 only £103 15s had been raised.

Although the service concentrated on providing hostel accommodation, at the third AGM in December 1957 Lord Longford made an appeal for £24,000 to finance an extension, which would include additional sleeping, dining and recreational facilities and a chapel. The hostel renovations took nine months and were completed in November 1965 at a cost of £4,980, excluding furnishings. It was now able to accommodate fifty young men rather than the original thirty-seven. In that first year, 609 people stayed there. There was an irony in that the existing residents of no. 51 Camden Square, next door, were being removed to North Villas to allow their rooms to be converted to the new hostel accommodation.

47

It was agreed that the further extensions and refurbishments were necessary for the Centre to fulfil its clear potential. However Fr Derek Worlock reminded everyone at the AGM that there must be more to offer than the provision of accommodation. The important task was to help the new emigrant to adjust to conditions in England. In 1957 the income and expenditure account at this AGM showed a deficit of £259, very different from what would become alarmingly normal figures five years later.

The integration of work in the original buildings with the proposed extensions to the rear in Murray Mews, where there had once been a garage spray shop owned by a Mr Lakis, meant they were not used properly until late 1958. Planning permission had been granted by the London County Council, but the work was finally completed in 1960, when Cardinal Godfrey reopened the buildings on 11 July.[30]

Word of these developments, in every sense, had got back to Dublin. It was not long before Erskine Childers, the son of the Irish nationalist and a future President of Ireland, visited the Irish Centre in February 1956 to see for himself what was happening. He brought with him an RTE recording unit, which interviewed Tom McNamara. This was to be the first broadcast of many from the Centre. Later in the year there was also a visit from the

The inaugural meeting of the Council of Irish County Associations at the Irish Club. (No date). Front row, left to right: T MacCavanagh (Armagh), James Conway (Cavan), Frank Biggar (Irish Embassy), Eamon O'Donnell (Donegal), Fr Tom McNamara, Dr Tom Tangney (Cork), Dr Freddie Boland, the Irish Ambassador, Dr J Canning (Donegal), Fr Tom Moore (Cavan). Back row, from base of stairs: Tadgh Feehan, Tony Murphy (Cork), Fr Cremin, Simon Breen (Tipperary), W. Gleeson (Limerick), Jack Steacey, Harry Bolger (Tipperary), J Carr (Donegal), J Moriarty, Paddy White (Kerry), J McAvinchey (Armagh).

Taoiseach, John Costello, with Dr Freddie Boland. Unfortunately, in spite of the previous appeals for funding from his government, he brought no money with him.

While construction activity on the site was continuing, the welfare work of the Centre was never forgotten, and the building did not neglect its commitment to the bringing together of Irish people in a social setting. The confirmation of their Irish identity was also vital to those who were struggling to obtain a foothold in a foreign environment.

In due course, the Council of Irish County Associations, as it became known, had taken on the raising of money for the welfare fund. It had moved its headquarters into the Irish Centre Club, named thus to avoid confusion with the Irish Club in Eaton Square, and was established to draw together the social activities of the building. The Irish Centre Club soon became a focus for the associations' bacon and cabbage dinners, ceilidhs, ballad sessions and other recreational activities. Membership was open and at a very nominal fee. Parish reunions, at which a visiting priest from Ireland came to London to meet members of his congregation who had emigrated, were another feature of the Centre.

The 1957 list of the County Association's officers reveal that James Conway (Cavan) was chairman, Michael Brazil (Waterford) was vice-chairman, while the hon. secretary was Patrick Byrne (Dublin) and hon. treasurer was W. J. Gleeson (Limerick). It is noticeable how many names (with their counties of origin, of course) recur in the history of personal contribution of time and effort to the Centre.

Its first Annual Dinner took place at the Café Royal in Regent Street on 5 July 1958. Its chairman then was Tadgh Feehan, a Corkman. The distinguished guest and recipient of the Toast was the Taoiseach himself, Eamon de Valera, TD. Another member of the Dail present was John Costello, who had remained the Taioseach until March 1957.

The associations were by now also flourishing outside London. John Leyden of the Clare Association in Birmingham described the coach-loads of Clare supporters that made the journey down to the annual GAA Games at Wembley. In 1959 they decided that they wished to stay together after the final whistle, and there was no better destination for them than the London Irish Centre. With some trepidation Tom McNamara made them welcome, until, as Mr Leyden says *"There was nothing to consume in the place but water."*[31] Satisfactorily refreshed, the Clare Association of Birmingham made use of the Centre on GAA Championship days for the next ten years.

By 1960 this Club was renamed the Carey Club after two founding members, Michael and Ned Carey who were not related, and was flourishing. Two years later its membership had grown to over 600 with people from across London. A sample programme, for September 1964, reveals a typical schedule, including meetings of the St Christopher's Cycling Club and the Gramophone and Recording Club, which enjoyed all types of music from *"Irish ballads to satirical and calypso."*[32]

This social or recreational aspect of the Centre continued to play an important part in its development. Much later, the excavations at the rear, onto which was to be erected the John F Kennedy Memorial Hall, commenced in 1964. While this was in progress, it was decided to alter the upstairs bar to create both a public bar and a lounge bar. These facilities were completed in April 1966.

There was of course a serious aide to all

the fun. The social side of the Centre was also in a position to raise much-needed funds. Subscriptions to the Club, payments for Bingo and takings across the bar were poured into the proverbial bottomless bucket, which would pay for extensions to the service and the buildings. Volunteers, many of whom enjoyed the social facilities, formed the backbone of the service. Those who were willing to fundraise were indispensable. Others with management, book-keeping, and typing experience or committee and chairing skills were vital if the Centre was to run smoothly. A large proportion of those seeking help arrived after office hours, so volunteers who were prepared to work into the night were invaluable.

Many had other, normal jobs and gave long hours of their spare time. A few were like Mary Kenny, from Ballinasloe on the Roscommon and Galway border, who arrived in 1955 and with extraordinary dedication is still volunteering at the centre. Her early working years were in Dublin before moving to London in 1953. Unsure about England, she returned home, only to come back in 1955. She has been heard to whisper that she is "married to the Irish Centre", and a long, supportive relationship it has been over nearly fifty years.

On the management side, the contribution of Tommy Dunne, who was a senior executive with Aer Lingus, really benefited the Centre, as did that of Dr Larry Morton, a local GP, who assisted in setting up the welfare service. A committee had been first established in 1955 to monitor and develop the service. Chaired by Dr Morton, who was from Dublin, it made a strong contribution towards more rational and effective work.

Regrettably, much of the energies of volunteers and even the part-time social workers was given to fund-raising. At the fourth AGM, which was held at Westmin-ster Cathedral Hall, the new Archbishop Cardinal Godfrey said, "The Irish Centre is for Irish people, and it is, therefore, up to the Irish in London to support it. I know that we are not a wealthy community as a whole – immigrants rarely are. But nevertheless there are many amongst the Irish community in Britain, captains of industry and commerce, those who have been successful in the building trades, men who have achieved considerable success and wealth – some of them in a relatively short period. With nearly a quarter of a million Irish-born people living in the London area alone, it would be a grave reflection on the generosity and Catholicity of which we tend to be so proud if the Irish Centre should not be able to achieve its aim because of insufficient support from the Irish here."[33] The new ambassador, Hugh McCann, was in attendance.

In his eloquent way, Cardinal Godfrey alerted his audience to the most pressing task for the Centre over the years to come. Unfortunately the need to pay the bills sometimes distracted attention from the immediate task of attending to the welfare of the Irish emigrant.

Yet after the campaigning and lobbying of the post-war years, something vital had been achieved: the establishment of a building to which Irish people in London could turn to on arrival and when in need. Father Ambrose Woods could be very content.

1   Fr Tom McNamara's successor, Fr Owen Sweeney, was also appointed as a senior chaplain, until it was pointed out by Paddy Keegan that the title 'director' perhaps carried more authority.

2   *Review of work of Emigrants' Section*, Catholic Social Welfare Bureau, Dublin, 1945.

3   'Safeguards in England for the Irish Immigrant', a speech delivered at the *Christus Rex* Conference, Rostrevor, Co. Down, 5 April, 1956.

4   Letter from Fr Ambrose Woods to Fr Carroll, 29 February 1948.

5   Letter from Fr Ambrose Woods to Cardinal Bernard Griffin, 13 March 1948.

6   Report of Irish Workers in London and Proposed Plan.

7   From the Connolly Association website.

8   Letter from Fr Ambrose Woods to Cardinal Bernard Griffin, 2 April 1948.

9   Letter from Cardinal Bernard Griffin to Fr Ambrose Woods, 21 April 1948

10   Oblate papers, London.

11   Letter from Fr Ambrose Woods to Archbishop John McQuaid, 26 April 1950..

12   Letter from Fr Tom McNamara to Fr Ambrose Woods, 24 March 1954.

13   Letter from Fr Eamonn Gilmartin to Fr Ambrose Woods, 11 November 1954.

14   Meeting in London between Cardinal Griffin, Bishop Andrew Beck and Ambassador Freddie Boland and the Archbishop of Tuam and the Bishop of Ferns, 1 April 1955.

15   Hierarchy Minutes, Dublin Diocesan Archives, 21 June 1955.

16   Pastoral Letter of Cardinal Griffin, Archbishop of Westminster, for Trinity Sunday, 1955.

17   *The Men who built Britain*, Ultan Cowley, published by Wolfhound Press, 2001.

18   Report on Emigrant Congress, 22 April 1976, Holy Cross College, Clonliffe, Dublin.

19   A postcard from George Bernard Shaw to the Irish Club. *The Irish Club Bulletin*, no. 105, October 1971.

20   *Irish Independent*, 25 February 1956.

21   Letter from Fr Tom McNamara to Fr Ambrose Woods, 24 March 1954.

22   LIC Minutes.

23   Interview with John, March 2004.

24   *Ibid*.

25   The Plan, 1948

26   *Helping Hands*, published by LIC, 1965.

27   21st *Annual Welfare Report*, 1975.

28   Interview with Mary Allen and Bridie Shaw, January 2004.

29   *Irish Press*, 19 December 1956.

30   *The Irish in Britain*, John Archer Jackson, published by Routledge Keegan Paul, 1963.

31   Letter in the *Irish Post*, 3 April 1976.

32   Carey Club programme, September 1960.

33   *Cork Examiner*, 11 March 1959.

CHAPTER FOUR

We would rather that they didn't come here

Father Tom McNamara
Father Owen Sweeney

The London Irish Centre was now firmly in business, making connections with others in the same field and with the local authority, St Pancras Borough Council. It also contributed to an understanding of how the needs of Irish emigrants to England might be better acknowledged and fulfilled.

By the end of 1956 the patrons of the Centre had been reduced to two by the death of Cardinal Griffin. He was replaced by Cardinal William Godfrey, so there were three again. Another of the original three, Bishop Andrew Beck, had been appointed to Liverpool, but he was followed onto the Trust by Bishop Bernard Wall, the new Bishop of Brentwood. Bishop Cyril Cowderoy of Southwark still remained a member.

In parallel with the London experience, the Irish Immigrants' Association in Birmingham had begun to make its mark under the guidance of Father Liam Dowling, who had once been a member of Father John Dore's team in Kilburn. Father John Dore was a priest of the Oblate order, whose parish was centred on the Church of the Sacred Heart of Jesus in Quex Road. Jerry Kivlehan has described him as *"inspirational, an amazing man of vision."*[1] An Irish Centre along similar lines to London was acquired in Moat Row in Birmingham's Bull Ring, and it began to develop its services to the Irish community of that city.

The growing reputations in Ireland of these two Centres, while not yet persuading the Irish government to offer a grant, did however create expectations among those in Ireland who were considering emigration which, when they arrived, found that they could not easily be met. Available resources rarely matched the need. Nevertheless, this was a time of achievement for both Centres.

From 1963 until the London Centre's 21st anniversary in 1975, a total of 23,596 people were recorded as having presented themselves at Camden Square for the first time. Numbers varied year by year, for example there were 776 in 1964 and 2,356 in 1975. During these same years 12,087 applicants were found jobs, which was a remarkable achievement by the welfare office in placing so many in semi-skilled and unskilled employment.

The hostels were a vital element of the service. Accommodation was needed as a base from which to look for work, although at that time the search was often not lengthy because the London economy was buoyant. This meant that the welfare service could place individuals in jobs with contractors or hotels fairly speedily. However, new arrivals needed an address, because certain employers required this before they took them on, or because they were paid a week or even two weeks in arrears. It is to Tom McNamara's credit, and in particular to that of his former parish priest George Groves, that they had long before recognised the importance of housing. Canon Groves, however, was something of an entrepreneur: the hostels at Tollington Park and Hornsey Lane Gardens were now leased to the centre at a peppercorn rent.[2] Marie Harrington, from Cork, which was Tom McNamara's county, was engaged to manage Hornsey Lane Gardens, which became known as Marian House.

In parallel with the work based in centres such as in London and Birmingham, the Irish Chaplaincy had diversified into more specialist forms of activity in the 1960s, particularly in the development of new tenures in housing, but also in an apostolate to 'travellers' and another to those from institutions in Ireland who still needed help. In London these people were assisted by the Benburb Base, a centre for young ex-offenders which was located near the Holloway Road.

The Marian Employment Agency, established in Kilburn in 1963 by John Dore, had the support of the Irish Chaplaincy. There had been a number of unscrupulous agents in Kilburn, recruiting men to work for building contractors but taking a cut from their wages. This alternative agency, with Fr Michael Buckley in charge, was set up to counter this. Recognising also that there was a need to put job-seeking on a more efficient basis, the agency offered an opportunity to those who were professionally trained and who could avail themselves of interviews in Ireland by matching them with available vacancies in England. It then also tried to pre-arrange accommodation before their arrival. By doing so it hoped to persuade at least some prospective emigrants to make a responsible decision before leaving home.

This system needed co-ordination on both sides of the Irish Sea. Father Eamonn

Casey, a far-sighted priest from Firies in Kerry, and an early enthusiast of the Marian Agency, travelled throughout Ireland with colleagues spreading the slogan of 'Responsible Emigration', while they helped to open local emigrant offices linked to the agency. The intention was to open one in every diocese if not county, so that each could distribute useful information locally and could maintain channels of communication with any emigrant's family. They could perhaps even provide financial assistance to those emigrants who needed it, either to help them return home or to receive necessary aid in England.

Later, Eamonn Casey, by then a curate on loan from Limerick diocese to Slough, Berkshire, realised like George Groves that the most pressing need for an emigrant was the provision of secure housing. He developed the Slough Savings Club Housing Aid Scheme. The club would rent or buy a property, and then rent it out to

Fr Eamonn Casey (centre) at a Galwaymen's Association dinner at the London Irish Centre in 1969.

needy families. A larger proportion of the rent would go to the club to repay the acquisition cost, and the remainder would be invested and later returned to the tenant with interest. In a short while this would enable the tenant to raise a deposit for a purchase. It was called a 'bank-your-money and buy-your-house' scheme.

A man of tremendous energy and notorious driving habits who rarely wore a clerical collar, Eamonn Casey's commitment to affordable housing led to his directorship of the Catholic Housing Aid Society. He promoted the concept of Housing Associations, particularly those which were sensitive to ethnic minorities. In 1966 he became a founder of Shelter, the national campaign for the homeless.

The Marian Agency also assisted those who had arrived unprepared. Twice a week Jim Casey, the agency's manager from Ennis, Co. Clare, was at Euston Station at 5.30 in the morning to meet the Irish Mail from Holyhead with its load of sleepy, some probably still sea-sick and bewildered emigrants who had crossed overnight. Although they had invariably been advised to bring enough money with them to ensure at least two weeks' survival in London, many arrived penniless. For this reason Jim Casey also tried to arrange interviews for jobs immediately, on the day of their arrival, for which no fees were charged. This practice helped to explain why the agency ran at an annual loss of about £1,500 a year.

As he said at the time: *"We do not encourage Irish people to emigrate and try to persuade them to remain at home, if possible, but we accept that some have to do so for economic reasons. We are especially concerned about the young people, who could barely make a living wage over here. There is also the fact that the Irish at home live in close-knit family groups, and when they come here they have to stand on their own feet for the first time. Many find themselves in small, dingy rooms and are extremely lonely. They cannot bring their wives and families until they are reasonably well established, so much of their time off work is spent in the pub."*[3]

At its height, the agency handled something like 2,500 cases a year, offering career guidance, placing applicants and even providing information on emigration to England from the offices across Ireland that Eamonn Casey had tried to set up.

With the Marian Agency also willing to take referrals from the Centre, and its own welfare or advice service now established, Tom McNamara was not willing to rest on his or anyone else's laurels. The reputation of the London Irish Centre's work was spreading to the towns and villages of Ireland itself, increasing the numbers who would travel first to Camden Square when they arrived in London. This reputation was not lost on the Irish government.

The search for funds

After careful consideration, the administrative committee agreed to send a deputation to Dublin to lobby for funds. Led by Dermot Kilgallin, one of its members, it arranged to meet the Minister for Foreign Affairs, Frank Aiken who was also the Tanaiste. Tom McNamara was a part of the deputation when they left in December 1961. Dermot Kilgallin was received by the President, while Tom McNamara met Sean Lemass, the Taoiseach. Their pleas for funding were heard with sympathy, but little action followed.

However the visit and its publicity did gain some small successes. Some churches and places of employment such as factories now made regular donations, and it was noted that a five pound cheque was received from a certain 'Mr De Valera' but whether he was the former Taoiseach and current President was never discovered.[4] This was most unlikely, but caused some speculation when the cheque was received.

The need for financial help was brought to the Irish government's attention again in 1963. Members of the committee conferred with the ambassador in London on the proposal that government funds should now be more available because of the increasing number of Irish centres beyond London and Birmingham, in cities such as Manchester and Leeds. The sum suggested was £200,000, *"a drop in the ocean in the context of government spending".*[5]

Frank Aiken visited the London Irish Centre with two other ministers, but in February he announced in the Dail that his government could not set up *"Duplicate social services in Britain, where one million Irish-born people were living. There was no substitution for the voluntary worker in helping the Irish in Britain. There were innumerable Irish clubs doing that work magnificently, and one of the best such organisations was the one in London."* In reply to questions from deputies, he said that *"If the Exchequer gave financial help to any one of these organisations, all the others would expect the same assistance."*[6] This view concealed the fact that Ireland was exporting its unemployed, which was of great benefit to the country's economy. There were also stories of Irish people escaping from justice at home before appearing in court, either on their own initiative or after advice, and even people discharged from mental institutions finding their way onto the boat.

Optimism that some financial targets were at last beginning to be met prompted Larry Morton and the committee to consider advertising for a female welfare officer at a salary of £800 a year, rising to £1,000. Up to then, all the advisory work had been done by the chaplain and his collection of volunteers, some of whom could only manage one day or one weekend or a few hours in the evening. As a result, 1962 saw the appointment of a full-time officer.

After some false starts, the committee interviewed Catherine Anne O'Sullivan from Blackrock, Cork, who accepted the job. With a degree in archaeology, she became the Centre's first professional social worker. She applied herself assiduously. Her full report on male clients for the short period 1 December 1962 to 11 January 1963 is fascinating: *"The 32 men which I saw in this period came from 18 different counties, with the greatest number coming from Dublin and Kerry. 12 men came to the Centre in December and 20 in the first 11 days of this month. 4 men were sent to the L.C.C. Reception Centre in Gordan Road, 4 to the Night Refuge in Crispin Street, 1 to Arlington Road (Arlington House), and 2 to other accommodation. I got 2 men jobs, 2 others said friends had promised them jobs, and I tried to get employment for 4 others. The only work at the moment is with London Transport on the Underground or on the buses but there are so many people trying for it that it is very hard to get taken on. 6 men were sent to the Labour Exchange. 6 men got financial assistance of a 1/- or more and 2 men had vouchers from the National Assistance Board. 1 man got his fare to Cork because his Mother was ill in hospital and he was unemployed. I telephoned to the police in Co. Mayo about a boy who had been over a few days and who insisted that he was 16° and that he was born on the 8th December 1946 or 1947. He did not know where he had spent the last two nights. He wanted money to go to Birmingham to join his brother but he had not got his brother's address. He was most annoyed that the police had been contacted. I also telephoned his Lordship (sic) Eugene O'Doherty, Bishop of Dromore, for a man whose flight to America had been delayed by a week and he had run out of money due to paying more than he expected for his visa and medical tests. His Lordship sent a cheque for £10 and the man has paid for the phone call and is staying at the Centre."*[7]

The hostel service

In the early 1960s the numbers of people arriving at the door looking for accommodation or employment had slightly dropped, in line with the drop in emigration from Ireland. One who did arrive, Ned Fogarty, was from Cork but had spent time in Wales.*"I wanted a change"*, he says, *"I knew all about the Irish Centre and the people who met you off the train at Paddington."* When he arrived in Camden Square, he was delighted. *"It was wonderful. It was a meeting place. You were among your own."*

Once he had checked into the hostel, his delight was not to last long. *"No one stayed for nothing. It cost £3.10 shillings a week. For that you got two meals a day and three on Sunday. You had to be out by nine in the morning."* He found Tom McNamara, *"a bit on the strict side. If he saw you fooling around you were out the door. He barred people for playing cards on a Sunday. We were gambling for half-pennies, playing 'twenty-five'."* Similar to pontoon, this was the favoured game, and was also called 'forty-five'. However, in Wicklow it is apparently known as 'thirty', and in Kerry for some reason as 'thirty-one'. Ned Fogarty says that he always slept in his underwear. *"Once someone stole my underwear. There were a lot of thieves about."* In spite of this he says that the hostel was clean and warm.[8]

Living upstairs at no. 52 Camden Square, Tom McNamara enjoyed his favourite drink in the bar, a gin and tonic, and a smoke of his pipe. He used to say that his job was enough to drive anyone to drink. He was a sociable and well-connected man, know-

Fr McNamara at a presentation.

ing everyone who was involved in the welfare of Irish emigrants. Apart from within the Dublin government, his influence was considerable, and he also had a supportive administrative committee now chaired by Dominic Donnelly and with Michael Casey as secretary. They were both also on the committee of the Irish Club

The welcome of the hostel for Ned Fogarty also met contrasting criticism from a few of its clients. Among the press cuttings of the Centre there is a long letter written to the Irish press, and although it is of this era it is without a date. It is right that the views of its author, which may or may not be typical, are quoted, because it gives an insight into the Centre's procedures at the time, and reveals that not everyone was content with the service provided.

"Sir – The London column of various newspapers gives an abundance of publicity to the activities of the Irish Centre at Camden Square, NW1. The emphasis is on the extensions being built, the grand dances and othe

social events being held, and the fund-raising etc. I have never read any testimonial from any Irish arrival who stayed at the hostel. I was there for four days last year, and I was not very impressed.

At Westland Row (station) I was approached by a young lady who gave me a leaflet with addresses of hostels throughout England where accommodation, advice and guidance were to be had. Being married, and in possession of a modest amount to see me over the initial days in England, I took it.

On arrival in London I went to the Centre's hostel. The entrance was impressive but what about the reception? At the desk a pleasant young lady with a Cork lilt in her accent told me I could have the last bed, and that the tariff was £3. 3s. for four days. Then she filled up a file card – age, date of birth, next of kin, etc., all the paraphernalia of being taken into a spike. No advice about employment, financial situation or domestic anxieties was referred to at this stage.

Money and receipts having been exchanged, I was taken to my bed. It had just been vacated, and the male porter seemed a trifle annoyed when I enquired about fresh linen. I never got any. The ensuing days were fraught with anxiety about employment and family worries (my wife and baby were in Ireland). The worry of meeting the cost of another four days in the hostel was never out of my mind, as my resources were running out. The pleasant girl in the office, who I found was the welfare officer, and the reverend father director never enquired about the obvious anxieties of arrivals, including myself.

The night before another four days' rent was due, I told the reverend father that I was leaving. Again he asked me nothing about my circumstances. I left the following day, and while I certainly expected nothing from them, their complete lack of interest in the arrivals from Ireland left me wondering just what their function is. Their tariff rates compare with what most landladies in London charge: no more, no less. I admit that the food is reasonable, the recreational facilities are good, and there is a fair social life with dances and a good bar (if you have the money). But when one is worried about a job, finance etc., they hardly make up for practical advice.

I wonder whether a centre could be built where emigrants could get the practical advice, assistance in genuine cases, and other help they need, and which the Irish Centre was ostensibly built to give. I am sure that other arrivals would testify that these things do not appear to exist at the centre's premises at Camden Square.

Yours etc. Anthony Fanning.

Whether the views of Anthony Fanning were widespread is unlikely, but he was also relatively fortunate that he had brought some money with him. Some people did not pay anything at all. At that time, the Centre was unfunded, and of course the stress of its circumstances could have meant that some callers were unhappy.

The welfare service

The service was stretched by extreme cases of social need, covering the entire spectrum of welfare work. These included people described as 'inadequate persons'. This expression is often seen in contemporary records, but simply means those who did not have the personal skills or resources to cope with life in London. Other clients included ex-prisoners, drug-addicts, alcoholics, psychiatric cases, missing persons cases and juveniles. Heroin addiction was a serious problem in London in the early 1960s. On a voluntary basis, Larry Morton came in each day from his doctor's practice to help those in the hostel who were dependent on this and other drugs.

The Centre also spent a great deal of time assisting Irish offenders. Some were referred by probation officers or came for help when they had been discharged from prison, or had been visited in prison by volunteers from the Centre. Nearly all had been convicted of petty crime. It was said that in Ireland a court would either sentence a man to a term of imprisonment or hint that he if left for England swiftly, he would be out of the way and his crime forgotten. Owen Sweeney describes it more delicately. *"People coming out of prison who couldn't face going back into their local community. People sadly coming out of mental hospitals, there would be a stigma attached to that. People in that condition, especially younger people, wouldn't have a single penny on arrival."*[9]

There were also intriguing monthly reports under the headings of 'Families'. Families presented some of the greatest concerns, either because they were in housing need or because they had marital problems. The former were referred to the local authority or a Housing Association or, if nothing else was available, sent into emergency hostel accommodation or bed and breakfast. The latter, who were often under huge stress because of their emigrant status or other factors, were given guidance and counselling in efforts to restore relationships which were under strain or had broken.

This work was echoed in the prosaic minutes of the welfare committee in the 1963 report. Under headings such as 'Any Other Business' on the 2 February administrative committee Tom McNamara reported that 1,034 girls had arrived at the girls' hostel during the past year. Of these, 395 were under the age of eighteen and 280 were "practically destitute" on arrival.[10] Unfortunately the records of the welfare service lack continuity or comprehensiveness, so that accurate analyses of trends and forecasts is difficult.

Some girls and women were pregnant. They had come to England to give birth, and were often found in conditions of poverty by the Crusade of Rescue,[11] which had a base at the St Louise hostel in Victoria, later to be acquired by the Centre. In the 1960s the Irish government was willing to bend its rules and fund, with a voucher or travel warrant, any pregnant girl's return. However the reception at home was sometimes unpleasant, so, predictably, they did not prefer this option. They had already chosen to escape the stigma by coming to London, but were often unaware that they were unable to obtain maternity grants or free hospital care in England. The welfare service also tried to persuade pregnant girls to have their babies in Ireland. When they did not wish to return, the workers recommended sympathetic households or landladies in London, and would also try to refer them also to local authority Social Services Departments.

A number of Irish people were also repatriated because of their mental health problems, or because they were young people who were particularly vulnerable. But the Irish government was unwilling to help repatriate those who found themselves in England without jobs, accommodation or money. *"The movement of the Irish between the two countries is so great that this would be impossible"*, a spokesman said, ignoring the fact that the movement was largely one way, *"Government policy is to develop employment opportunities in Ireland, so that people will not emigrate. We would rather they did not come here."*[12] The embassy was quite firm about this.

Although this position was later to improve during the time of Father Owen Sweeney, the exceptions made were all the help that the Centre received from

Ireland, whereas St Pancras Borough Council, which was shortly to be absorbed, together with Holborn and Hampstead, into the London Borough of Camden, made annual grants. From time to time grants were also received from Islington and Haringey councils. From the Dublin government there was nothing.

At a conference in Ireland Tom McNamara delivered a paper on the position and achievements of the Centre. He mentioned that it had recently affiliated to the newly-formed Camden Council of Social Services. The council, in recognition of its work, had *"recently voted a grant of £1,500 towards our funds – a big increase on previous contributions."* The paper ends with this stirring exhortation, *"As each emigrant is a representative of Ireland and what it stands for, we owe it to ourselves here in Ireland that each individual contributes his potential ability to a world in dire need of exemplary people. It is by working together and contributing towards a strong united body of workers that Ireland's name will flourish with pride at home and abroad."*[13]

Beyond activities at Camden Square, the London Irish used to come together for an annual fundraising concert on behalf of the Centre at the Queen's Hall, and over the years the number of venues increased with the spreading population. The Irish population was now more self-confident and more ambitious in its venues, with West End hotels regularly booked for county association dinners and dances. After a tentative start, the Albert Hall became the fixture for an annual fundraising concert on a date near St. Patrick's Day.

A new hall

A new hall was soon to open in the Centre, but before it was completed the AGMs took place in the Irish Club in Eaton Square or occasionally at a West End hotel. One of the latter in 1963 was a lavish affair which included a fundraising dinner and dance after. Aer Lingus, thanks to Tommy Dunne, provided the food, which was especially flown over from Ireland. The Joe Loss Orchestra performed the music, and Tommy Trinder was an excellent cabaret. A wine importer and Harley Street specialist, Dr Fitzpatrick, sold tickets, and the event raised £5,000. With a pang of socialist guilt, Lord Longford decided that he could not attend, because as a Labour peer he was concerned what might be reported in the *Evening Standard*. He obviously missed the fun.

The new hall, to be called the J F Kennedy Memorial Hall, was built by the contractor M J Gleeson. Jack Gleeson was on the early committees. Excavation work for its foundations began in May 1964 on the site of a garage and an adjoining patch of garden. The late President's brother, Senator Edward Kennedy, looked at the plans in London in June 1964, as a guest of Dominic Donnelly. It appears that this inspection took place elsewhere than at the Centre, because in a photograph there is a portrait of Churchill hanging on the wall, something most unlikely at Camden Square. Tom McNamara is also there, and this must have been one of his last formal engagements before his retirement. It is understood that Senator Kennedy came for the photo opportunity, said a few words, had a soft drink and then departed.[14]

Farewell to Father Mac

On 8 October 1964, after a grand farewell and presentation as a guest of the Carey Club at the Gresham Ballroom which 200 people attended, Tom McNamara left the London Irish Centre to become once again a parish priest at the newly created parish of St Mellitus and St Gabriel, in familiar

Senator Edward Kennedy being shown plans by Jack Gleeson for the Memorial Hall to be named after his brother, the late President, John F Kennedy, June 1964.

Upper Holloway, near Archway. At one time Catholic worshippers here had used a Nissen hut in the rear garden of the Tollington Park premises, but a nearby Evangelical Church found that by 1959 it had less need for its larger building and offered it to Canon George Groves who was pleased to acquire it. In due course a new church was built here, with its foundation stone laid in May 1967. *"He done a marvellous business there. He was well able to wheel and deal"*, was Mossie O'Riordan's description of the transaction.[15] Mossie O'Riordan, who was Operational Director of Joseph Murphy and Co, then based at a depot near the Centre off Agar Grove, became a loyal friend and benefactor over many years.

Tom McNamara's parish was a short distance from Camden Square, so he was able to return to the Centre for particular occasions. One of these, in February 1965, was a deserved presentation to him by Dominic Donnelly of a silver salver and a cheque. Having been one of those who had argued the case for the Centre's existence from the late 1940s, and then had worked as its chaplain or director for nine years from 1955, 'Father Mac' left an almost indelible mark on the Centre, and on welfare provision for Irish emigrants to London. His foresight had placed hostel accommodation as a major priority for the emigrant, and his network of contacts ensured that many were placed in digs or lodging houses when there was no available space in the hostels. Yet in his time it was estimated that no fewer that 5,600 men had stayed at the hostel at Camden Square, and more than 6,000 women had been accommodated at Hornsey Lane Gardens.[16] Other networks, such as the Marian Agency, were able to offer employment, and it also is a tribute to both the Centre and the agency that employers came back again and again to fill their vacancies.

Nevertheless Cardinal Heenan at the Westminster Diocese felt that he had completed sufficient time at the Centre, and his request to Archbishop McQuaid in Dublin produced Father Owen Sweeney to follow him into Camden Square.

A few years later, after his retirement from St Mellitus and St Gabriel, Tom McNamara returned home to Ireland. One evening in January 1976, on his way to visit a curate in Tipperary, he felt a pain in his heart. As Mossie O'Riordan, a fellow Corkman, says, *"He pulled into a lay-by near Bandon and snuffed it."*[17] He was fifty-nine years of age.

Father Mac's funeral, at Newtown, near Charleville, Co. Cork, was a huge affair. Bill Cagney, the director of the Centre at this time, arranged a coach from Camden Square. The funeral was also attended by the Irish Ambassador, Eamonn Casey now Bishop of Kerry, Michael O'Halloran, MP for Islington North and other civic representatives.[18] It was said that, *"if any man burned himself out working on behalf of the Irish in London, it was Tom McNamara."*

His portrait in oils was commissioned by the Council of Irish County Associations. The artist was Maurice Litten, a member of the Royal Society of British Portrait Painters. A photograph was used to assist in the likeness of his face, but Dick Butler, then chairman of CICA and a well-known Tipperary man in London, had to wear a suit and a clerical collar to pose for the artist. It is said that he looks decidedly uncomfortable in the costume. The painting was unveiled on 4 November 1976. Known as *Father Mac*, it is now severely stained by nicotine, but still hangs in the hall which is named after him.

Father Owen Sweeney

Tom McNamara's successor was an interesting assignment.

Father Owen Sweeney was originally from Falcarragh, Co. Donegal. After his ordination in 1952, his first appointment was as a curate in Rathdrum, Co. Wicklow, where he made a name for himself with amateur dramatic entertainments in the parish. In Drimnagh, Dublin, he ran talent competitions for two years, and with the money raised built a parish concert hall. As if by a perverse fate, he was assigned by the Irish Chaplaincy from a quiet parish with a penchant for aspiring entertainers to a position as 'camp chaplain' in heavy industry on sites in Britain, for many of which the main contractor was McAlpine's. Owen Sweeney was a resourceful man, and willing to serve the Irish worker away from his home and local parish. At the vast steelworks site at Llanwern in Wales there were 11,000 employed, of whom 6,000 were estimated as Irish. The men lived near the site in prefabricated huts, which were laid out as miniature towns, with other huts designed as shops, cinemas and a post office. They made it seem like home, but the hardest time was for the married men.*"What really cut them up"*, he has said,*"was when their children did not recognise them when they returned, they had been away so long."*[19] As chaplain on this site, Owen Sweeney lived in a 'terrapin' provided by McAlpine's who also adapted a prefab hut next to one of the hostels as a chapel.

The construction company, Sir Robert McAlpine, had been founded by 'Con-

Fr Owen Sweeney at a Christmas celebration. Cllr Charles Ratchford, the last Mayor of St Pancras, is to the right.

crete Bob' McAlpine in the 1880s. He had been at one time a bricklayer from Scotland reputed as being able to lay 2,000 bricks in a day. The firm's management passed from father to son. More recently chairman Sir William McAlpine has acknowledged the contribution the Irish labourer had made: *"Since the late eighteenth century the Irish have played a major role in the expansion of British industry and of the country's canal, road and rail network. The success of the British construction industry owes a great deal to Irish skills in excavation, and construction, and their contribution to the development of the industry has been immeasurable".*[20]

From Llanwern, Owen Sweeney was moved to the Oldbury nuclear power station site in Gloucestershire, where again

he ministered to many thousands of Irishmen on the site. *"I came to appreciate the inestimable value of their contribution to human well-being",* he said. *"I came to regard them as the true nobility of society, humble hard-working men who rarely complained about their lot."*[21]

In 1963 he was recalled to become chaplain for a year at University College, Dublin, before Cardinal Heenan, Archbishop of Westminster, hearing of his work for the Chaplaincy, requested Archbishop McQuaid to send him to the London Irish Centre. He arrived in July 1964, not really having known London before.

Cardinal Heenan visited the Centre just a week after Owen Sweeney's arrival and saw something of the plans for extension. Before he left he presented Owen Sweeney with a cheque, who later said, *"It was a very big donation at the time."*[22]

The four trustees of the Centre were a distinguished group. Two were Cardinal Heenan, Archbishop of Westminster, and Lord Longford, by now the Lord Privy Seal in Harold Wilson's cabinet and Leader of the House of Lords. Owen Sweeney has described Lord Longford as, *"A thorough gentleman. He was a good socialist, concerned for people in need. He was also absent-minded, and would get in his car and then turn to me to say 'Where am I going'?"*[23] With them were also Lawrie Arnold, one of the founders of the Centre, and Jack Gleeson, the contractor. He now had the KCSG, or the award of the Knight Commander of the Order of St Gregory.

The administrative committee was still chaired by Dominic Donnelly, who also was a leading figure at the Irish Club, and described as "a self-educated, self-made man who had done well in business in England but never lost his humility". Owen Sweeney was made Hon. Treasurer, as had been Tom McNamara before him.

The raising of funds was never far from the minds of the committee, and of course its 'senior chaplain'. Paddy Keegan had noticed that Owen Sweeney had been signing all his letters with this title. He suggested that he should style himself instead as 'director', because this was a better description and carried more authority.

Within a few weeks of Owen Sweeney's arrival, the Centre sponsored in November 1964 a screening of the documentary film *Years of Lightning, Day of Drums*, in the unlikely setting of the Empire Pool, Wembley. The exhibition rights had been offered in order to raise funds for the John F Kennedy Memorial Hall then being built. A general appeal had only brought in a disappointing £1,165, so events of this sort to raise further funds were important.

Narrated by the actor Gregory Peck, the film showed the exuberant life and tragic death of President Kennedy. It included his achievements for civil rights, the Peace Corps, the conquest of space, the Berlin crisis and his presidential visit to Ireland.

The evening was made complete by the singing of the Gaelic League Choir of some of the late President's favourite sings, including *The Boys of Wexford* and *Kelly, the Boy from Killane*. The auditorium of the Empire Pool was filled with not only Centre guests, but also with US servicemen who were stationed within travelling distance of north-west London. Senior US diplomats and the Irish Ambassador, John Molloy, who had met President Kennedy in the USA, attended along with Owen Sweeney and Mayor Charlie Ratchford of St Pancras Borough Council.

Owen Sweeney's first Christmas in London was marked by an event that could have been embarrassing. A man living nearby, known as Bobby or 'the Bull' Flanagan, was returning home to Navan for good. He needed some money and offered his neighbour, Ned Fogarty, his television set for ten pounds. That was a week's wages for Ned Fogarty, and he could not afford it. Bobby Flanagan then sold the set to Owen Sweeney, for twenty pounds. Two weeks later Rediffusion came to Flanagan's address to repossess the set, and followed directions to Owen Sweeney at the Centre. Eventually the debt was paid, but as Ned Fogarty says, *"The parish priest got caught."*[24]

Camden was formed in 1965 from the old boroughs of Holborn, St Pancras and Hampstead. At the ceremony to mark its formation, the Marquis of Camden *said "I was rather surprised they called the place Camden ... I suppose I'm sentimental and pleased about it. Camden Borough Council might also look good on the dustcarts."*[25] The first Mayor of Camden was Sammy Fisher,

A county association in a party mood.

later Lord Fisher, who had been a head teacher. Owen Sweeney has described him, *"… as a close friend. I had great respect for him. And in the very beginning, when he came in, he assured me that if there was anything in the world that he could do to help, he would. He came to several functions in the Irish Centre."*[26]

New halls and activities

Functions at the Centre were important for social and revenue reasons, but there was nowhere really suitable to hold them. The building of the Kennedy Memorial Hall extension was intended to be a solution.

Initially, a three storey building had been envisaged, but the second storey had to be halted while planning permission was obtained. Because this hall was classified as a public building, facilities such as fire exits had to be incorporated. Negotiations with the council dragged on from months into years. In the meantime,

wet weather damaged the temporary roof, which resulted in even more delays. There was also flooding in the basement. Finally, planning permission for the third storey was not forthcoming, and so a decision was made to keep it at two. However the district surveyor later condemned part of the second storey roof, and it had to be replaced.

A second phase of refurbishment, which fell under different headings but included the hostel accommodation, began in 1964. This was completed in November 1965 at a cost of £4,980. Camden Council grant-aided the Centre at some £1,500 a year, but as Brian Duggan, the secretary of the administrative committee, remarked with dubious confidence, *"Only God can say where the rest of the finances come from."*

Whether or not God could predict this, the screening of *Years of Lightning, Day of Drums* did raise some much-needed cash, but even before the hall was com-

The construction of the John F Kennedy Memorial Hall, on the corner of Murray Street and Murray Mews, 1964.

pleted it became clear that this would not be enough to meet the demands likely to be made on it, and so another phase of fundraising had to be contemplated.

The year 1965 saw the opening of the ground floor of the hall by Archbishop Walsh in the presence of the US Ambassador, and also the opening of a new lounge bar upstairs, although they were not fully functioning until 1969. The lounge was later named the Douglas Hyde Lounge, after the poet and founder of the Gaelic League, who was the first President of Ireland. The Irish Centre Club based itself here. When it finally opened, the chapel within the roof structure of the Kennedy annexe heard three Masses every Sunday.

A portrait of the late President Kennedy was commissioned by the Claremans Association, to be displayed in the Kennedy Memorial Hall. Unfortunately the artist, Paddy Marrinon, had included in the background the famous Cliffs of Moher, a majestic feature of Co. Clare's coastline. This did not endear the painting to members from the other thirty-one Irish counties, each with claims to majestic features.

To ensure that the hall was used as much as possible, parish reunions and any other activities which brought in letting fees were encouraged. Almost every night of the week there was a counties' activity of some sort in the Irish Centre Club, which had reverted to its original name in 1965, from a Derry Association Dance, to a Galway bacon and cabbage supper, to a Corkman's Social with music by Pat McNamee and his band. In the early days, the associations were known as 'mans' associations, and it took a few determined women from among their memberships to change this to the much more inclusive name, 'county' associations.

On other nights there was bingo at

8.15 pm and a social until 11.00 pm. The bar was open all day on Sundays. Mary Kenny used to run a whist drive. Ned Fogarty remembers the singer Michael O'Duffy, 'The Golden Voice of Ireland' but said to be even more popular in Russia, performing at a charity recital. Another singer was John Downey, *"a beautiful tenor like John McCormack."*[27] However, Owen Sweeney, who certainly knew O'Duffy well, did not for some reason appreciate singing in the bar, and tried on occasion to prevent it.

These events and performances helped to increase income, but also created certain tensions. Some of the residential neighbours near the Centre were not altogether pleased with its arrival on their territory, and from time to time protests and objections were made to the director or to Camden Council about its noisier activities. Following a court case in June 1970, double-glazing in the Kennedy Hall was installed at a cost of £1,000. This in turn led to further problems over the resulting lack of ventilation, and an air-conditioning system had to be included which cost a further £23,151. The second storey would eventually add another £10,000 to the cost.

These difficulties meant that the cost of the new hall escalated sharply and expenditure and the regular payments of wages and services far outstripped the Centre's revenue. Fund-raising consultants O'Byrne and Hawker were invited to propose ideas to meet this debt, but the committee decided after all not to engage them. In later years firms of fund-raisers were employed by the Centre with no success.

There was never enough money for the needs of the welfare service, and almost every Sunday Owen Sweeney visited Catholic parish churches in London to make an appeal. He always found the response to be generous. However, by 1965 the debt had risen to £26,956 12s. 5d and by 1967 to £46,803. Inflation, which was rising fast in the 1960s, made the debt increasingly difficult to contain. Hard economic facts faced the Centre over the next few years.

Living upstairs at no. 52 Camden Square, Owen Sweeney has described the daily routine. *"There was a sameness about the Irish Centre all the time. Every morning when you come down from upstairs there would be a line of people sat waiting for the welfare social worker to come on duty. They would be looking for employment. Others would have psychiatric problems, drug problems and things like that. The social workers would try to do as much as you put onto them for what they were qualified to do, a lot would ask to see the priest."* He described some of the other callers. *"You would be told they had received a telegram saying that the mother was dead and they should come home immediately. Now you never give money in that case, you would ring the parish priest and find that the mother had been dead for the last twenty years. I remember one day ringing way down in Galway, because a man said that his mother was seriously ill. I rang the Garda and he said that the woman had passed his window just five minutes ago."* He also recalls the gang in Dublin, and there may have been more than one, which would send the telegrams. *"Every week they would go round from church to church, welfare agency to welfare agency and convent to convent"*, hoping that the fare home would be later collected.[28]

Paddy Keegan recalls that within weeks of his arrival Sweeney had considered appointing an order of Sisters, the Ladies of Mary, to carry out tasks such as managing the upstairs hostel. They visited, but found that the Green Room downstairs was in such a mess that they declined. To assist Miona Hanly, who had been appointed in 1964 from Dublin, with the welfare service, he recruited a professional social worker called Tessa Honeywell. He regarded this as a bit of a breakthrough because she was English, she knew the British welfare system backwards and was the first non-Catholic on the professional staff of the centre. Ruth Duffy, a second qualified social worker, also joined the team.

Because of the amount of work, the Westminster Diocese also found it necessary to assign a second chaplain, Father Paddy Murray, who arrived in August 1965. Born in Kildare, but living in New Ross for most of his life, Paddy Murray was ordained at St Peter's, Wexford. He had spent the last two years at St Joan of Arc, in Highbury, north London, as Irish emigrant chaplain.

To accommodate the additional staff, a property at no. 12 Murray Street, across the road from the Centre, was purchased in 1966 for £3,600.

The welfare staff continually tried to persuade all those under eighteen who arrived at its door to return to Ireland, and for this a formal scheme was finally developed with the Embassy that if the Centre provided a ticket the Embassy would refund its value. This was grudgingly supported. In Dublin, Owen Sweeney met Frank Aiken at the Ministry of Foreign Affairs in St Stephen's Green, and had dinner with him at his home the next day. *"I had many meetings with the Irish Embassy and the Minister for Foreign Affairs in Dublin, to try and get the Irish government to give grants towards the welfare of Irish emigrants, and they were very, very reluctant to do that".* However, he did achieve some concessions. *"The problem that we had was that very young people were arriving in London, 15 or 16 and completely unprepared. I remember getting the government to agree to get the young people back*

to Ireland. The Irish government would pay their fare back, that was the first step."[29]

Within the Centre itself small improvements had begun to make a difference to its clients. Many people could not obtain employment convincingly because of their unkempt appearance. A pool of clothes was therefore established from which items could be borrowed. Lockers were also installed to reduce the problem of petty theft. By September 1964 a washing machine had been purchased. Another obvious improvement was that the route from the front door to the welfare office through the veritable maze inside the building should be sign-posted, so that visitors would not become lost or sit waiting longer than was necessary.

Owen Sweeney had a reputation of being a bit of a prankster. The amateur dramatics at his previous parishes in Dublin were obviously an inspiration for him. He would often display his talent to discover what new arrivals might feel about the Centre by joining them in disguise in the queue. He described one man as a layabout, who used to come into the Centre for what he could take. *"He had a hot temper too, but one morning before he arrived I dressed up in old clothes and put an old wig on and makeup and sat down on the stool that he would sit on. He came in and sat down beside me and said 'What are you doing here?' I said, 'I am doing here for the same reason as yourself'. He said 'You shouldn't be interfering with these decent people here', meaning me, the priest. I said 'It's the likes of you that causes all the trouble in this place'. He then got up and took off his coat and had his fists up for a fight. I had to quickly tear off my wig and makeup."*[30] This was one ingenious way that Owen Sweeney researched the condition of the callers at the Centre.

One of those who arrived at this time was Sally Mulready, from Dublin, who was looking for a job with accommodation provided. The first person she met was Mary Kenny, in her usual position near the door as a volunteer receptionist, who gave her the address of the Strand Palace Hotel. From then, Sally Mulready has maintained contact with the Centre in many beneficial situations, and is herself one of its success stories.[31]

Throughout these years the debt of the Centre continued to climb. In 1964 it reached £32,000. A year or so later there screamed an ominous headline in the *Irish Independent*. 'Irish Centre may close'. The story that followed offered a grim picture: *"The Irish Centre in Camden Town is preparing to face the worst crisis in its history. The British government's stringent financial measures threaten the future of the Centre and it may be forced to close its doors within a few months. An urgent appeal for aid is now going out to all Irish organisations and societies in Britain. The Centre, already in debt to the tune of £50,000, is unable to raise a further loan. 'Whenever we appeal for funds in Ireland the reply is that contributions go only to those charities originating in Ireland', New Ross born Fr Paddy Murray exclaimed. 'My God, surely our charity originates in Ireland'. Running costs at the Centre are at £1,000 per week, including salaries at £300 per week."*[32] There were few ideas of how to deal with this.

The fiftieth anniversary of the Easter Rising of 1916 was commemorated by an event in the Kennedy Hall. Politically, the London Irish Centre tends to adopt a nationalist position, which reflects the views of most of its users, but with a sense of moderation. Over the years its halls have been host to all sorts of meetings, with the building available, as its constitution asserts, for Irishmen and women of all persuasions.

Within a year or two of the new hall's opening, however, it became the source of bitter controversy. Some in the Council of Irish County Associations felt that its charges were too high, particularly as the counties contributed so much to the income of the Centre. Sweeney pointed out that these contributions had been *"Largely negatived (sic) by the privilege of free associate membership of the Irish Centre Club, a privilege terminated at the last AGM of the club."*[33] However, after strong protests the committee decided to take action, and a donation was sent to the Michael Collins Memorial Fund in Ireland.

Paddy O'Connor

After Councillor Fisher in 1966, the second Mayor of Camden to be elected was Cllr Paddy O'Connor, a Wexford man who was also Camden's first Irish Mayor. Almost as soon as the Mayoral chain was placed around his neck, he changed the colour of the Mayor's notepaper from Camden's corporate orange to green. He had strong political views, forged in his upbringing, and was among the defiant St Pancras tenants who erected street barricades during the rent strikes of the late 1950s. Even while Mayor he was arrested by the police for obstruction in Robert Street during a protest demonstration.[34]

Paddy O'Connor had arrived in London from Bray, Co Wicklow, at the age of fifteen looking for work. The year was 1931, and there were no jobs. For a few years he managed to commute between England and Ireland, never staying long in either country, but six years later he finally decided to settle in London. One of his first jobs, at a salary of nineteen shillings a week, was selling vegetables and flowers. He also worked as a barman, waiter, kitchen porter, navvy, dishwasher and engineer. *"You name it, I've done it"* he said, before he later settled into the job of a bus inspector.

As first citizen for a year, Cllr O'Connor was Camden's most famous Irishman, and was invited to speak at the centre's AGM. Obviously relishing his status, as Mayor and also Vice President of the Centre, he described himself as *"The only Irishman aware of the importance of public relations"*, and in that role managed to make the wider council environment well aware of its obligations towards the large and relatively well-organised Irish community in Camden. He also maintained that the basis for the row over the charges of the Kennedy Hall was really about whether people would rally around to keep the Centre going. In his forthright way he reminded the Council of Irish Counties and others that it now cost at least £36,000 a year to run the Centre.

In 1967, his year as Mayor over, he joined the council's Immigration Problems Steering Group. *"When I came to this country"*, he said, *"It was very much a case of coming and going, but now people are settling down in family groups. In the old days they were usually poorly educated. They used to say that Ireland's main exports were beef and men. Unlike other immigrant groups, they often went home because they lived near enough to do so. The whole situation for the Irish immigrants has changed since I came here. There is a much larger cross-section of people who are doctors, lawyers, nurses and building contractors. Many of the immigrants now have houses, families and children at school in this country. They are also taking a much greater part in social organisations, politics and trade union work."* Nevertheless, Paddy O'Connor was able to sum up the attitude of the Irish as very much like, *"Today is here and the devil take tomorrow."*[35]

When he finally stepped down, he retained his links with the Centre by becoming a member of its administrative committee.

In January 1965, for greater efficiency,

Cllr Paddy O'Connor, at the Camden Arts Centre when Mayor of Camden.

and on the advice of Cardinal Heenan, the Marian Employment Agency opened a branch office in Camden Square, managed first by Maurice Twomey and then in 1967 by Austin Fields. Of 846 people seeking employment that year, 556 were placed in jobs. It also sponsored courses for clergy from the Irish Chaplaincy and others who would have to work with new emigrants in offering welfare advice and other facilities. The one-week course involved visits to building sites, clubs, pubs, dance-halls and also to hostels, so those who enrolled were introduced to the background and pressures which faced their work, and shown what problems to expect. No doubt some of the more austere students were a little surprised.

By 1968 the agency's manager in Quex Road was John Murphy. It continued to operate on the two sites until 1975, and by the late 1960s about 3,000 people had obtained employment through using its services. But by 1971 only 592 job appli cations were made through the agency, and it closed the following year. At one time it had been envisaged that the agency would have become self-financing by charging introductory fees to potential employers, but in practice only a minority paid their fees.

The welfare report for 1966 revealed evidence that many emigrants had limited education and lacked self-confidence. *"Responsible and planned emigration"* was the only way to lead towards a reduction of welfare cases dealt with at the Irish Centre. Such a positive approach would also ensure that the Irish, *"who have so much unrealised potential – will offer their full contribution to Britain."*[36] The same report stated that extensive improvements were carried out in the men's hostel at Camden Square. Similar work was initiated at the girls' hostel in Hornsey Lane Gardens.

Income was reported at £24,000 during this year with expenditure running at £36,000, with the capital debt rising to £43,000. *"With the purchase of a valuable adjoining property* (no. 12 Murray Street) *under way and its development a vital necessity, the Centre must face capital expenditure in the region of £200,000 over the next five years. The sources on which the Centre depended for revenue until now cannot just provide the money that will be wanted for the future, as, apart from capital development, running costs will rise to at least £50,000 per year. New sources must be explored."* Since then, this search for new sources has echoed around the London Irish Centre.

Owen Sweeney's retirement

The Centre was seriously in debt and, partly because of the resulting stress, Owen Sweeney was in bad health. *"I had bad chest problems, and had to leave London because of the smog."*[37] He was posted by the Archdiocese and Hierarchy back to Ireland, away from London's pollution, in January 1967. His chaplain, Paddy Murray, remained in Camden Square, but he left later in the year to take up an appointment as Dean of St Peter's College, Wexford.

On his retirement, Cllr Paddy O'Connor presented Owen Sweeney with a St Pancras Aldermanic Badge on behalf of the council. In a letter which followed the presentation, he wrote *"I know you will treasure the Badge and long may it remind you of the happy times you spent and the many good friends you made in Camden."* The badge now has pride of place in Owen Sweeney's Dublin flat.

He returned to a succession of posts in Ireland. He first worked in Clondalkin as a curate, and from there to Clonliffe Seminary as president and then to Athy, Whitehall, Tallaght and Sandymount. Believing that the age of retirement for a parish priest should be at sixty-five rather than seventy-five, he has chosen to drop a rank to become a curate at Sandymount. Paradoxically, he was appointed Monsignor, *"I have never allowed anyone to call me that, I am always called Father Owen."*[38]

His departure left the Westminster Diocese in something of a dilemma as to who might replace him. In spite of the experience of Paddy Murray at the Centre, it was felt there was no priest from the diocese able to take on the challenge.

Meanwhile, the Oblate Congregation up the road in Kilburn, under the leadership of John Dore, was creating something of a reputation. As early as 1966 Cardinal Heenan had considered the Oblates a good choice to take on the Centre. They had ministered to parishes in England and Scotland for over a hundred years, and were experienced in a wider involvement with the emigrant community. It was clear that the work at the Centre had developed beyond ministry and advice into the areas of cultural and social activities. With an order such as the Oblates supporting the Centre, Cardinal Heenan believed that they would also bring some stability to its future.[39]

[1] Interview Fr Jerry Kivlehan, June 2004.
[2] Interview Paddy Keegan, July 2004.
[3] *Hampstead and Highgate Express*, 25 August 1967.
[4] Irish Welfare Fund minutes, 2 March 1962.
[5] *Cork Examiner*, 15 February 1964.
[6] *Irish Press*, 25 February 1963.
[7] LIC Archives. Welfare Service Annual Report, 1963
[8] Interview Ned Fogarty, April 2004.
[9] Interview Fr Owen Sweeney, October 2003.
[10] Irish Welfare Fund report, 2 February 1963.
[11] The Crusade of Rescue was founded in the 19th century by the Society of St Vincent de Paul to locate and assist young people and families in need. It is now subsumed by the Catholic Children's Society (Westminster).
[12] Irish Welfare Fund minutes, 2 March 1962.
[13] Paper of Fr Tom McNamara, undated.
[14] Interview Paddy Keegan, July 2004.
[15] Interview Mossie O'Riordan, March 2004.
[16] *Cork Examiner*, 9 October 1964.
[17] Interview Mossie O'Riordan, March 2004.
[18] *Cork Examiner*, 5 February 1976.
[19] Interview Fr Owen Sweeney, October 2003.
[20] Sir William McAlpine, 18 May 2000.
[21] *Irish Post*, 10 March 2001.
[22] Interview Fr Owen Sweeney, October 2003.
[23] *Ibid.*
[24] Interview Ned Fogarty, April 2004.
[25] *Hampstead and Highgate Express*, 29 May 1964.
[26] Interview Fr Owen Sweeney, October 2003.
[27] Interview Ned Fogarty, May 2004.
[28] Interview Fr Owen Sweeney, October 2003.
[29] *Ibid.*
[30] *Ibid.*
[31] Correspondence Sally Mulready, June 2004.
[32] *Sunday Press*, 31 July 1966.
[33] *Kilburn Times*, 8 August 1966.
[34] *Local Government Reorganisation. The first years of Camden*, Enid Wistrich, published by the London Borough of Camden, 1972.
[35] *Hampstead and Highgate Express*, 25 August 1967.
[36] LIC Welfare Report, 1966.
[37] Interview Fr Owen Sweeney, October 2003.
[38] *Ibid.*
[39] From *The Phantom and the Phoenix*, the memoirs of Fr Frank Ryan, November 2000.

CHAPTER FIVE

Do the job that has to be done

Father Paddy Hackett

John Dore, a Limerick man, was an influential figure among the Catholic clergy of north London. As a priest in the Congregation of the Oblates of Mary Immaculate, he could therefore also put the initials OMI after his name.

Father Gerry French, who was director of the Irish Chaplaincy from 1996 to 2000, and not an Oblate, has said: *"The Oblates had a great way of working with people. They went to the front line – whether it was the camps in Wales, Chelmsley Wood when it was the largest housing estate in Britain, or to Camden or Birmingham. They had an empathy with ordinary people and a special feel for the most vulnerable. They get on with the job. There's no grandeur about them."* Their commitment to the poor often means that they are in direct contact with emigrant communities.

John Dore's parish church was the Church of the Sacred Heart of Jesus. It was so popular, it is said, that he and his assistant priests were officiating at thirteen packed masses each Sunday for no less than 12,000 people. Loudspeakers were wired up in the yard outside so that Mass could be heard there by those unable to get into the church. Even the neighbouring Methodist church was sometimes used as an overspill for particularly large congregations.

There were also so many wishing to make confessions, rather than there was so much to confess, they would continue the whole day. Where most churches might handle them in a few hours, six of the priests from Quex Road presbytery entered their confession boxes at 10.00 am on Saturday mornings and, in shifts, were still hearing from 'sinners' at 9.00 pm.

Father Paul Byrne, who had started as a teacher at Belcamp College, the Oblate school at Malahide near Dublin, and then served as a student priest at Quex Road, says that John Dore *"was perfect for the time, a big man, a great teacher, a very good businessman, he took risks."*[1] Byrne little realised then that his own career as a parish priest and provincial would be almost entirely dominated by issues of housing and Irish emigration. He developed Catholic Housing Aid across England, and was the first director of Shelter in London in 1969. Its success encouraged the formation of the Housing Corporation by the British government in 1974. Returning to emigration, he later became Executive Secretary of the Irish Episcopal Commission for Emigrants, and in this position tackled the Irish government over its lack of commitment to Irish men and women scattered across the world and, of course, also in Britain. He was eventually awarded an OBE for his achievements in housing. He received from the Labour Party the James Larkin Award for Services to the Irish Community in April 2004.

John Dore also had an entrepreneurial sense of what attracted people to his church.

He arranged the sale of twenty-eight different Irish county newspapers outside its entrance every week, collected by the Legion of Mary direct from Heathrow airport before dawn. The value of such a service to his parishioners should not be under-estimated, because it helped create a cultural identity among newly-arrived emigrants as much as it brought them together for Mass. The priory also chartered its own aircraft to fly parishioners home to Ireland for Christmas and the summer holidays, and also of course for the unmissable all-Ireland final at Croke Park.

The Quex Road priory helped many people to buy their own homes by using its savings bank scheme, similar to that which Eamonn Casey had pioneered in Slough. The scheme was set up to beat the profiteering in housing which had started to take hold in Kilburn, and it later became a part of the range of services of the Catholic Housing Aid Society. The Oblates were also involved practically in housing, by managing some small hostels in the area. In addition, they had a good knowledge of the local Irish landladies who were willing to accept the referrals from a local priest if they had the room.

This commitment to help the homeless, the disadvantaged and the poor, was part of a long tradition. The Church of the Sacred Heart had been founded by Father Robert Cooke, Provincial Superior of the Oblate Order, who had ridden in a horse-drawn omnibus from east London to Kilburn in 1864. He wrote in 1865, *"I have heard my brother, who is a priest of great experience, say that there was no suburb in London where a new mission and church were required more than in Kilburn."*[2] There were few dwellings there at the time, and even fewer Irish people or Catholics, although there was some multiple occupation of houses by Irish emigrants in Kilburn Lane.[3] It is thought that perhaps there were Irish communities living in camps, although this was unrecorded in the census. In Kilburn Robert Cooke noted that *"All around were extensive fields, trees, wild flowers and a few scattered houses."*[4] This must have been a pleasant contrast to the filthy slums of Tower Hill, where the Oblates were in ministry. He would also have been aware that the former Catholic Priory of Kilburn had been dissolved by King Henry VIII in 1536.

The Oblates returned to Kilburn, and on 1 February 1865 rented property at 1 Greville Road. The following day they celebrated Mass here with five worshippers. A year later they acquired four acres of the Cotton estate in Quex Road for what must have been an expensive £4,000. A temporary church was built, but Father Arnoux, the parish priest, was now in competition with those whom he called 'the ritualists', or the Anglo-Catholics, who were building huge churches in London such as St Augustine's in nearby South Kilburn.[5]

The order played a part in the Catholic revival inspired by Cardinals John Newman and Henry Manning in the late 19th century, of which the building of the Church of the Sacred Heart is regarded as one expression of the order's achievement in creating magnificent spaces for worship. It was designed by the architect Edward Pugin, who was also responsible for Southwark Cathedral and for Maynooth Seminary, Co. Kildare. After a relatively short period of construction, the church was opened in 1879 with a ceremony and a blessing from Cardinal Manning, who was then Archbishop of Westminster. He was a man for all the people, as familiar with the poor parishioners of Kilburn as with the gossip of Mayfair drawing-rooms, the demands of the striking dockworkers when he heard them in Bermondsey in 1889 and the atmosphere of High Mass at the Oratory.

Because the records of local fund-raising do not reveal many names with an Irish origin living in Kilburn at that time, it is believed that the Irish population was attracted to the district by this great church, rather than that it was built to serve those already resident.

The founder of the Oblates was Charles Joseph Eugene de Mazenod, a priest from an aristocratic and wealthy background, who was born in Aix-en-Provence, in France, in 1782. His family fled the French Revolution of 1798 and its subsequent Reign of Terror by travelling to Italy. An acrimonious split took place there between his parents and, on his return to France alone in 1802, the shock of seeing the condition of post-revolutionary Catholicism invited a call to the priesthood. In 1811 he was ordained in Amiens.

De Mazenod returned to Provence, and started to exercise his calling among the needy, the prison population, and the peasants in the remote countryside. This incurred the opposition of the local clergy, who tended to be from upper or middle-class families with little real contact with the ordinary people who spoke a different dialect. He persevered by seeking similarly committed priests who were prepared to work outside what they regarded were out-moded structures. They described themselves as 'Missionaries of Provence', preaching in the local provençal dialect, and travelling on foot from village to village. Between these public forays they withdrew into a quiet communion of intense prayer, study and worship.

So that they could be assured of some continuity of purpose, de Mazenod went directly to the Pope to beseech for formal recognition of the group as a Religious Congregation of Pontifical Right. His

St Eugene de Mazenod.

persistence paid off, and on 17 February 1826 Pope Leo XII approved the new Congregation as the Oblates of Mary Immaculate.

By 1856, de Mazenod's stature in France was such that Napoleon III appointed him a senator. At his death in 1861 he was the country's most senior bishop. Pope John Paul II declared him a Saint as recently as 1995, and in recognition of de Mazenod's own unhappy family life he is regarded now as the Patron Saint of dysfunctional families. The Oblate Congregation began to spread beyond France to Switzerland, England and Ireland. Because of his missionary commitment, de Mazenod was likened to a 'second Paul', and bishops came to ask him to provide Oblates for their expanding overseas missions. Despite their small numbers he responded with enthusiasm, and in due course OMI priests spread to Canada and the USA, to Ceylon, Basutoland and South Africa.

The seal of the order bears the inscription: *Evangelizari pauperibus misit me,* which translates from the Latin as 'He sent me to evangelise the poor'. It was then an evangelising congregation, in particular "to proclaim Christ and his Kingdom to the most abandoned", and Oblates from Dublin followed the waves of Irish emigration of the 1840s to England and Scotland for fear that separated from home they might lapse into heathenism.

In Chambers' dictionary, the adjective oblate means 'dedicated' or 'offered up', and its adherents now dedicate themselves to ministry across continents. The Oblate world is divided into geographical provinces, with each province administered by a provincial, described by Paul Byrne, who was a provincial himself from 1988 to 1994. *"What we have is about 5,000 men in the Oblates from the far north to New Zealand. The boss if you like is the Superior-General in Rome, with a council or board underneath him, and then under that are the geographical units called provinces, and the boss man of that is called a provincial."[6]* The Anglo-Irish Province surprisingly includes Brazil, because its spiritual neglect was causing concern in Rome, and Pope John 23rd asked the Oblate Order to found a mission here. Oblate priests started to serve in this South American part of the Anglo-Irish province as recently as 1961.

The priorities of the province, at least in England, have now moved more towards practical support for the Catholic community. Paul Byrne describes the Oblates as *"Hands on. They prefer to act intuitively, and get on and do the job that has to be done."[7]* Using the familiar language of the building industry Father Paddy Sheridan describes Oblates as *"You have one main contractor who is God, and*

he sublets the work out, and you have the Jesuits who would be involved in the details of administration and we would be doing the groundwork, the foundations, the earthy communities."[8] Father Tom McCabe puts it more bluntly, *"I think being close to the people is what we have to be about, that's what we learnt from St Eugene. I don't think we have any raison d'être for being anywhere else except with the poor."[9]*

Many churches and other buildings in cities across the world now bear the name Eugene de Mazenod. In Inchicore, in south-east Dublin, is the headquarters and also accommodates the Missionary Association of Mary Immaculate for the Anglo-Irish province. The Retreat here is accompanied by another imposing Pugin-designed church in grey stone, which later received a sort of recognition as a location for the film *Angela's Ashes.* In Kilburn in London, the Mazenod Community Centre and, on the floor above it, the Eugene de Mazenod Primary School, which is part of the Local Education Authority provision of Camden Council, are located. The community centre was built as a result of the energy and commitment of John Dore and his parishioners, who had negotiated with the Inner London Education Authority to see their ambition reach reality.

One of Dore's extended team of priests, Paddy Sheridan, was the first Oblate to be sent to the London Irish Centre. *"I had been sent from Liverpool to the East End, for the Irish of the East End. Now, I didn't know what that meant, nobody else seemed to know either, but then in February I was over in Quex Road. Fr Dore came back from a meeting with Cardinal Heenan, and he said the Cardinal has asked the Oblates to take over the Centre, we're going to take it over. He said 'Paddy Sheridan, you're chaplain in the East End, you will now have to go over to the Irish Centre'."[10]*

Fr Paddy Sheridan.

Perhaps resenting his arrival, Paddy Murray, who had remained at Camden Square after the departure of Owen Sweeney, informed Paddy Sheridan he was not altogether welcome. Paddy Sheridan explained that he had been sent by his provincial, Fr William O'Brien, and was not now going to pack his bags. He describes the accommodation at the time, *"I lived in the Centre. It was rough. The facilities at that time were crude and we were, if you like, embarrassed by the whole thing, but what could we do?"*[11] He was not a man to be deterred.

The arrival of the Oblates
From Killinkere in Co. Cavan, and ordained at Pilltown Seminary in Co. Kilkenny in 1960, Paddy Sheridan held the fort as the priest at the Centre until the arrival of Father Paddy Hackett as director in late February. Paddy Sheridan says of Paddy

Hackett, *"He was a wonderful fellow. We had a great policy. If there was any difficulty I met the difficulty, and by the time that people got to Hackett they were out of breath, and the thing was nearly solved."* Typically, Paddy Sheridan undersells himself. *"I was the first dogsbody. I was in charge of nothing. I was not even in charge of myself."*[12]

A native of Birr, Co. Offaly, who was also ordained at Pilltown but ten years before in 1950, Paddy Hackett is remembered as being immensely popular, with a warm personality. He was a superb diplomat, listening to all and giving as much consideration to the most needy as he did to the most exalted. Tall and thin, and not always in good health, he has been described as a *"lovely, saintly man."*[13]

In another account Paddy Sheridan says that running the hostel and the centre was *"tough, constant, endless and always rewarding"*. It was a seven day a week, sixteen hours a day job, where a major crisis might suddenly burst upon the routine. It was, he said, *"The most demanding place I have ever been in. Real Oblate type of work. One had to be a strong as an ox, as patient as Job, as energetic as St Paul and as foolish as a saint"*. There was no job demarcation and everyone did everything. The facilities were poor at that time and the resources were minimal, but this was more than compensated by the enthusiasm of the professional staff and the voluntary workers.

The running debt at the Centre was now £60,000, and the Douglas Hyde Lounge still needed a proper roof. However, it was finally opened on 16 January 1969 by the new Ambassador, John Molloy, and blessed by Bishop Eamonn Casey. There was a slight problem when the holy water for the blessing was almost forgotten.[14] The lounge became the Friday, Saturday and Sunday centre for members of the Irish Centre Club. Soon realising that he had other attributes beyond administration, the committee offered Paddy Sheridan the challenge of creating an attraction on quiet Monday nights in the lounge, and it soon became the venue for Irish music from Finbar and Sean O'Dwyer and others. One of those who sang ballads with as much passion as anyone else was Paddy Sheridan, who had already invited such star traditional musicians as Tommy McCarthy and Bobby Casey to perform at Sunday morning sessions.

As Michael Murray, an enthusiast, has said, *"On Mondays I would make for the Lounge. Jimmy Power was standing at the microphone saying, "Testing, testing". And Father Sheridan was bustling about, moving things around and singing "All Kinds of Everything" to himself. 'You're great Father, how do you manage to fit it all in?' I ask. 'Sure I enjoy every second of it', is the reply, 'That's what we're here for, to look after people's welfare. And that includes singing and dancing, and a drink if they want one'. At this point I ask him if he wants one. 'I never touch it', came the reply. I wondered how any man could work that hard without a drink in him, and say so. 'Hard work never killed anyone. Smile at life and it will smile back. And no matter where you go, always give yourself a big welcome'."*[15] In the first year, the Monday night ballad sessions made £10,000, and sensing that management was perhaps not Paddy Sheridan's strongest card, the committee invited him also to take charge of the sessions in the Lounge at the weekends.

Although the decision to invite the Oblates to take over the Centre had been made by Cardinal Heenan, a trustee, it seems that no-one bothered to explain the situation formally to the Congregation. Its official account, the *De Mazenod Record*, did not report the work at the Irish Centre until the next year, when it states, *"It is not certain if (the) Irish Centre is an Oblate House. The Oblates are considered Irish chaplains working for the Archbishop of Westminster. The property is not owned by the congregation and there is no parish."*[16] The relationships between its unwieldy council and its committee, the chaplain or director and the diocese of Westminster needed some clarification.

A procedure developed in which a new Oblate director was first assigned by the current provincial, then appointed by the Cardinal in Westminster and the other trustees and later confirmed by the Annual General Meeting of the Centre's council. The director, under his oath of obedience as a priest, had to accept the posting, or 'obedience' as it was actually called, although in more recent years a degree of discussion is permitted. Once appointed, the committee inevitably strengthened the link by making the director also its treasurer, thereby giving him some control over finances.

Maureen Greaves, from the Falls Road in Belfast, started work at the Centre as a receptionist in July 1967. Living just around the corner, she had been coming to evening Mass, and on one occasion Paddy Sheridan was standing at the door. As she entered he asked her if she would like a job. She became the youngest member of staff, and says that she was treated like *"the child"*. She started work at 10.00 am, when her first task each day was to take the names and addresses of those who were in the waiting area.

The staff used to have their meals together in the downstairs Green Room, in which there was a large oval table. Everyone working at the Centre was welcome in this room. Larry Gosling, who had been a cook in the Army, did the catering. If Maureen Greaves did not like the cabbage, Paddy Hackett told her to eat it. She was respectful of him because he was the boss. *"He was a no nonsense type of man"*. His humour

Fr Paddy Hackett.

Northern Ireland

Paddy Hackett's arrival at the Centre in February 1967 almost coincided with the emergence of the Civil Rights movement in northern Ireland on 29 January, which brought to the surface many of the struggles over inequality of opportunity in the north. These had been dormant for many years, but were remembered only by sporadic outbursts of 'old' IRA activity. However, there was a sharp reminder of sectarianism during the months from February to June in 1965 when the first petrol bomb attacks on Catholic homes had been perpetrated in Belfast.

The arrival of British troops in northern Ireland in 1969 was welcomed by the Nationalist community which regarded them as support against the injustices of the Unionist majority, while in the House of Commons measures were voted through which were intended to reduce the inequalities between the dominant Protestant and the minority Catholic populations. It was not long, however, before the situation deteriorated. As riots and killings spread in northern Ireland over the next few years, the power of the British state consolidated itself, by both statute and by practice, in the field.

A new science of 'intelligence' was quickly developed, usually based on informers and surveillance on both sides of the Irish Sea. Priests and other leaders of the Irish community in Britain, whether involved politically or not, soon became aware that they were being watched. Some who were stopped and questioned at points of entry were surprised, and in some cases perhaps even flattered, at the extent of the information that had been collected about them. Father Frank Ryan, who was to join the Centre in the 1970s, describes this as creating an uncomfortable feeling, even though he and others were operating entirely within the law.

was very subtle. She says, *"All the problems of the world were solved around that table."*[17] Members of staff, who might have had time for lunch, and the volunteers sat here. Paddy Hackett's first secretary was Ann Kenny, a cousin of Mary Kenny who was already working as a volunteer. She was then followed by Therese Healey, who had obtained the job through a recommendation from her doctor, Larry Morton of the welfare committee. It was well known that the day after Therese Healey returned from holiday was the day to avoid her. She would be so full of memories and photographs of the wonderful time she had enjoyed in Ireland that no work would be done. She did, however, have a good singing voice.

The Centre had already gained a reputation as a place of refuge for those who were struggling to make a life in London. This haven began to attract those who were evading problems back home, or escaping from the more threatening aspects of the Troubles. Local people responded. As Maureen Greaves says, *"People brought in clothes to be sent to northern Ireland to those who had been torched out of their homes and were homeless."*[18] In 1969 the Relief Fund for the Victims of Northern Ireland began to use the Centre as a base for fundraising events.

Departures and Arrivals

With words of farewell in the introduction to the Albert Hall concert programme,

Paddy Murray wrote, *"This affords me the final opportunity of expressing my thanks to you all personally, especially the various Committees and members of the Irish Centre for your support to Father Sweeney and myself during our time in London … my prayers and thoughts will always be with you the 'exiles'."*[19] He left Camden Square to return to the diocese of Ferns, Co. Wexford. The provincial, Fr William O'Brien, believed a replacement was needed to assist its developing service.

In May, another professional social worker was recruited. She was Sr Anne-Marie O'Boyle, of the Holy Sisters of Bordeaux, who was a trained nurse. Although she was originally from Leeds, she had been working at Hope House, the

Fr Paddy Hackett in the welfare office with Sr Anne-Marie O'Boyle and another worker.

nursing home run by her order in Quex Road. She was known to John Dore and Paddy Sheridan, who asked her if she would like to join Miona Hanley, who had been at the Centre since 1964. In a piece for the *Irish Times*, Eileen O'Brien describes Miona Hanly as *"working like a galley slave. She could scarcely speak to me as she was continually interrupted by telephone calls. Almost every call meant that a bit of Irish wreckage had been washed up somewhere in London."*[20]

Of the total of 1,966 people interviewed at the Centre in 1967 by the welfare service, only 95 of the men and 38 women were over 45. There were also 11 boys and 38 girls under 17, and 504 boys and 111 girls aged 18 to 20. A third of the total arrived with no money at all, and very many more had not even £25, which was considered to be the minimum for the survival of a week or so in London.

The annual report for that year was packed with warnings and advice. It suggested that no one should consider emigration without at least £25 in their pocket. For those who suffered from mental and physical disabilities, it stated, the prospect of accommodation or employment was extremely slim. Those approaching pensionable age should not even consider coming over to England to find employment. The housing shortage in Britain also made it very difficult for families to find adequate accommodation. Young people under eighteen years were likely to be paid so little that accommodation in London would not provide them with homes.

In spite of this Maureen Greaves recalls young people, under sixteen, who were running away from home, some of whom were pursued by their parents. The poor, the mentally or physically disabled, pensioners, families, and the young, almost every category, were warned off. Yet still they came.

A fairly common category were the pregnant girls. Anne-Marie O'Boyle remembers one who was eight and a half months' pregnant who arrived with her boyfriend. She could sense that the baby might be born prematurely, and the girl would soon be in labour, so she persuaded Paddy Hackett to jump in his car to rush them up to Highgate, where there was the Good Shepherd Mother and Baby home.

The 1967 report stiffens its advice by adding, *"Some who emigrate seem to suffer from a lot of wishful thinking and a lack of common sense. Those who have responsibly decided to emigrate, should, if they have properly prepared for this big and important step, reach worthy positions in Britain. Those who come on the off-chance of an easier life, or because they do not fit in at home, or merely because they are dissatisfied in their own country, should think again before leaving their familiar surroundings."*[21]

Some, however, fell outside these categories. Joseph Crowley was from Co. Cork and twenty-one years old when he arrived at the Centre one Saturday morning, looking for accommodation. Unlike many others, Joseph had quite a bit of money with him, and his main reasons for coming to England were not economic. *"He had worked in the family business at home as an invoice clerk, and hoped to find similar work in London. He also came to London to widen his experience so that he might be able to write novels or poetry. 'I hope that I can find the inspiration I am looking for in London', he said, 'And in any case the libraries are better'. It was an unusual reason, but Joseph Crowley was one of the many young people who felt that London could offer them something extra, however indefinable, than they could find at home."*[22]

From left: Frs Claude Malone, Paddy Sheridan and Paddy Hackett outside the London Irish Centre in Murray Street.

Father Claude Malone

By September Father Claude Malone, a Kildareman from Naas, had arrived to replace Paddy Murray. While a student priest the year before, he had already been assigned work experience in the parish of the Sacred Heart in Kilburn. Part of this was to accompany the volunteers of the Legion of Mary to Euston Station to meet the hundreds of Irish men and women who had crossed the Irish Sea the night before. Some were as young as fifteen, he remembers.

In 1967 he received his first 'obedience' from the provincial, and arrived at Camden Square as a junior chaplain, walking through the door with a brown suitcase. As Paddy Sheridan says, *"Claude was only a young priest when he came down. He was very good at figures and book-keeping, and I was not. I was utterly useless, but get me up on a stage in front of people and I am at my best. It was a nice balance if you like. Paddy Hackett, Claude and I used to be called 'The Father, the Son and the Holy Spirit'."*[23]

Each morning Claude Malone remembers sitting with the book-keeper, Bridie O'Loughlin, who was about to return to Dublin to take up a job with one of the banks. *"It was an A to Z course on how to keep the books. No training had been provided in this field during the previous seven years of formation. However, under the very watchful eye of Paddy Keegan, volunteer professional skills were acquired."* He adds with foreboding, *"Little did I know that this training was laying a foundation for what lay ahead."*[24]

Among the Centre's archives there is a surprising collection of newsletters published by the Irish Centre Club. Their survival in the random manner in which all the Centre's archives have been collected and stored in different parts of the building over the fifty years is itself a surprise. These newsletters commence in January 1968 and continue, monthly but with some gaps, until October 1974.

As Roneo'd stencils onto foolscap paper, they provide in faded print an account of the activities of the Centre. The style of writing is endearing. The earlier ones are signed off with a cheery "God bless you all", but with no name below, although it is safe to assume that they were written by one of the two chaplains. The identity soon becomes clear with the name that appears at the foot of the November 1968 newsletter, Fr P Sheridan, OMI. Intriguingly, one month later this author signs himself as Rev P Sheridan, OMI. By August 1969 he has reverted to Fr P Sheridan. However, whenever he signs off there is always a cheery "God bless you all" or, at the right time,"Beannactai na Nollag". Whether on a stage or writing a newsletter, Paddy Sheridan did both very well.

The January 1968 newsletter is headed by a typical list of forthcoming events, from the Dublin Association Dance, the Crean School of Dancing Children's Party, the United Ireland Association, a Benefit Dance for Joe Reilly, to the Carrigallon Reunion in January 1969. Then follows the regular programme: Bingo Night (Sundays, Wednesdays & Fridays) and the Weekly Tote Draw (every Sunday). Bacon and cabbage dinners are also a regular feature. A year or two later, Irish Song and Dance replaced Bingo on Mondays, and Country and Western arrived on Thursdays. Bingo, however, survived three times a week on Wednesdays, Fridays and Saturdays. These events were organised by the social committee.

Sally Mulready, who had arrived in 1966, remembers the bingo. The callers were then only men. *"I remember being firmly put in my place when I stood up to read the bingo numbers of the person next to me wh* had called 'house'. 'The men do all the calling here', one of them said, and he snatched the card and read all the numbers out again".[25] Women's Liberation was then making strides everywhere but in Camden Square.

In the newsletter of January 1968 a gently humorous text with information of past events and announcements of those to come is placed lower down the page, usually overlaid by a subtle Christian message. The text consists, for example, of news for members of an ambitious Christmas dinner for 220 Irish boys and girls, and states optimistically, that "the building extension is well on the way to completion". However, in almost every issue, fundraising of one sort or another dominates, as it is to dominate the Centre for most of its fifty years.

The next month's newsletter begins with the reminder, as if one was needed, "It is now 12 months since the Oblates took over at the Irish Centre. Our coming was at the request of the Cardinal and, like many acts of obedience, it was not without its difficulties. I'm sure that all those members who have had put in such hard work over the years were wondering what these Oblates would be like. Would they pull down? Would they build up? Would they dismiss? Well, you have had 12 months to weigh us up and likewise we have had time to meet you. For our part we are the happiest men in London - all three of us love the Irish Centre."[26]

Love it they might, but Paddy Hackett, Paddy Sheridan and Claude Malone were never far from the mounting debt. The Irish are, of course, as inventive in raising money as they are in other activities, and every weekend Paddy Sheridan helped to reduce the debt by visiting some twenty-five different pubs across London with a football pool. "I only go to pubs which have Irish guv'nors, and I always come back with something worthwhile", he said. He also claimed that in every pub he visited he

was offered "a drop of the hard stuff", but as a good Pioneer he chose to stick to milk.[27]

Concerts and Visitors

The Annual Report for 1968 was a glossier document than had previously been produced. The Welfare Office that year helped 2,010 applicants, as opposed to 1,568 the previous year. A proportion of them were from 'other nationalities'. It also includes a report on the Irish Centre Club. By now its banqueting, conferences and dances were booked into the Kennedy Memorial Hall. Above, the Douglas Hyde Lounge was a spacious room where ballad sessions could take place on Mondays, traditional Irish music on Wednesdays and Country and Western on Thursdays. Paddy Sheridan was a talented Master of Ceremonies at the weekends.

The chairman of the social committee was Pat Hegarty, from Glencolumbcille in Donegal. Throughout the Centre's history, there have been devoted volunteers, people for whom it was more than just a building, who committed their time and their own resources in making it a success. Whether it was painting and decorating, washing the curtains, helping in the kitchen or contributing to the fabric of the building, the London Irish Centre would not have survived without them. Pat Hegarty, for example, was instrumental in erecting a rail at his own expense around the flat roof overlooking Murray Street, after Fire Brigade concerns about safety.[28]

Fund-raising was forever the challenge. Concerts staged each March at the Royal Albert Hall had started relatively modestly, but in time grew more lavish. Paddy Sheridan booked the artists. In 1967 they included Joe Lynch, Dermot O'Brien and the Clubmen and Kathleen Watkins. The Producer was always T. Leslie Jackson, who staged This is Your Life with Eamonn Andrews for the BBC. Dana, the singer from northern Ireland, was so keen to appear at another that she gave Paddy Sheridan her private number, rather than that of her agent. The wider esteem of the Centre was reflected by the fact that Terry Wogan was booked as the compère at more than one concert. However, the efforts by the administrative committee to organise these events and sell tickets, which usually began just after Christmas, and the comparative cost of the hire of the venue, meant that these concerts were never a huge financial success. When they began to produce less and less income they were finally abandoned.

Nevertheless, arriving to discuss an appearance at a future concert, the singer Bing Crosby visited Camden Square in August 1968. Maureen Greaves was frantically trying to tidy up before his arrival, but he crossed the road from the Murray Street house with Paddy Hackett before she had finished. She remembers with great embarrassment that she shook his hand while holding a brush and a wet cloth in the other.[29] Bing Crosby was taken on a tour of the building, but unfortunately Paddy Hackett forgot to ask him to sing a song or even sign a cheque.

The receipts from the Albert Hall concerts, divided with the Irish Chaplaincy, were to meet the ongoing expenses of the Centre, but from Paddy Hackett's time the saga of the new hall took hold of the imaginations of directors. This venture involved huge capital sums. After the difficulties with funding, planning permissions and regulations related to the Kennedy Memorial Hall, it might have been wiser to have been more cautious.

The public reputation of the Centre continued to spread. Gay Byrne's *Late Late Show* visited the premises to record its programme for audiences back home. This was on the welfare of Irish emigrants. On the panel were Eamonn Andrews, the writer Mary Kenny and a journalist from the *Irish Times*. Gay Byrne was host and chairman. His audience included members of the Centre and parishioners from Quex Road, who were often one and the same. John Dore, who was among them, had invited Brendan O'Connor and others to join him.

The discussion soon turned to the early morning arrivals from Ireland at Paddington and Euston stations, and in particular to the Irish girls who came with just a few shillings in their cheap handbags, some of whom were pregnant. Brendan O'Connor was active in the Legion of Mary, which met them and other emigrants every morning on the platforms. They would offer advice and help, sometimes in direct competition with the spivs who were offering them something different. In this effort the Legion was discreetly supported by the police. Its members also visited Soho clip joints at night in order to persuade those that may have fallen by the wayside to think again. In so doing, they persuaded many girls to return to Ireland, their fares paid for by collections at the church in Quex Road.

Unfortunately, the writer Mary Kenny used the programme to launch into *"a tirade of abuse against the Irish"*, blaming everyone for allowing this situation to happen. Brendan O'Connor was offered a microphone and told her, in forceful terms, that as she was working for the Beaverbrook Press she was now no friend of Ireland. He says deprecatingly of himself, *"With the language I used, I would never be a member of the Irish diplomatic corps."*[30]

With no doubt a diplomat or two for company, in March 1968 the Taoiseach Jack Lynch, paid a visit to the Centre. Anne-Marie O'Boyle showed his wife the upstairs accommodation, while the Taoiseach no doubt discussed weighty matters such as funding with Paddy Hackett in the Green Room. Paddy Sheridan remembers Jack Lynch saying that when he returned he would see his Minister, *"but that was no good."*[31]

It is also recorded that in June 1969 a group of Leeds United footballers visited, among them one Jack Charlton. They went into the Douglas Hyde Lounge to have a drink and enjoy the ballads. Jackie Charlton actually paid a membership fee for the Irish Centre Club, and to think that some people years later imagined that he had no Irish connection!

Tom McCabe

An Oblate student who came to the Centre in 1968 was Tom McCabe. *"This was my first visit to London, so I was very like the young people coming to Euston Station. I had no idea what to expect, except that I did know Claude Malone. I didn't know Paddy Sheridan, but I knew he was from Cavan. I found my introduction to it was like being thrown in at the deep end of the pool. I found it a very exciting place, with people coming at you from all directions."* He recalls how he helped to assist young people without housing to become stabilised and sufficiently confident to move on. Their accommodation was arranged in the upstairs rooms with two, three or four beds to each room. The days were long, and in the office downstairs things often did not quieten down until one o'clock in the morning. There was little backup available, and a lot of work was done out of hours. *"We had many dramas with the young men in the hostel in trouble, getting drunk and having accidents, suicide attempts, we had it all. I have memories of nights being down at University College Hospital with people, waiting to see what would happen, bringing them back in the car to the hostel and hoping they would be alive in the morning. You had the social side of the centre*

A room in the hostel upstairs at the London Irish Centre.

and you had the hostel, and you had the interaction between the two, which was often difficult."[32] However, *"There was a great buzz to the place"*, he has said. There was not a great deal of space in the rooms of the hostel, and because many of the young men had been working on building sites during the day, *"the smell in the middle of the night would knock you over."*

Tom McCabe later returned to the Centre as a chaplain. Another student priest was Frank Ryan, who after he was ordained took charge of Hope House, the hostel that was later purchased in Quex Road.

Extensions

At that time, Hope House was not under consideration. The new hall certainly was. This 'saga' proceeded slowly, in phases,

over many years. It included the opportunity to develop beyond no. 51 next door
along the frontage of Camden Square, the
consequent sale of this land to a Housing
Association and the transferral of funds
into the acquisition in 1974 of the nursing-
home in Kilburn which was to become
Hope House. The decision to extend on
the remainder of this land to the rear, by
building a larger new hall on the open
space and across the railway tunnels
became a fundamental element of a story
which cast a shadow over the Centre for
many years.

It dated back to 22 September 1964,
when the property agency for British
Railways contacted Owen Sweeney to say
that their clients were considering disposal of nos. 49 and 50 Camden Square.
This was later extended to include nos. 44
and 48, which had been built above the
tunnels. In between was the open space.
In February 1965, Owen Sweeney informed the committee that these premises
and the land between might be available
to the Centre for £47,000 on a 99-year lease.

The committee was interested in the
purchase because it meant that an entire
complex could be designed for the site.
At one time it even included the demolition and rebuilding of nos. 51 and 52
Camden Square. The architect was Vernon
Gibberd, of Gore, Gibberd and Saunders,
who had first outlined the project with his
colleague, the civil engineer Noel
O'Connell, in 1966. He described how, by
linking nos. 44 to 50 Camden Square with
nos. 51 and 52, it would be possible to
redesign the welfare block, provide private rooms in each of the two hostels and
make more rational use of the existing
club facilities. The cost was estimated at
£197,875.

The prospect of an extension prompted
an examination by the Centre of the best
use of this additional space. The committee at first considered an expansion of the
Kennedy Hall, which was always solidly
booked, with two additional forty-bed
hostels alongside Camden Square. Also
involved was a property company called
Studio Co. Ownership, with whom British Railways wanted a joint development,
but negotiations with this company ultimately broke down. On 6 November 1969
British Railways offered the Centre the
sole option of developing the site.[33]

On 1 July 1969 the Centre met Camden
Council, which as well as being the planning authority was obviously interested in
additional temporary housing accommodation to help relieve its own problems.
Fears were expressed about the difficulties
of building across the roof of the tunnels,
something which was to haunt the Centre
for many years. On 17 September 1970
outline planning permission was requested. The Centre would undertake
responsibility for the safety and maintenance of the tunnels.

Paddy Hackett was interviewed about
this on RTE, where he said that negotiations with British Rail, the new re-branded
name for British Railways, were at an
advanced stage, and although the fund-
raising would be a challenge the development would be worth the effort.

Plans were again submitted to Camden
and had final approval in 1971. The cost
was now given as £395,000, in comparison
to the original scheme which was
£420,000. Camden itself would contribute a significant amount. A National
Collection at churches throughout Ireland
already in the planning stages of the
Episcopal Commission for Irish Emigrants
and the Irish Bishops' Committee, would
raise the rest.

In order to facilitate the development
the committee decided that it would be
advantageous to be registered as a Housing Association, and could therefore apply

for housing grants. As a result, Irish Centre Hostels Ltd was formed in July 1969 as a separate entity from the London Irish Centre, although there was an overlap among the members of their management committees.

British Rail accepted the offer of £47,500 for the site made in 1970, but progress toward the the sale was slow. The Centre had still not formally agreed the purchase. On 11 December 1972 British Rail pressed it to close the deal, still at the original price. However the Centre was reconsidering its original plans, and wondered whether the site could be used for flats or other dwellings rather than hostel accommodation.[34]

Eventually, ten years after the first contact, Irish Centre Hostels Ltd bought nos. 44 to 50 Camden Square from British Rail on 4 February 1974 for £49,883. It was acquired on a 120-year lease, but the ideas of the 1960s were never to be achieved. The land at the rear was on a free lease.

By now a new architectural practice had appeared on the scene. This was led by Keith Roberts, who had the advantage that he was living in Camden Square, with offices in Murray Mews at the rear of his garden. Apart from an occasional workshop, this mews had been hardly built upon, but the arrival of professionals and middle-classes into this neighbourhood encouraged them to commission young and adventurous architects to design their homes here.[35]

With what some might describe as a possible conflict of interest, Keith Roberts also became secretary or chairman of the Camden Square Neighbourhood Association. Despite the Association's difficulties with the Centre over issues such as late night noise, he managed to persuade its director and committee to engage Keith Roberts Associates as the Centre's architect. This of course did not please Vernon Gibberd, who made a formal complaint to the Royal Institute of British Architects. In the meantime no development took place while proposals were made as to how to raise the enormous capital sums required.

Keith Roberts had a connection with Joan Jarosy, a founder of Community Housing Association (CHA), who acted as a consultant to this housing association. His persuasive powers convinced the Centre to pass its interest in nos. 41 to 49 Camden Square to CHA, which had the right management experience to develop these as flats for people in housing need rather than a hostel.

An agreement between all parties including the new architect, the Centre and the CHA was finally drawn up. The possibility of building development along Camden Square was regarded as a real prize.

With his growing practice, Keith Roberts engaged a young architect, David Ashton-Hill, with whom he worked in the office in Murray Mews. An early job of his was the restoration of the 19th-century moulded decorations on the front of the Centre building. David Ashton-Hill was able to take casts from a house across the square and transfer them to the façade of no. 52 Camden Square.

Upstairs in the Hostel

Meanwhile, the daily routine of the Centre continued. Claude Malone remembers collecting the rents from the young men in the hostel. Residents were asked to "move on" after four weeks. If they were not working they were generally claiming benefits, and this enabled the Centre to arrange lodgings with approved landladies. He recalls looking after the 'savings' of many of the residents, which were locked away in the safe. Many even returned after they had left the Centre in order to continue to place their savings with him. His book-keeping skills were to come in handy.

Christopher O'Brien arrived at the door in 1969. He had no idea what he would do. Back home, he had picked cockles from the strand near Castlemaine in Co. Kerry, and then worked in the bars of hotels in Killarney. Once he reached Euston Station he walked up the road to the Centre with £10 in his pocket. He met Paddy Hackett at the door, who offered him a bed in a room with three others. *"Fantastic, the lads were"*, he remembers. There were showers, and the cost was £2.10s a week for bed, breakfast and dinner. It took him a week to land a job. With his previous experience in hotels he was sent by the welfare service to a pub in the Elephant and Castle area in south London, which was a live-in job. After he had succeeded in finding his way there, the manager asked him if he could fight, *"It's a tough pub"*, he said. He lasted just a week.

When he returned to the Centre the experience was not quite so fantastic. He came back from the Buffalo one night with five shillings in his pocket, which was stolen by the morning. *"The Dubliners in another room were a rough crowd. They threw their mattresses out of the top windows, but Paddy Sheridan threw them out at five in the morning."* On the third stay he met Paddy Sheridan at the door, and was asked *"Have you got money?"* Christopher O'Brien replied with a nod. Paddy Sheridan then advised, *"If I were you, I'd go back to Ireland."* He did in fact find accommodation for him.[36]

The 1969 welfare report retained the usual headings of welfare advice, accommodation and employment. Some 2,299 people had arrived at the Centre that year to seek help. However a new element had entered the story. The situation in north-

ern Ireland was beginning to be reflected in these records, with nine families from the north arriving at the Centre in search of help. As Paddy Sheridan puts it, *"It was an amazing thing, but there were people from northern Ireland, and they'd tell you 'If I was back in northern Ireland I wouldn't talk to you as a priest, a Catholic priest'. But they wanted a job and they wanted a place to stay."*[37]

The end of the 1960s saw riots in Derry which became known as the 'Battle of the Bogside', and further riots in the Shankhill Road in Belfast. These reverberated in London. The Centre could not avoid the waves of feeling that were sweeping the country, often exacerbated by foolish press reports. One Saturday evening, when the building was full, its halls and bars busy with people enjoying themselves, a telephone call was received by the volunteer receptionist Deirdre McDermott. She later told Claude Malone that someone with an English accent had asked, *"How would you like to have a big, fat English 'bum' planted at your Irish Centre?"* She instinctively replied that there were quite a number already planted in the bars there that evening. After she had hung up she realised that the caller had said 'bomb', and not 'bum'. Although this was not funny, she and Claude Malone could do little more than laugh.[38]

Paddy Sheridan is remembered as a jovial sort of priest, *"full of devilment, clowning about"*[39], and fond of the ballad sessions after a normal day's work. However, he also had a committed, serious side. In a later newsletter, he wrote that he had recently visited northern Ireland, *"I was in Belfast and the physical state of that city is desperate – soldiers, tanks, guns, barbed wire, boarded and burned shops and houses, even many of the footpaths are torn up, but above all the fear and suspicion in the people. All these things add up to create a foul atmosphere. This is especially true of Belfast, but true of many other towns in the province. It is a sad situation. There is only one solution for it. Ireland is one country and will have to be ruled as such. There is hardly any doubt but that is how it will be; but in the meantime how many lives will be lost. When they speak of extremists they have associated that to mean the IRA, but the extremists who are causing most of the trouble are those within the Unionist Party who do not want to let go of their power. We have all been asked to storm Heaven during the month of October. It will take God himself to solve the problem of Northern Ireland. Ask and you shall receive!"*[40]

One who arrived from Ballygowan, near Belfast, was Tom Greaves. Unlike others escaping the Troubles, he had followed his girl-friend Maureen, the Centre's receptionist, to London. When they were later married, with Claude Malone officiating, the Centre gave them the Kennedy Hall for the reception. Paddy Sheridan suggested to the young couple that their honeymoon destination should be Lourdes.

Before they were married Tom Greaves spent a year in the hostel. He paid £2 10s for bed and breakfast and an evening meal. He found it noisy at times, with fellow residents playing music in their rooms, but there was a TV Lounge. *"I made a lot of friends, so I did"*, he says.[41] In later years Maureen and Tom Greaves gave great support to the directors.

The Council and the neighbours

It was during Paddy Hackett's time that the Centre invited the Mayor of Camden to an annual dinner. This politically expedient invitation, which may have helped to ensure a regular grant from the council, continued for many years until it finally faded. Nevertheless, as a result of the contacts of Mary and Bill Allen of the Waterford Association, for eleven years Mayors of Camden were invited on a brief exchange to that county, which for many was a welcome break from mayoral duties in a busy London borough. The annual dinner, on behalf of the Mayor's charity, has been recently revived by the Mayor of Camden of 2002, Councillor Judith Pattison.

The first dinner was to honour Camden's first woman Mayor, Cllr Millie Miller. In her response to the toast and in reminding her audience that the recent formation of the larger borough of Camden had been a shotgun marriage between the former boroughs of Hampstead, St Pancras and Holborn, she said: *"The borough as it has developed could never have achieved such sufficiency if it had not been for the various communal groups which have taken it to their hearts and certainly not least of all because of the co-operation here of the Irish community. Something like forty per cent of all the heads of households in Camden today were born overseas, and this includes across the Irish Sea, and I think that the greatest percentage inside that 40 per cent is accounted for by the Irish community. We have to thank the Irish for their great work in building houses, roads, the new tube line, their help in the hospitals and catering establishments. We thank Father Hackett for the wealth of services that the Irish Centre provides. For a great burden would be placed on the statutory services if it was not for the fact that when Irish people, particularly young people, coming over to London for the first time, find themselves in difficulties, everybody knows that the Irish Centre is here to give them a hand, and this does relieve our council services considerably."*[42] This annual event helped to cement the links between the Centre and the local authority.

Constant minor improvements and additions to the building attracted larger numbers of callers and evening visitors to

A county association dinner in the new Kennedy Memorial Hall.

the Centre. The more exuberant activities sometimes had an impact on the adjoining houses. Unfortunately this led, particularly in the summer of 1970, to complaints from the neighbours, led by the Camden Square Neighbourhood Association. It is said that a petition to actually close the place down was supported by Keith Roberts, the Centre's architect, who was also at the time the association's chairman or secretary.

A summons was issued in June 1970, which created some anxiety. However, the case was adjourned pending the installation of double-glazing on the windows of the Kennedy Hall, from where much of the noise was perceived to emerge. This work was quickly completed at a cost of £1,000, but gave rise to another problem of fresh air supply in the building. One thing led to another, as always,

so the next fundraising target was an air-conditioning system. However, noise and disturbance remained an issue with the neighbours over a number of years, before it was finally ended by more stringent bookings policies and a more careful management of those who left the building at night.

Workers and Volunteers
In September 1970 Claude Malone departed for a post as assistant Novice Master at the novitiate in Ardagh, Co Limerick. Paddy Sheridan, the author of the Irish Centre Club members' newsletter, described him generously as the one *"who looked after the money and the books as well as a lot of the welfare work. He did it all efficiently and apparently unnoticed, but we knew and appreciated what he did for the Centre."*

There were other staff changes at the Centre at this time. After many years, Miona Hanly left the welfare office for Cardiff University. Her place was taken by Maura Dorgan.

There was also a small army of volunteers who assisted the Centre and also helped to improve its facilities. Teams of painters and decorators were at work, led by Luke Kennedy, Chair of the Sligo Association, Tess Moroney, Bridie Shaw, Michael and Bridie Lahiff and Martin and Tess Doyle. At the end of an evening's work, Paddy Sheridan would invite them into the kitchen for tea and the inevitable craic. Brigid Hegarty says of her husband, Pat, that *"Most of our courtship was spent at the Centre as he continued his chairmanship of the social committee, and helped the volunteers."*[43]

The welfare volunteers soon met with a challenge. White collar emigrants flooded into England as part of the fall-out of the Irish bank strike in June 1970. This caused financial chaos in Ireland, although people improvised with IOUs and private bartering arrangements. No one expected that bank workers, without a strike fund, would hold out for so long, but many of them were able to pick up other employment. Bank strikes now appear to be a recurring theme in Ireland, but this encouraged a different category of caller to the Centre. It is said that they were put up for nothing.[44] They certainly made good use of the Marian Employment Agency.

Paddy Hackett's health, which suffered from diabetes, deteriorated. He was fortunate that there was a supportive administrative committee and a trained nurse, Anne-Marie O'Boyle, on the staff. In 1971, he retired and went as a parish priest to the Church of the Sacred Heart in Quex Road. This was not far from Camden Square, and he would return to attend committee and other meetings. Among the Irish population of Kilburn he was never far from the effects of the disturbances in northern Ireland, and was regarded as someone who could offer help or advice to those who were in distress or some trouble.

One of these was Kenneth Lennon, from Newry, who on Good Friday in 1974 called on him in the Quex Road presbytery desperate for help. He had wanted to see Brendan Magill, who had an Irish record shop in Kilburn and was a well-known member of Sinn Fein, and thought that Paddy Hackett could arrange this. He was extremely disturbed by the fact that he was under an obligation to the Royal Ulster Constabulary Special Branch who had used him as an IRA informer. Two days before, he had told his story to Larry Grant, a legal officer at the National Council for Civil Liberties, and even to George Melly at Ronnie Scott's Jazz Club. The police had been using him, he said, but now that he wanted to escape from their grasp they would not let him leave. Unfortunately Paddy Hackett could not give Kenneth Lennon the immediate help he wanted, and with Easter looming he suggested that they met again on Monday. Lennon told him that as soon as he left the presbytery he would be walking into the arms of the police. On the Monday morning Paddy Hackett was shocked to read of his death. He had been shot in the head three times, and his body had been dumped in a ditch in Surrey.[45]

Meanwhile the diocese of Westminster had been in contact with the current provincial, John Dore, about a replacement for the Centre from the Oblates.

Long before his time, Paddy Hackett died in Kilburn in April 1982. As the first Oblate at the London Irish Centre he will be remembered. His funeral, at which Cardinal Hume said a Mass, was *"a massive send-off, with standing room only."*[46] It is said that the whole of Kilburn closed down in his memory. The police had to escort the thousand or so mourners as they walked in procession to the cemetery.

In December 2001, one of the hostels of Irish Centre Housing, in Kingsgate Road, Kilburn, was named Hackett House in his honour.

[1] Interview Fr Paul Byrne, January 2004.
[2] From Missionary Record of the Oblates of Mary Immaculate, 1930.
[3] Census of 1851, quoted in 'The Irish in Kilburn' by Michael Alpert, *Camden History Review*, Vol. 25.
[4] From *Reaching Out: The History of the Anglo-Irish Province of the Missionary Oblates of Mary Immaculate* by Fr Vincent Denny, OMI.
[5] 'The Irish in Kilburn' by Michael Alpert, Camden History Review, vol 25.
[6] Interview Fr Paul Byrne, January 2004.
[7] *Ibid*.
[8] Interview Fr Paddy Sheridan, October 2003.
[9] Interview Fr Tom McCabe, October 2003.
[10] Interview Fr Paddy Sheridan, October 2003.
[11] *Ibid*.
[12] *Ibid*.
[13] Interview Bridie Shaw and Mary Allen, January 2004.
[14] LIC Newsletter, February 1969.
[15] *Irish Post*, 23 January 1971.
[16] (DMR 36, 1968).
[17] Interview Maureen Greaves, April 2004.
[18] *Ibid*.
[19] St Patrick's Festival Concert programme, 16 March 1967.
[20] *Irish Times*, July 1967.
[21] Annual Report, 1967.
[23] *Hampstead and Highgate Express*, 25 August 1967.
[23] Interview Fr Paddy Sheridan, October 2003.
[24] Correspondence with Fr Claude Malone, April 2004.
[25] Correspondence with Sally Mulready, June 2004.
[26] LIC *Newsletter*, February 1968.
[27] Interview Fr Paddy Sheridan, October 2003.
[28] Correspondence with Brigid Hegarty, June 2004.
[29] Interview Maureen Greaves, April 2004.
[30] Interview Brendan O'Connor, May 2004.
[31] Interview Fr Paddy Sheridan, October 2003.
[32] Interview Fr Tom McCabe, October 2003.
[33] *Helping Hands*, published 1975.
[34] LIC minutes, 11 December 1972.
[35] Camden Square Conservation Area Statement, published by the London Borough of Camden.
[36] Interview Christopher O'Brien, May 2004.
[37] Interview Fr Paddy Sheridan, October 2003.
[38] Correspondence with Fr Claude Malone, April 2004.
[39] Interview Maureen Greaves, April 2004.
[40] LIC Newsletter, September 1971.
[41] Interview Tom and Maureen Greaves, August 2004.
[42] *Cork Examiner*, 3 May 1968.
[43] Correspondence Brigid Hegarty, June 2004.
[44] Interview Ned Fogarty, May 2004.
[45] From *The Phantom and the Phoenix*, the memoirs of Fr Frank Ryan, November 2000, and an interview with Fr Ryan, October 2003.
[46] Interview Maureen and Tom Greaves, April 2004.

CHAPTER SIX

Don't worry, the money will come

Father Liam Fanning
Father Paddy Mee

By 1971, with the recruitment of more professional staff, the London Irish Centre was consolidating its welfare work much more efficiently. The numbers arriving at the Centre also appeared to have stabilised. A report from the welfare office by Sr Anne-Marie O'Boyle and her colleague Maura Dorgan stated that 1,630 persons (1,243 males, 339 females and 48 families) were interviewed by the welfare service. In 1970 there had been 1,694, and as the authors stated, *"The trend is hopeful, and may mark the turning of that tide that has robbed Ireland of its greatest wealth – its own young people."*[1]

Someone with personal experience of that tide was Cllr Brian Duggan, the ninth Mayor of Camden in 1972, who had arrived in England in 1961 from Thurles, Co. Tipperary, because he was a bit *"fed up".* He felt that he could achieve more in London than was possible with his job back home with an insurance company. It was a late decision, because he had taken the boat at the age of forty-one with his wife and their two children. However he had secured a job in the aircraft industry, and within a year was visiting the Irish Centre Club and soon had become its secretary.

In 1968 Brian Duggan retired from this post in order to concentrate on local politics. *"I was selected by St Pancras Labour Party to be forwarded for election to the council, and I was elected in the same year.*

My first job was as Deputy Mayor, and to tell you the truth I didn't even know where the Town Hall was, but I got on alright in the job". Always the shrewd political observer, Paddy Sheridan wrote, *"He used to roll his own cigarettes, but in later years, since he really became involved with the Labour Party, he has got himself a pipe. Harold Wilson is seldom seen without a similar mouthpiece. I wonder is there some magic in a pipe?"*[2] Brian Duggan was later elected as Mayor, following Paddy O'Connor as Camden's second Irish Mayor. *"Paddy was a great man, who was afraid of nobody",* he said. *"He really did fight for the Irish as things were a lot tougher for us in those days. He was the Irish rebel who would take to the streets if necessary."*[3] This period followed the only three years of a Conservative administration in Camden.

After his year as Mayor in 1972, Duggan returned to his job in the aircraft industry, but he continued as a councillor. *"I was up at 6.30 am for work, and I would have to go straight from there to a council meeting. It was difficult in that sometimes I would not see the children for days."* In those days council meetings often dragged on until the early hours.

Perhaps to avoid this pressure, he left the Labour Party in 1982 to join the new Social Democratic Party. He stood down from the council a year later, after having lost his seat. He had already spent some years working at the Centre as a volunteer, and he now took charge of the Missing Persons section, which had been set up by Sr Joan Moriarty who had joined the welfare service in 1974. With support from the authorities in Ireland and contacts made during his time on the council, he ensured that this work was valuable. Many of the missing people whom Brian Duggan was attempting to locate were young men and women on the run from threats in northern Ireland.

Before Brian Duggan had joined the Centre's staff, John Dore, the provincial who had now succeeded Father William O'Brien, made perhaps a surprising choice to follow the well-regarded Paddy Hackett at the Centre, when Father Liam Fanning was assigned the post.

Originally from Rathvilly in Co. Carlow, Liam Fanning arrived with some reluctance. However, the oath of obedience was important, and he had to go to where the provincial instructed him.

His chaplain was Paddy Sheridan, an almost permanent but welcome fixture at Camden Square. Frank Ryan, who also knew Liam Fanning when he was a student, now says, *"He didn't like the Irish Centre at all."*[4] Maureen Greaves remembers him as *"a bit odd. I never thought he was right for the Centre."*[5] In spite of his unwillingness to serve here, Liam Fanning did enjoy the regular quiz nights ias a member of the Carlow team. He used to sit sucking his pipe and answering the questions that flummoxed others. Carlow won the Guinness Cup while he was there. His useful memory in quizzes was contradicted by his constantly forgetting where he had parked his car. Anne-Marie O'Boyle says he would very often walk to the wrong place, and come back to ring the police to say it had been stolen.

In January 1971 Cardinal John Heenan visited the Centre to meet the architect, Vernon Gibberd, who was then still com-

Fr Liam Fanning.

missioned to carry out the development proposals and to inspect his plans. He brought with him a £1,000 cheque. In thanking him, Liam Fanning said this was *"a great start to our year"*.

The National Collection

The National Collection, which was being organised by the Irish Episcopal Commission for Emigrants, was scheduled to take place a few months later on 14 March at Sunday Mass in parish churches throughout Ireland. The amount raised would be used for projects for the emigrant community in Britain, in particular the Irish Centres in London, Birmingham and elsewhere, and the Benburb Base for ex-offenders near the Holloway Road. The Centre's Albert Hall fund-raising concert that year was booked for the previous

The leaflet promoting the National Collection, to be held in parish churches across Ireland in March 1971.

Saturday evening. The receipts for this would provide much-needed revenue for the Centre.

But it was not clear if the income from the Collection could be used for clearing

debts, paying staff or for capital development. Father Frank Lewis, who assisted Eamonn Casey, wrote to Paddy Sheridan, *"This money is to be used to ease the task of emigrant chaplains. The Birmingham Centre and the Benburb Base will both have to leave their present premises during the coming year and will need considerable help to get suitable alternatives. The Irish Centre in London needs renovation and extension if it is to continue to do its work effectively. It is also hoped to have some money for a central fund which will be used by individual chaplains who have a particular project that they wish to get off the ground but are prevented from doing so for financial reasons."*[6] Paddy Keegan's memory was that it was for capital development only. The purchase of Hope House, when it became available, was eventually offset by by the National Collection funding.

A public relations firm had been hired in Ireland to promote the Collection, but it was to be some time before there was any news of its success or otherwise. Speculation was wild. When the news finally arrived, the Collection was seen as a huge achievement, with a response as high as £263,000.[7] There was even the hope that, now shamed, Jack Lynch's government would match the amount collected, pound for pound.

The National Collection had been first proposed by Bishop Eamonn Casey as long before as 11 November 1969. Successive Irish governments had been challenged by him and a number of other, bolder priests to support with more enthusiasm their 'exiles' abroad, and in particular the Centres in England which were serving them. In the absence of such support, it was decided that a National Collection at parish churches across Ireland on a particular Sunday, might help fill the gap and at the same time shame the government. In his persuasive way, Eamonn Casey had

95

managed to convince the Irish Hierarchy of bishops to support this initiative. In spite of the lack of government support, a Bishops' Committee had been formed in order to progress the project.

If Dublin was showing little concern for emigrants in Britain, there were entrepreneurs who saw in this growing community a viable business opportunity, and who believed that there was a need to bring them together by means of information and news.

The *Irish Post*

The *Irish Post* was the idea of Tony Beatty, an accountant in north London who was from Co. Waterford. A mutual acquaintance had introduced him to Brendan Mac Lua, and they first met in Dublin in August 1969. Secure in the knowledge that the Irish in Britain now had sufficient buying power to attract advertising, the first issue of the *Post* was launched on 13 February 1970, with a headline that stated 'Irish vote should be put to good use'. At the launch, George Colley, who was Irish Minister for Industry and Finance, pointed out that the Irish community in Britain, then estimated at two million, *"Could flex some formidable political muscle."* This was a General Election year.

Brendan Mac Lua became one of the most influential Irish voices then in Britain. As first editor and managing director of the new weekly newspaper he has said, *"One achievement over-rides all others. The newspaper played a very large part in creating a sense of community which involved all the Irish in Britain."*[8] More important, under his at times brave editorship, and that of other editors who followed him, the *Irish Post* ensured that events in the north of Ireland were properly covered. He also kept alive the memory of Irishmen and women wrongly arrested and imprisoned in Britain during the long years when

they might have been forgotten by the other British media.

Building on the cohesion and identity that the *Irish Post* had fostered, the Federation of Irish Societies was founded in Portsmouth in 1973. This is now a national umbrella organisation, which draws together Irish clubs and societies across Britain to promote *"The interest of Irish people through community care, education, culture and arts, youth and sports activities and information provision."*[9] The Federation now has its headquarters in Camden Square, and rarely does an issue of the *Irish Post* pass without a mention of some activity in the building.

If an *Irish Post* reporter had attended the meeting of the Centre's administrative committee in April 1971, the topics under exhaustive discussion would have been very familiar. They included the subject of new carpets and redecorations, questions about the Albert Hall concert the month before including a critique or two of the performers, and another debate on the redevelopment of the adjoining land.

The committee decided to split the proposed uses of this development. The Camden Square frontage would become hostel or housing accommodation, and to the rear there would be a new hall or dining facilities. Camden had already given outline planning permission. Things were looking promising, although the capital funding had not yet been identified. The estimated cost was £395,000. It was thought that the housing would be easier to fund than those for the social element. Advice was sought from financial experts and the Catholic Housing Aid Association. Meanwhile, Liam Fanning's cool words of optimism were, *"Don't worry, the money will come."* He anticipated that there might be adequate funds raised by the National Collection.

'Adequate funds' had different mean-

The rear of the London Irish Centre premises from Agar Grove, showing the new Kennedy Memorial Hall at the left and the workshop to be later demolished to make way for the McNamara Hall.

ings as time passed. The schemes for the development were continually changing and throughout the length of this saga, it was extremely difficult to keep accurate track of costs and estimates. Different prices may have been quoted at different times for different reasons.

The day-to-day accounts of the centre were another matter. These were prepared by Paddy Keegan, as the volunteer accountant. He remembers giving them regularly to Liam Fanning before a meeting, so that the director could check them and come back with any questions. Unfortunately Liam Fanning would put them away in a drawer, and weeks later Paddy Keegan would discover that they had not been touched.

Tom McCabe remembers Paddy Keegan as an important figure. *"He was the one who was on your side, night, noon and morning, at your beck and call. He was the*

trouble-shooter. He did so many jobs that nobody else wanted to do there, hiring and firing. I personally found him a wonderful support, because I knew nothing about accounts when I went there, and of course Paddy had the task of turning me into a sort of junior accountant in a short time." Paddy Keegan had no interest in an official appointment as accountant, but was content to represent the Gaelic League on the administrative committee. This body, which was then strong in London, had little respect for the Centre because it felt that it exposed the problems of the Irish to the British. Nevertheless it had its official place on the committee, and Paddy Keegan took the opportunity to fill it.

In June 1971, Dominic Donnelly decided to stand down. He had been chairman for ten years. From Lisduff in Co. Roscommon, he was a successful businessman in London who was prominently identified with Irish culture and politics, and had given his support to the young Northern Ireland Civil Rights movement. His relationship with Liam Fanning was not productive, however, and he had visited John Dore in Dublin to say so. But Fr Dore was a stubborn man, and insisted that Liam Fanning should complete his three year 'obedience'.

In a farewell letter to members published in the July/August 1971 newsletter, Dominic Donnelly described the progress of the development next door: *"You know that the committee has been negotiating for some time to acquire further land, so that we may build new hostels, modernise the kitchen area and increase the size of the Hall. I am pleased to tell you that negotiations have now been successfully concluded and legal formalities are with the solicitors to be finalised. So this clears the way for the building programme. Architects have been instructed to prepare detailed drawings, and when they have got the approval of the local authority, we will then be in a position to start the actual building work. To carry out this programme will require a lot of money – something in the region of £400,000 to £500,000."*[10]

He was succeeded by Charlie Gallagher, another former chairman of the Irish Club, who was from Tubbercurry, Co. Sligo. The *Irish Post* wrote, *"The Irish Centre is very lucky to get him at a time when it is planning expenditure of approximately £500,000 over the next seven to ten years. And when these days you see a maroon Rolls Royce outside the Irish Centre in Camden Town you know that a man is at work – a man who could instead be playing golf on the most exclusive course."*[11] As chairman of Abbey Homesteads and a director of the property company Abbey Group, Charlie Gallagher had a string of enterprises ranging as far afield as Cyprus. It is a measure of the respect that the London

Irish Centre received, that successful businessmen such as Dominic Donnelly and Charlie Gallagher were willing to give it their time.

A few years later, Dominic Donnelly was killed tragically in a motorcycle accident in Co. Longford. Charlie Gallagher said of him, *"He was a great social worker, a great Christian and a great Irishman. A good man is always missed"*. Cardinal Heenan later said a Funeral Mass for him in Westminster Cathedral.

The distribution of the National Collection had been delayed, but Liam Fanning's time as director became dominated by the need to raise funds, large and small, simply to meet ongoing costs. Sponsored walks, often organised by other bodies onto which groups could attach themselves, were one way, and he, Paddy Sheridan and a few others including Tess Moroney memorably walked the thirty miles from Harlow Old Town to Camden Square. *"I was never so glad as to see Holloway prison as in all of my life"*, Liam Fanning said.[12] One of these walks raised the considerable amount of £1,600. Walks around the Inner Circle of Regent's Park were a more favoured and less exhausting alternative. Liam Fanning attended all the weekend socials and dances, often persuading the distinguished ecclesiastical guests to part with a donation. On the Monday mornings he would tell his secretary that he had secured the money, which kept the creditors at bay.[13]

In order to help the fund-raising process, the indefatigable Paddy Sheridan also approached a number of county associations, and quickly raised £1,000 from Clare and his own Cavan.

Father Tom McCabe

In September 1971, Paddy Sheridan says *"another Cavan man"* arrived. This was the return of Tom McCabe who was from

Fr Tom McCabe.

Ballyjamesduff, and who had been at Camden Square as a student in 1969. He now returned as a chaplain to replace Father Phil Kennedy, a Thurles, Co. Tipperary, man who had joined in September 1970, and had then moved on to London University. Phil Kennedy's stay at the Centre was short, but he was remembered for his enthusiasm for the game of hurling.

Tom McCabe had studied for five years at Belcamp College, an Oblate boarding school at Malahide near Dublin. In 1964 he had obtained a BA at University College, Dublin. His ordination had taken place in October 1970 also in Pilltown, Co. Kilkenny, after he had completed his theological studies in Dublin. With an ambition to serve as an Oblate in Brazil, McCabe had written to the Superior-General in Rome to request this assign-

ment. However, his student experience in Camden Square had been so fascinating he said that he would also like to serve at the London Irish Centre.The provincial, John Dore, confirmed his assignment. As an ordained priest Tom McCabe's duties now included an extra dimension.For example there were the Masses, for which he now shared responsibility. *"There was a little chapel upstairs.There were two Masses a day, one in the morning and one at night. I think we had two more Masses on Sunday."*[14]

On 13 July 1971 Bishop Eamonn Casey visited the London Irish Centre and informed Liam Fanning and his staff that the distribution of the National Collection would commence in the near future. The task of allocating the funds, which now were to be used only for capital expenditure and not to meet debts or for running costs, had been assigned to the Bishops' Committee, led by Eamonn Casey.

There was no word for months. The administrative committee then learned in February 1972 that a consultancy, Annan, Impey and Morrish had been appointed to investigate the individual merits of the potential recipients. The consultants' report, on 24 March 1972, examined six London projects and recommended that the London Irish Centre should receive £84,000. The total London allocation was £150,000, and approximately £100,000 would be spent outside London.

There were in fact serious doubts about the ability of the Centre to manage its own finances. The development plan of the hall, without a proper feasibility study, had been making people on the Committee somewhat nervous. Some members recommended that the Hammersmith Irish Centre and another in Tooting, south London, should share an equal allocation. Quite naturally, the London Irish Centre objected to this view, and argued that as the first and biggest centre it should receive the greatest allocation. In May 1973 the administrative committee learned that although the £84,000 had finally been allocated, it had still not received it.[15]

Some months later, in September, Eamonn Casey confirmed that there would in fact now be a grant of only £75,000 towards the purchase of new hostel accommodation. This smaller amount was not greeted with pleasure. Some of it must have been paid in 1973, because in January 1974 the administrative committee's minutes report that "the balance" had not been received.

Among those who knew him, Liam Fanning was regarded as popular and outgoing. He was good at delegating and people liked working for him. He had a misleadingly relaxed exterior presence but did not seem well suited to the stresses and complexities of managing the Centre or indeed of practical welfare and advice work. As Paddy Sheridan generously wrote in the newsletter for that month, *"Being head chaplain at the Irish Centre is about as complicated a job as any priest could have. It has its pleasant moments, but it has its frustrations. One great characteristic which Fr Liam Fanning had was his kindness to his fellow chaplains."*

Liam Fanning remained as long as he could, but in December 1971 he was most relieved to return to parochial ministry at Coleford, in Gloucestershire, to enjoy the quiet of country life once again.

During this period there had been a growing awareness of the Irish who were resident in Britain, much of it negative, as a result of the escalation of the problems in northern Ireland. At the end of the 1960s, on the advice of the Metropolitan Police, the annual St Patrick's Day Parade in Westminster was discontinued because of the fear of reprisals. While it was discontinued in London, an excursion was organised by the parade committee to join the one in Dublin. It was welcomed there for two years, carrying a banner made by the Poor Clare Nuns in Arkley, north London. The parade was eventually restored to Westminster when the police, wisely, realised that its purpose was entirely religious, and to prohibit it could further inflame tensions.

Meanwhile, the Troubles in northern Ireland were escalating. On 9 August 1971, internment without trial was implemented. As many as 342 nationalist suspects were arrested in a series of overnight raids, but with no arrests from the loyalist side. This policy was much later shown to be a failure when finally the Home Secretary, Merlyn Rees, signed the papers for the last of the detainees to be released in December 1975.

In this period the shootings of 'Bloody Sunday' took place in Derry, on 30 January 1972, when thirteen people died. A week later, seven local priests conducted a Requiem Mass at the Centre. The sermon was given by a minister of the Church of Ireland, a Protestant. One of the priests, Father Colum McDonnell, who was director of Benburb Base, appealed to Camden Council to pressure the government into bringing 'sanity' to the Ulster crisis. *"I beg the Camden people to listen to Fr McDonnell's plea"*, said Jock Stallard, MP, St Pancras North. A priest in Somers Town, Father Patrick Dillon of St Aloysius Church, reported that many people took the day off work on Wednesday – the day the Derry dead were buried – in sympathy.[16] The following week there was a letter of support from Sister Sarah Clarke, of the Order of La Sainte Union, writing on behalf of the Northern Ireland Civil Rights Association. It was clear that in places like Camden, where there was a large Irish community, there was also a sense of identification with the cause of civil rights in northern Ireland. From 1969 the Centre had been aiding the relief of distress in the north with cash collections and donations of clothing. The recipients were fairly ecumenical, and included Irish Unity, the Civil Rights Committee, the Falls Road Relief Fund, the *Belfast Telegraph* Relief Fund and the Derry Internees Dependants' Fund. Distribution was often through politicians such as John Hume and Eddie McAteer.

Tess Hutchinson, the daughter of Martin and Tess Moroney, describes how northern Irish children came to England for respite holidays away from the bombings and riots of Belfast or Derry. They were invited by the Centre and placed into the homes of members.*"I remember my parents playing host to three boys who were about eight years of age. One of the boys insisted on wearing pyjamas over his day clothes when he went to bed at night. This, he explained, was in case there was a raid by the Army or the RUC on the home. One of the other lads was amazed that the floorboards in our house were nailed down, because he said back home his Dad had not nailed them down because they had regular visits from the Army or the RUC to look beneath them."*[17] It is clear that London must have been quite a pleasant shock.

However, a wave of anti-Irish sentiment was also sweeping across Britain, which was to increase when the IRA began its mainland bombing campaign in 1973. There was a supposition in some sections of the press that all Irish people had connections with the IRA. Many British people were also concerned by attacks on British soldiers, but at the same time felt that northern Ireland was a place across the water, far away, and wondered aloud why lives there were being wasted, let alone taxpayers' money. They did not fully understand Irish history or its sectarian politics. *"Let the Irish fight it out among themselves"*, was often heard.

Meanwhile the *Irish Post* was now bringing the community in Britain together on a weekly basis, commenting on the news while fostering a deserved sense of identity. The situation also acted as a catalyst. A proliferation of political groups was also gathering. The Troops Out Movement was founded in 1973, the Anti-Internment League soon followed and the Irish in Britain Representation Group came together in 1983. They and others grew in membership, even although the British authorities, while watching them, ignored what they had to say. Tom McCabe had already noticed a creeping politicisation in the more moderate activities at the Centre, *"There was one particular county association, Armagh, that people felt had an undue degree of IRA influence within its membership. I could not be absolutely sure that this was true. Many of the County Associations from the north did have their quota of people. Then you had the prisoner aid groups. It was a very raw time, and in a way we were all influenced by what was happening."*[18] Even the Council of Irish Counties did not escape politicisation.

Father Paddy Mee

One person who was caught up in this was Father Paddy Mee, the next director. He was born in Drumgowna, Carrickmacross, Co. Monaghan, in April 1915. Educated at St Mary's, Dundalk, he was ordained at Daingean, Co. Offally, in 1940. He was first assigned to Glencree in 1940, before moving on to Belcamp College in 1946. By 1966 he was the parish priest at Holy Cross, Liverpool, before coming directly to the Centre in December 1971.

It is said that there were two sides to Paddy Mee. He had a gruff, even authoritarian exterior, behind which hid a man of understanding and sympathy. He has been described as *"really a gentleman, as soft as butter. His bark was always worse than his bite."* And he had a sense of hu-

Fr Paddy Mee.

I ever worked with. He allowed you your head and never questioned you. Paddy was always considered political but was for truth and honesty, all the time and no matter. He loved his country and if an injustice was done it didn't matter who did it. Paddy condemned it."[20] He was staunchly republican, yet shrewd enough to prevent the IRA or others from ever compromising or manipulating the integrity of the Centre. This was usually attempted with some subtlety, but occasionally with pressure. Bomb threats were one way."*The police would be regularly in checking toilets*", says Tom McCabe, "*You know we went through this drill, we had to get people out of the building, we also had to put security on the door at night. I would say that when I came for the second time this was definitely the background against which we were working, and you felt it in your stomach. We couldn't do anything about it, it was an open space.*"[21] Though the Centre continually rejected approaches from the para-militaries, the police still took a great interest in its activities and in who was staying at the hostels.

Police Interest

Apart from helping to clear the premises after bomb threats, more than once the police returned for their own purposes. They came to scrutinise the admission cards, kept in a filing cabinet of those seeking help. However, Anne-Marie O'Boyle ensured it was always locked, and the key went home in her purse every night.

On one occasion Paddy Mee was awakened from his sleep by a violent banging. The police at the door asked him to open up the office, examining any letters or documentation that they came across. What caused real interest was a list of names, found on a desk, which appeared to reveal suspicious international links

mour. Many people commented on what an inspiring person he was to work for. As Tom McCabe said "*He gave people the sense that they were running the place. And in truth you were.*"[19] Shy by nature, Paddy Mee was cautious and slow to embark upon major schemes or projects unless things had been carefully considered beforehand. A real conservative in matters of everyday life as well as in his Catholicism, he had a suspicion of professionals, preferring the advice of those he knew best.

Paddy Sheridan, who was still there when Paddy Mee arrived, is typically direct in his comments."*Paddy Mee was before his time. He was one of the best men*

The names included Dietrich Bonhoeffer, Hans Kung, Michael Quoist, Karl Rahner and Edward Schillebeeckx. They were obviously not Irish names, but possibly a sinister network of international conspirators. When the Metropolitan Police were finally informed who they were, they were most unwilling to believe that these were some of the century's leading theologians.

On another raid, they came into Mee's bedroom. *"Paddy Mee would have under his bed all these crucifixes made out of matchsticks by the prisoners in Long Kesh. He was a very hard-working, honest-to-God man. I didn't enter into his politics"*, said Joan Moriarty, who joined the staff in 1974. The crucifixes were never found.

Tom McCabe tells of another visit. *"I had six or seven Special Branch people come into my little flat. I wasn't thinking of making them a cup of tea, I was furious. I hadn't been long in bed and they were pounding the door. I thought that the house was on fire or something. These guys all came in and they were all spruced up, they looked as if they had been up for ever in their Armani suits. They turned my room upside down and went through my diaries, all that stupid stuff, really crazy, nonsense. While they were doing the Centre itself I began to get my thoughts together, and I thought 'Paddy Mee is going to lose it'. So I went over the road as quickly as I could, and there he was having coffee with them, charming the man in charge of the raid. The funny thing is that they went upstairs to his office and they looked everyplace. He had the Prisoners' Aid names stuffed in a drawer. It was a very shallow drawer in the middle of the desk, and they never saw it."*[22]

During this raid another officer burst into a bedroom in the upper floors of the Centre. He saw someone in bed, with long blond hair across the pillow. Extremely courteously the policeman muttered *"Excuse me, Miss"*, without realising that this was in fact Oliver Barry, who was then a student priest at the Centre. Despite such raids over a number of years nothing of value was ever found.

New staff

Following an appeal from Paddy Mee to the religious orders for new staff, Sister Thecla Cleary applied to work in the Centre as a part-time volunteer for several months. She came from the Sisters of Joseph of Peace, based in Hanwell in Middlesex, although her origins were from Shinrone, Co. Offally. Active in the Pioneer Association, she had worked in Scotland at Carstairs with people who had learning difficulties, and then later at St Peter's College in Cardross. In a few months she agreed to move to the girls' hostel in Hornsey Lane Gardens to take over from the formidable Marie Harrington on her retirement.

Tom McCabe recalls that during this time the welfare team was young and enthusiastic, and the work was unpredictable with a different human crisis almost every day. The report published in 1972, by Ann-Marie O'Boyle and a new colleague Hilary Murnane, who was from Skibbereen in Co. Cork and who had joined the Centre in March 1972, gives an analysis of the statistics of that year.

The number of boys and young men accommodated at the hostel at Camden Square was 497, but the number of girls at Hornsey Lane Gardens was only 275, because of redecoration. At the welfare office in the Irish Centre itself some 1557 clients were interviewed, comprising 1120 males, 340 females and ninety-seven families. Dublin, Cork, Limerick and Tipperary tended to be the counties from which most of the callers came. A drop in figures was continuing, partly as a result of the Irish economy picking up, but there was a significant proportion coming through the doors from northern Ireland. *"Northern Ireland refugee families, driven out of their homes by intimidation or frustration, have arrived in London during the past year to find that the odds are against them in an overcrowded city, with its own serious housing problems."*[23] Like others before them had found, London was no easy option.

One arrival in 1973 was Frank, a gay man from Dundalk in Co. Louth. He left because of homophobic persecution. *"I cried my eyes out leaving the port of Dun Laoghaire, watching the lights of Ireland disappear. I thought I would never see Ireland again"*, he said. When he arrived in Camden Square, he was immediately reassured. *"I loved it when I went in, I was with my own kind. There was drink. The food was good. It was Ireland away from Ireland."* The rent at that time was £4 a week. Very soon he met someone working as the Centre. *"John handed me my dinner"*.

Describing the working routine, John says he was offered a job as a cleaner at £14 a week, and also served the meals. He would have to clean up after the dinner dances, which would sometimes take all night. In the evenings he had to go around with a book checking who was in the hostel, and heard young, homesick men crying in the toilets. The TV Lounge was closed at 10.30 pm. He says that once the building itself was locked a particular member of the staff who enjoyed a dangerous prank would wait inside an open window on the first floor with a bucket of iced water ready to throw over the first person who climbed in. Occasionally there were *"… wild boys staying, who smashed toilets and cleaned their shoes with the sheets"*. Away from home, *"they threw chips under the bed and fag butts on the floor."* At night he says that the priests *"used to have a coffee and milk, and grumbled about the takings."*

Frank and John have now lived together as a couple for thirty-two years. As two young men who had fled severe homophobia and abuse in Ireland they now say that if it was not for the Irish Centre, *"I don't know where we would have ended up."*[24]

Many people first met at the Centre, and in spite of the Troubles, or because of their tendency to throw people in adversity together, the social life of the Centre was thriving. The regular Sunday evening sessions with the Waterford fiddle player, Jimmy Power, were an attraction. He played there for years until one of the priests disapproved of a relationship that was discovered between a married member of his band and a woman.[25] Joe Davis used to go there for a drink, where Mary Kenny asked him to help move the chairs. He says, *"Mary epitomises the whole Irish Centre. Her heart is the Irish Centre, she is the Irish Centre."* He was soon asked by Paddy Mee to run its social committee. *"I spent most of my time, and most of my money, there"*, he says.[26] One of the more enjoyable tasks was finding musicians who could play at the sessions. Mary Kenny thought he could book a band for £10. Instead, Joe Davis travelled on the pillion seat of Paddy Sheridan's motorcycle across London to listen to those bands that had been recommended.

"The Sunday sessions always drew a big crowd", remembers Sally Mulready. *"There were some fine floor singers. Curley Sullivan from Cork sang, and everyone loved him. And in his 'country and western' style voice Paddy Sheridan used to launch into 'Come back, Paddy Reilly, to Ballyjamesduff,' as only a Cavan man can sing it. There was a great atmosphere, home from home."*[27]

This was also the time that Tommy Maguire arrived, at the invitation of Paddy Sheridan. With colleagues, he took children's classes for traditional music in fiddle, whistle and piano accordion on weekday evenings and Saturday mornings. His

Sally Mulready fourth from the left, with Jimmy Power, the fiddle player, and others.

concerts were extremely popular, in spite of the pipers each wanting a room to tune up, and the proceeds went into the Centre's funds. He also organised at least two marching bands.

In those days, the Kennedy Hall was so busy that for their dinners and dances the county associations were only allowed two Saturday nights at this venue in a year. Bookings were made twelve months in advance. Inevitably there was a deal of horse-trading that went on between the county secretaries to obtain the most convenient Saturday.

In August 1973 Tom McCabe left the Centre to return to Dublin, to be replaced by Father Patsy Carolan.

Father Patsy Carolan

In his thanks at the end of his 1973 report Paddy Mee drew attention to his two chaplains, Paddy Sheridan and now Patsy Carolan, for *"their hard and unremitting work*

– especially in the 'after hours demands'. They and the voluntary staff who man the reception desk every evening and make possible a 16-hour working day at the Centre." The report ends with a thought: *"Is emigrant still a dirty word, or is it the material from which a better Ireland could be helped on its way?"*

Patsy Carolan had been assigned to parishes in England before, to Norris Green in Liverpool from 1964 to 1969 and to Chelmsley Wood from 1969 to 1974. Originally from Grousehill, in Co. Cavan, he had been through the novitiate and the training before his ordination, but his first introduction to the London Irish Centre was unusual. *"I played football for Cavan in the Ulster Final in 1960, and I wasn't supposed to play"*. He played under an assumed name, since the Oblates did not permit their members to take part in public sports. This has since been reversed, it seems, by their eagerness to enjoy the game of golf. *"Father Paddy Mee happened to be at*

Fr Patsy Carolan with two members of the Irish Centre Club.

the game and saw me play. He came to me afterwards and said 'You are in trouble, but tell them I told you to play, and stick to that', which I did."[28] Some years afterwards, Paddy Mee asked him whether he could manage the potential new hostel, Hope House. He was in Chelmsley Wood when the provincial, John Dore, prompted by Paddy Mee, contacted him.

The nursing-home known as Hope House was located very near the Church of the Sacred Heart at nos. 20-22 Quex Road. Tom McCabe describes how he used to go running over Hampstead Heath with a priest from that church, Father Pat Burke, who told him that the Holy Family Sisters, a sister organisation of the Oblates, would welcome an interest in the building from the London Irish Centre. He passed this news on to Paddy Mee, who had been actively looking for new hostel premises, and had already viewed two alternatives. But when the Sisters decided to discon-

tinue their nursing-home at this address *"It seemed like a gift from Heaven."*[29] Although built in 1884, with a chapel added in later years, it was in an excellent state of repair, but needed to be adapted to its role as a hostel for young men.

Patsy Carolan admits to knowing nothing about housing, but in his innocence he said that he would accept the assignment. John Dore encouraged him. He spent over six months visiting housing schemes, attending courses and reading books on the subject.*"I knew nothing about it, to be honest. Trying to get a vision. I set up that vision, and the hostel was started."*[30] The Sisters were still in the building when he arrived to take it on, but eventually there were over a hundred 'young fellows' in the house.

He may have been modest about his experience of housing, but Carolan had a skill which might have come in useful. After a series of initiation tests, he had become a member of the Zodiac Society, which is affiliated to the Magic Circle. *"I had always been interested in card tricks as a child, and really got into magic when I came to this country. I worked in a youth club in Liverpool and the kids loved it"*, he said.

The Housing Act had extended the powers of the Housing Corporation in 1974 to help voluntary bodies, such as housing associations, undertake their own projects. The Irish Centre itself had already decided to form an association and to register this with the Housing Corporation. In July 1969 it had set up Irish Centre Hostels Ltd, which could apply for grant aid from the Corporation. Surprisingly, however, it was not the Housing Corporation which purchased Hope House.

Hope House

After some swift negotiation, Hope House was bought by Irish Centre Hostels Ltd on 31 January, 1974, for approximately £150,000. The National Collection finally donated £75,000 towards the purchase price, and Camden Council provided a helpful mortgage of £87,000. Planning permission for its conversion was duly granted. *"This is a very good and modern property, in fact one block containing 27 rooms had only been built in the last three years, and without any alterations is ideally suited to our purpose"*, stated a press release. *"There is a real need in this city of London for this type of accommodation. Many firms have vacancies for good jobs simply because men who would be willing to take the jobs simply cannot find accommodation. Our intention is to cater for these. We do not believe it is in the best interest of newcomers to London to start living on the state and just idling their time inevitably getting into trouble. This is in line with the general policy of the centre, which is preventative."*

Mossie O'Riordan tells a story of when the Irish owner of a hotel in Russell Square told Paddy Sheridan that she had some beds to dispose of, and she asked whether Mossie could send a truck there to collect them. Thinking that there would be just a dozen, he agreed, as he also had storage in his depot near the Centre. *"Sure, there were a couple of hundred beds and mattresses"*, he later said. *"And about a thousand mice with them. The mice got into the offices. One of the girls started screeching and she was up on a table. The mice had arrived"*. He says that he never really got rid of the mice until the yard was pulled

Hope House Hostel, 20-22 Quex Road, Kilburn.

down to make way for the Maiden Lane estate.[31] Many of these beds eventually found their way into Hope House.

The building was formally opened by Cardinal Conway, Archbishop of Armagh and Primate of all Ireland, on 27 March 1974, with Patsy Carolan appointed as its manager. Speaking at the opening, Bishop Eamonn Casey gave a broad hint that the Irish government may, at last, be persuaded to provide financial help for projects to aid Irish immigrants in Britain. As he said, *"The time is now right for my government to express its responsibility for the welfare content of newly-arrived Irish immigrants on the shores of any land. I hope the Irish government will come forward and repay the debt of decades, if not centuries."* Representatives of the Irish Episcopal Commission had met officials of the Department of Foreign Affairs of the new Liam Cosgrave government in May 1973 to press its claim, but ultimately with no success.

In this the Commission was supported by Cllr Paddy O'Connor, who demanded to know what the government was planning to do. *"It's a disgrace that we have an estimated 10,000 people sleeping on the pavements of London. And that's not counting those housed by organisations like St Mungo's in the old Marmite factory in Vauxhall, or those saved from homelessness by the Oblate fathers of the Irish Centre, without the slightest help from the Dublin government. Despite the fact that many years ago, together with many other Irish people in London, I approached the government and said 'Give us at least a grant to build a hostel'. We never got the grant, and it looks as if we never will get it."*[32] Again there was little response.

As if to emphasise the need, it was reported in the *Daily Telegraph* that Camden Council was alarmed by a sudden upswing in the number of Irish emigrants seeking its help. A spokesman was quoted as saying that they frequently became "a social and financial problem" within a few days of arrival. At Hope House, Patsy Carolan said, *"We are tremendously busy at the moment. The other night I was called out of bed five times between one o'clock and six in the morning"*. Father Frank Ryan occasionally had to step in at Hope House when Patsy Carolan was away.

Father Frank Ryan

Frank Ryan had also arrived in 1974. He had already been a student at the Centre, but now rejoined the team as a chaplain. After ordination in 1967, he had left *"the parish I loved"*, St Anne's in Birmingham, in 1969 to become priest in the bleak environment of Leith, just north of Edinburgh. Here he worked in the tradition of the Oblates unafraid to roll up his sleeves to assist the local community in youth work.

In the summer he received a call from John Dore, asking him to move down to the London Irish Centre. For Frank Ryan, a Portlaoise man who wears a Pioneer pin of abstinence in his lapel, the London position had little appeal. Arriving in October, he accepted the appointment out of his religious obedience rather than any wish to participate in the activities of the Centre. *"Mainly because I saw it as a kind of ghetto, where the Irish would drink, talk and carry on as if they had never left Ireland. I had little love of Irish traditional music, and since I did not drink had even less appreciation of the social scene, centred on many bars. Privately, I thought this was the last place I wanted to be sent."*[33] In spite of it being a tough assignment, he now admits that he even enjoyed it.

There was no job description, apart from 'junior chaplain', but there was plenty to do. He soon gained a reputation as a hard worker, doing odd jobs around the building, and would think nothing of sweeping up and cleaning the yard at the back. As Maeve Heath says, *"He was up to arms in muck."*[34] Frank Ryan describes his introduction as 'fierce'.

His first impression was of crowds constantly arriving, like waves, especially on Sundays when the Centre was home for a variety of activities. It also acted as a sort of information exchange. Personnel on the switchboard were expected to know everything of interest for an Irish person in London, including the results of the latest hurling or football matches. Every kind of question was likely to be asked, and the answers were expected to be definitive if not authoritative.

Occasionally humour intruded into the reality. Frank Ryan repeats a Paddy Sheridan story. *"People came to Murray Street from the back of nowhere. They had never seen London, they'd never seen a black person before standing on a corner, and couldn't believe they were real. Some of these guys were being exposed to things they had never witnessed before. There was this fellow who was having a shower upstairs in the hostel, so Paddy Sheridan found water coming down the stairways, so he went up to investigate. And there was your man with his foot on the drain and Paddy said 'What are you doing?' He said I'm having a bath, and I'm waiting for the water to come up."*

Unlike Paddy Sheridan, he concentrated on the welfare, rather than the social, activities of the Centre, and found it practical if for most of the time he was not wearing the clerical collar. Calls and callers came in twenty-four hours a day, seven days a week. In dealing with these, he remembers a great spirit of commitment among the staff in the welfare office. Each person was listened to, and the repeated pleas of "I need a job" or "I need somewhere to stay" were predominant. Sometimes also there was a request for food or

for clothing, and occasionally, from those who had realised that London was not for them, "I want to go home". In some cases they had little or no money, but in others whatever money they had once possessed had been lost in the pub or the betting shop.

Sister Joan Moriarty

Another arrival in 1974 was Sr Joan Moriarty, who joined Anne-Marie O'Boyle in the welfare office. They each gave many years to the Centre. Joan was originally from Cloghan on the Tralee side of the Dingle peninsula, and was of the Daughters of Charity of St Vincent de Paul. She was a professional social worker, having worked in child guidance at the Child Study Centre on the Navan Road in Dublin and later in London with the Catholic Children's Society, where she said, *"The set-up was not suited to my temperament."*

She says that she had read an article about the London Irish Centre and about Paddy Mee, whom she describes as *"the best of men"*, and so she picked up the phone. She was answered by Paddy Sheridan, *"and true to form Father Sheridan said one thing and he was gone like lightning. So I duly arrived up for the appointment, and Father Sheridan was not there and had told nobody"*. Her second call was to Paddy Mee whom she met, and he asked her when she could start. *"I just loved the Irish Centre. In those days of course we had a very small office and it was used by everybody. There were two of us working in that office. You came in on a Monday morning and all your records were pulled out. It was used for everything over the weekend, all the Irish societies used it and the beer was spilt all over your desk."*[35]

Her work was centred on young people. As she reported, *"Some had fallen out with their parents and were on the run from them. Some boys were on the run with their girlfriends. There was quite a number of preg-*

nant girls who had nowhere to go and needed counselling and help. There were people who had grown up in institutions who had wandered away. There were a lot of disturbed people. There were gay people who couldn't face the situation in Ireland and sought refuge in London."

The 1974 welfare report, written by Anne-Marie O'Boyle and Joan Moriarty, included details of the two hostels. Hornsey Lane Gardens was now supervised by Sr Thecla Cleary, and the new men's hostel, Hope House in Quex Road, was "very efficiently managed" by Patsy Carolan.

As an institution, the London Irish Centre was regarded as an authority on the Irish in Britain, and one that was consulted or even provoked for comment. Sometimes it made the national headlines. With the heat of anti-Irish feeling sweeping the country, Lord Arran fanned the flames with an article in the London *Evening Standard* newspaper under the heading 'May the Irish rot in Hell'. In the article he described all Irish as "savage, murderous thugs", which created a storm of protest. He was denounced as racist by various Community Relations Councils and by the National Council for Civil Liberties. When approached for a comment, Patsy Carolan told the *Hampstead and Highgate Express* that Irish people he had been in contact with were "appalled and annoyed" by the article. Jock Stallard, MP, tabled a question in the House of Commons, asking if the Attorney General would be implementing proceedings under the Race Relations Act against Lord Arran.[36]

Farewell to Paddy Sheridan

After what seemed like many long years at Camden Square, it was Paddy Sheridan's turn to move on, to Birmingham. One of the last of the rediscovered newsletters was not written by him, their author for years. But with equally charming prose, his colleague Frank Ryan described the "façade" of the Irish Centre as now "weathered". "In losing Father Patrick Sheridan, OMI, it has lost its greatest PRO man. Father Sheridan became so involved with the Irish Centre that the two became almost synonymous. He worked here for eight years. His parting may make the beginning of a legend, let us hope it is not the end of an era."[37]

After a splendid send-off in the company of the Ambassador, Donal O'Sullivan, during which Paddy Sheridan gave a farewell performance of his favourite ballads on the stage of the Douglas Hyde Lounge, he left to join the Welfare Centre in Birmingham as its director. A journey from London to Birmingham was relatively easy, and he drove up the M1 motorway listening to cassettes of Irish ballads in his car. His departure from London coincided with the day that the IRA bombed two Birmingham pubs.

He later described the London Irish Centre. "Looking back, it was savage. Because you never got to bed. At the earliest it was two o'clock, and you were up at six. Every six or seven weeks you just had to get away. It was savage work. What people do not understand is that we were never paid, we lived on the smell of an oily rag. We saved the Irish Centre an enormous amount of money, and we worked for nothing, we worked from hand to mouth. That's our way of life. There's no big deal about it."[38] But the Centre was not to know that he would return a few years later.

For many who were thinking of emigration, London was a totally foreign place. Paddy Mee recounted a favourite story to describe one of the people he had met in London, an Irishman who had just arrived at Victoria. The man was advised that there might be accommodation in a hostel

110

in Quex Road, and he decided to walk, asking the way as he proceeded. Soon he found himself crossing a park. When he finally arrived at Hope House he asked someone at the door who it was who owned the fields back there, because he could get a job milking the cows. He was gently informed that the 'fields' were in fact called Hyde Park. Frank Ryan ended the story, *"We later got him a job minding cattle on a farm in Kent."*[39]

Families were deterred as much as possible from emigration by the offices and advice bureaux which had been set up, and by the voluntary bodies within their parishes such as the Legion of Mary, but all too often this effort was unsuccessful. *"All our propaganda"*, said Paddy Mee, *"is aimed at telling families that there is little hope for them here in London."* He added, *"The real tragedy today is the changing type of homelessness. Before, we all knew we had a problem with the older Irish over here. But now, more and more people are coming in from urban areas in the south. We can never solve this problem, because the roots lie in Ireland. But as far as I can see, not only is the Irish Government not doing anything to get to the root of the problem, they are even refusing to help us deal with the effects of it here in London."*[40]

While welcomed, the purchase of Hope House had changed the Centre's plan for the redevelopment of the adjoining site in Camden Square. With its resources now diverted to Kilburn, the Centre finally passed the opportunity for this hostel redevelopment to the Camden-based Community Housing Association. However, the ambitions to build a hall on the land behind it remained as potent as ever. As Tom McCabe later remembered it: *"During my time the hall was being dreamed about, very strongly dreamed about. This was by Paddy Mee and he really persuaded, or they persuaded each other,*

Charles Gallagher, the chairman. The hall was always an issue, because we knew this land which was owned by British Rail was available cheaply. It depended on good vision as to what to do with it. It was there for the taking. We had been offered it. It was very, very tempting. We knew that our building was weak. We knew that we needed development on the site. We knew that, and this was a big site, and would we be able to do it and where was the money coming from?"[41]

There were continuing anxieties about what was happening to the income that was being earned. *"We were always trying to make ends meet"*, says Frank Ryan. *"Running the bars we were turning over a lot, but we were always trying to figure out why they were not making an appropriate profit"*. He describes one of the reasons. *"We were all in the pub with the bar managers, and one manager disappeared. We then heard that he was locked in a cupboard, and the people who had locked him in got the keys and stole a lot of money."*[42] Frank Ryan was a tee-totaller, but the disappearance of income from the bars was worrying. It would be some time before some control was restored.

Across Camden Square, the house at 1 North Villas was no longer required, and was sold to Camden Council in September 1974. This helped to balance the books.

With the hostel at Tollington Park having been sold in July 1970, Hope House had now joined Hornsey Lane Gardens as the other one directly administered by Irish Centre Housing Ltd. The latter housed forty girls but was recognised as being somewhat remote from the activity based around Camden Square and now in Kilburn. There was another difficulty. As Joan Moriarty said, *"Hornsey Lane was not the safest place for young people to go at night. It was a little off the beaten track, and it wasn't safe for young people getting off buses if they were working late."*[43]

111

St Louise Hostel, Medway Street, Westminster.

Later in 1974, St Louise Hostel in Medway Street, Westminster became available. This was the ideal replacement of Hornsey Lane Gardens, and was purchased from the Daughters of Charity of St Vincent de Paul in 1975. It was reopened, after considerable refurbishment, by Cardinal Basil Hume on 5 May 1981.

The hostels under the administration of the Centre were only able to accommodate a fraction of those who arrived looking for a bed. With refurbishments also taking place, many callers were referred to approved lodgings. If this was unsuccessful there were other hostels such as the Salvation Army, the YMCA or Arlington House.

The Centre also kept a list of potential employers who were willing to take on labour. The Marian Employment Agency retained its links until it closed in 1975. During most of this time there was no shortage of work, and it only took one or two phone calls to find a job. West End stores, hotels and hospitals accepted many of the women. For men, no matter how incapable someone seemed, it was always possible to find a job for them, even if it was only making tea or sweeping up on a building site. Some building contractors, however, were more demanding. One firm would always ask on the telephone, "What weight is he?" as if it was buying

cattle, but meaning "Could he dig trenches all day?" Not everyone wanted men who were fourteen stone with prominent beer bellies, but some employers were glad to get them.[44] Employers such as Mossie O'Riordan, from Joseph Murphy's, would still drop in at the bar at the Centre, often to recruit workers. Joan Moriarty has an amusing recollection of his requests for staff, *"Sister, don't send me anybody with a crew cut. Or with pointy toes in their shoes. Or with cowboy boots".* As a helpful welfare officer, no doubt she delivered the goods.

As the reputation of the welfare service grew, more callers were attracted to it. There were many who had been in England for some time, but were now in middle age with little to show for their work. Even when they had been earning good money on building sites they had not the ability to save. The money was good but often earned under false names, so saving was not part of their language. Some could not survive the more damaging aspects of life in London.

The welfare and employment services required increasing funding, and more imaginative ideas were continually sought. The Albert Hall concerts continued, but the effort was seen to be counter-productive and audiences were dropping. It was an expensive place to rent, and the organising committee had to cope with everything from demo tapes by fledgling stars to trying to keep under control those who wanted complimentary tickets. In March 1975 the concert top-lined Brendan Shine and his Superband, with the tenor Frank Patterson and the television star Joe Lynch who was a stalwart in his support. Although the Centre finally ceased to stage the Albert Hall concerts a few years later, this method of fund-raising did not die. In due course it was adopted by the Irish Chaplaincy.

In poor health, Paddy Mee left in February 1975. The dedication required had taken its toll, not just on him but also on previous incumbents. He was quoted as saying, *"I don't know where I'll be going yet, but it couldn't be a nicer place than this."*[45] After Camden Square, he was assigned as parish priest in Stafford Road, west Kilburn from 1977 to 1983, and from there back to Ireland at Cahirmoyle from 1983 to 1984. He was then posted across the Atlantic to Whitehorse, a mission in Canada, until 1987 and returned to Daingean, in Co. Offaly, where he had been ordained, from 1988 to 1989. While using Belcamp College as his retirement base, he also spent time in Clogher diocese near his home parish in Co. Monaghan, serving as a priest in a voluntary capacity.

Before he left, Paddy Mee was having a cup of tea late one night with Paddy Keegan in one of the Centre's rooms. An unfamiliar priest entered. This was Bill Cagney, who had been asked take over as director.

Tom McCabe says, *"Paddy Mee was a wonderful man, a man with a great heart who often sold himself short. Because of the way he spoke in public I always felt he did sometimes harangue a bit, but that wasn't the man. He was very committed to justice and very committed to people, particularly the people who were coming to our hostel. I think he was an intelligent man who thought seriously about things, and was much more balanced in fact than sometimes his words or indeed the stereotype that has emerged of him might suggest."*[46]

He died on 28 September, 1996.

1. LIC Welfare Report, 1971.
2. Irish Club *Newsletter*, 1971.
3. *Irish in Britain News*, 20 September 1991.
4. Interview Fr Frank Ryan, October 2003.
5. Interview Maureen Greaves, April 2004.
6. Oblate papers, London.
7. LIC 17th Annual Report
8. *A History of the Irish Post*, published by the Irish Post, 2000.
9. Federation of Irish Societies website.
10. LIC *Newsletter,* July/August 1971.
11. *Irish Post*, 3 July 1971.
12. *Ibid*, 30 May 1970.
13. Interview Paddy Keegan, July 2004.
14. Interview Fr Tom McCabe, October 2003.
15. LIC minutes, 14 May 1973.
16. *Camden Journal*, 4 February 1972.
17. Correspondence with Tess Hutchinson, July 2004.
18. Interview Fr Tom McCabe, October 2003.
19. *Ibid.*
20. Interview Fr Paddy Sheridan, October 2003.
21. Interview Fr Tom McCabe, October 2003.
22. *Ibid.*
23. LIC Welfare Report 1972.
24. Interview Frank and John, July 2004.
25. Correspondence with Sally Mulready, June 2004.
26. Interview Joe Davis, May 2004.
27. Correspondence with Sally Mulready, June 2004.
28. Interview Fr Patsy Carolan, October 2003.
29. Interview Fr Tom McCabe, October 2003.
30. Interview Fr Patsy Carolan, October 2003.
31. Interview Mossie O'Riordan, March 2004.
32. *Sunday World*, 12 May 1974.
33. Many of Fr Ryan's remiscences are taken from *The Phantom and the Phoenix* by Frank Ryan OMI, privately published in 2000.
34. Interview Maeve Heath, March 2004.
35. Interview Sr Joan Moriarty, March 2004.
36. *Hampstead and Highgate Express*, 7 June 1974.
37. LIC *Newsletter*, October 1974.
38. Interview Fr Paddy Sheridan, October 2003.
39. Interview Fr Frank Ryan, October 2003.
40. *Sunday World*, 12 May 1974.
41. Interview Fr Tom McCabe, October 2003.
42. Interview Frank Ryan, October 2004.
43. Interview Sr Joan Moriarty, March 2004.
44. From *The Phantom and the Phoenix*, by Frank Ryan.
45. *Camden New Journal*, 28 February 1985
46. Interview Fr Tom McCabe, October 2003.

CHAPTER SEVEN

All that is best in our culture and tradition

Father Bill Cagney

There were more arrivals and departures of staff as the Centre took on further responsibilities and commenced, physically, to spread outwards. This long-expected expansion was to dominate much of the decision-making over the next twenty years.

Paddy Mee was followed into Camden Square a month later, in March 1975, by Father Bill Cagney. Frank Ryan, who was still here as a chaplain, describes him as "tall, bald, bespectacled and full of energy". A Kilteely, Co. Limerick man, Cagney was ordained in Kilkenny in 1949, after Belcamp College and a period in Cahirmoyle in Limerick. The Oblates had taken over the home of the Smith O'Brien family, a scion of which had been William Smith O'Brien of the 'Young Ireland' movement. Its 1848 uprising came to an inglorious but famous end in a skirmish in widow McCormack's cabbage patch in Ballingarry, Co. Tipperary. For his pains William Smith O'Brien was transported to Tasmania.

Bill Cagney had been an Assistant General of the Oblates in Rome for five years when he was informed that his next assignment was to be director at the London Irish Centre. *"I asked where it was. I had never even heard of it"*, he has said. During a brief holiday he visited Camden to have a look, when he met Paddy Mee and Paddy Keegan late one night.

In fact Father Jim Butler, who was to join him in London two years later as a chaplain, tells an intriguing story. *"Father Cagney was to be sent to me as a curate at Darndale, that was his first appointment when he came back from Australia. He visited London but his luggage arrived in Darndale, my parish in Dublin, but he went to London and found out that Fr Mee was leaving, and perhaps found a gap for himself. The next I heard was that he was head of the London Irish Centre. It was never brought to me, I was never consulted about it, just that his brother came and collected his luggage and took it off to London."*[1] This says something about the flexibility of the provincial.

Before Rome, Bill Cagney had spent the previous twenty-one years as a priest in Australia and New Zealand, eight of which as the provincial superior of the OMI. He was well-travelled and he regarded himself as a sort of clerical jet-setter, opening missions in Java and central Indonesia. When he finally reached Rome he was given special responsibility for the African, Asian and Latin American missions, but he later described his posting to Camden Square as *"the toughest mission of all."*

Florrie Darcy, from Limerick via Wolverhampton, was interviewed for the job as his secretary in October 1976. *"He is a great man to work with. He really works hard, but you might as well be talking to the wall as asking him to take it a bit easy."*[2] She remembers that he was always a man on the move. His breakfast was just half a grapefruit and a cup of black coffee. He was extremely articulate and never prepared a speech, preferring to talk without notes.[3]

One of the things Bill Cagney soon noticed was the lack of success the Centre had in employing capable catering and bar staff. Not long after he arrived, he asked Florrie Darcy if she would take over the management of the premises, including the catering and cleaning. She said that she would try it for a year.

New legislation brought an immediate crisis for the new director. The changes which were introduced in 1974 and 1975 had implications for all those in the housing sector. Landlords of lodging houses were unwilling to let rooms, because tenants' rights were now so much strengthened by the Act. This put an increased burden on the accommodation managed by the Centre, independent hostels such as Arlington House and the temporary accommodation run by the council.

"The situation is becoming more and more difficult", said Bill Cagney, recognising this. "Nobody should come over here and think that they are going to get a job or a bed. It's just not on. There will have to be some co-ordination in Ireland to hammer this message home."

The Troubles

The Troubles did not help. The Guildford and Birmingham bombings had taken place in October and November 1974, and the next year was marked by bombs in Manchester and London. Many people now were being turned away from accommodation elsewhere simply because they were Irish, whether they were from the north or south of Ireland. "Only last week a man with seven young children, and three more coming over soon after, walked into the Irish Centre. He had nothing. No job, no flat, nothing. He expected to find work. We had

a talk with him. He was sensible enough to listen and went back home the following day. We paid the fares", said a spokesperson at the Centre.[4] Unfortunately the IRA little considered what damage it was also causing to the Irish in Britain.

Rushed through Parliament in November 1974 as a result of the Guildford bombings was the Prevention of Terrorism Act. Its indiscriminate use was condemned by the Taioseach, Dr Garret Fitzgerald and others. "I remember an announcement on the radio saying that people listening to traditional Irish music should be reported", wrote Sister Sarah Clarke. "I became accustomed to stories of arrests being made in the middle of the night, or raids mounted during the day at workplaces, of vanloads of policemen with guns and dogs, of doors kicked in and families held in their own homes whilst walls were taken down and floors ripped up, of possessions taken away, letters, gramophone records, anything thrown into plastic bags, of children crying as parents were handcuffed and taken away."[5] Shortly afterwards, meetings to campaign against the PTA began to take place among Irish communities across the country, including in Camden.

At the AGM of 1975, just weeks after his arrival, Bill Cagney paid tribute to Paddy Mee, who had struggled against age and illness. He then addressed the meeting on what was to become his greatest priority. This was the potential for the site next door, which had finally been purchased from British Rail. The scheme that had originally been planned with the architect Vernon Gibberd had not been progressed, but another had been developed with the local architect Keith Roberts. Community Housing Association also wished to continue its partnership with the Centre, and this was confirmed in June 1975.

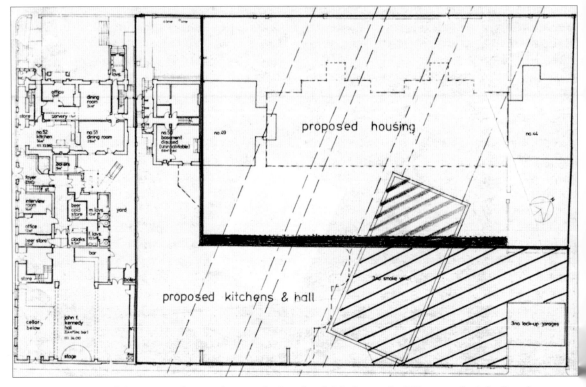

An early drawing of the proposed extensions to the London Irish Centre building, on the left. Camden Square is at the top, Murray Street is on the left and Murray Mews is at the bottom.

To be built across nos. 44 to 49 Camden Square, this would now become social housing run by CHA, because it was felt that its management experience was beyond the scope and skills of the staff at the Centre. Camden Council favoured these plans and the site was sold to the CHA for £100,000, with a further £25,000 to refurbish Hope House. Paddy Sheridan was not altogether pleased at the news. *"I disagreed with Fr Cagney selling any part of the land to another Housing Association. I thought it daft. There was a 99-year lease on that land. And because land is so precious, and here we were building a hall beside a Housing Association where you could have noise interfering with people living in those flats."*[6]

The minutes of the AGM preferred to describe, rather emotively, the vision of Bill Cagney. *"The Centre would be one of the finest of its kind. It will not just be an imposing edifice, but will embody all that is best in our culture and tradition and will throb with the pulse of the Irish nation"*. However, any grand designs for the hall would have to wait until other parts of the scheme had been accomplished.

A helpful start was provided by Mossie O'Riordan. At the prompting of Bill Cagney, he asked a number of his men from Joseph Murphy and Co. to work as volunteers over one weekend in order to clear the orchard and open space above the railway lines between nos. 44 and 49 Camden Square. With chain-saws and other equipment they made quick work of it. He says they enjoyed *"a good breakfast and saved the Centre £12,000."*[7]

The Murphy Brothers

A major figure in the fortunes of the Centre at this stage was Joseph's brother, John Murphy, who was himself keen to support the Centre. After all, it was now caring for people who were in the same circumstances as himself thirty years beforehand, and its employment service provided his firm with labourers. There is a story that during a foot and mouth outbreak, when meat was scarce, John provided the Centre with food sent over from Ireland to cook a Christmas lunch for a large number of people. His brother Joseph had a similar benevolent relationship with the Irish Club in Eaton Square.

John was the first to arrive in England, and Joseph Murphy joined him in 1946. From Cahersiveen in Co. Kerry, they were no different from the tens of thousands who took the boat before or after, but they were early enough to spot the opportunities for rebuilding Britain, and obtained their first big contract for removing wartime obstacles from the English Channel. In the years since, theirs is probably the most sensational rise in influence and in personal wealth of anyone in the construction business in Britain. As former navvies, it is perhaps regrettable that neither of the two brothers has shown any interest in recording their history.[8]

After ten years they separated their businesses, with Joseph specialising in cable-laying and subterranean work, while John tended to concentrate on work above ground. Because of this difference they became known as the 'Grey' or 'Green' Murphys respectively, and their transport fleets and plant later reflected these colours. Men were sometimes asked whether they wanted to work for the Grey or the Green. With the third local firm, RSK, a song developed with a chorus ending in the Green and the Grey and the RSK'.

The construction of British homes and infrastructure was a major challenge facing the post-war government. At that time there was also little regulation and as a result, corners were cut in the race to compete for and complete contracts. Few building companies looked after the men who worked long hours for them. In the 1960s many were willing to take workers from the lump, without insurance and union representation. It was a truism that for the men, it suited them at the time, but when they didn't get their social insurance they repented at leisure. Some men were paid without divulging their real names; some companies preferred to pay the men by cheque even though they had no bank accounts. Pubs would cash the cheques less a commission. Subbies and agents took their cuts. Many could never make enough money for a deposit or the week's rent in advance to a landlady, and were forced to 'skipper out' or sleep rough. In Camden, there was the once a week a shave and a bath in the public baths in Prince of Wales Road and less often the purchase of a second-hand suit from Alfred Kemp's in Camden High Street before tanking up to meet the colleens in the Buffalo.[9]

People are divided about the nature of the Murphy empire, beginning as it did in the days when there was little regulation. Although the pubs were said to honour their cheques, there is no doubt that it was in some ways a brutal system. The Murphy brothers probably employed more Irishmen than any company in Ireland.

John Murphy had a colleague who might have been less than pleasant, known as 'Elephant John' O'Donoughue, *"A frightening man who roared. He was like a sergeant major"*, says Christopher O'Brien.[10] Six foot two inches tall, and weighing seventeen stone, he was probably the most infamous of the gangers or agents from the post-war years. From the same small town as John Murphy he began his working life as a labourer alongside his fellow Kerryman. *"There's a story that once in a pub he saw ten men from Green Murphy and generously offered to buy then a pint each. Having seen the barman begin to pull them, he went to the gents' toilet. The toilet had a window, through which even this big man could wriggle in order to avoid paying for the pints.*[11] When he died in 1999, after forty-five years with the company, there were conflicting memories of him in the *Irish Post.* His friend, 'Concrete' Mick O'Sullivan said, *"He was quite simply a legend and a great character. He had a wonderful sense of humour, loved playing practical jokes, and was very generous if one of his men came into bother or needed money for an emergency".* On the other hand, in the same newspaper D. Casey wrote, *"He became notorious, not for his generosity of spirit to his fellow man but for the manner in which he abused and humiliated his fellow countrymen on behalf of his boss. These Irish contractors were used to build Britain after the war. They are now competing to be among the richest families in these isles. Where is the generation of Irishmen that worked for them? Many got maimed and killed at their work places. Those that survived can be seen in Camden Town, Cricklewood and Kilburn, suffering from rheumatism, bronchitis, arthritis and other diseases that have arisen from not being provided with protective equipment."*[12]

Joseph Murphy, who died in 2000 in Guernsey, had also been good to the Irish Centre. With Mossie O'Riordan's help, his company was able to carry out some of the refurbishment at Hope House. Without charge he provided vehicles to transport furniture and the men to shift it. Jim Butler, who experienced this a year or two later, says of the Grey Murphy's, *"They were extremely good at loaning things. If you needed a lorry you got a lorry, and as many men as you wanted in the lorry. You'd get whatever you wanted on a Friday evening, because the boys who were working the lorries were on double time."*[13] Mossie O'Riordan would often visit the Centre for a quiet drink in the evening, sometimes with his boss's chauffeur-driven Bentley waiting in Murray Street.

Joan Moriarty says, *"Mossie would come to me at Christmas time. 'Joan', he said, 'What do you want?' If I said I wanted fifty chickens to help give the elderly a Christmas dinner, Mossie would have the fifty chickens or whatever else I wanted. He would provide that, he was one in a million."*[14] It seems Christmas charity was common to both brothers.

'Big' John Murphy now lives in Hampstead, a few miles up the hill from the Centre, and has been seen at Mass at the Sacred Heart in Quex Road. It is said that until fairly recently he would be at his yard in Kentish Town each morning at 7.00 am. *"He looked after his men. There was a big restaurant at the yard. You could have steak in the mornings. And he always gave out the right clothes for the job, including the green Wellingtons."*[15]

In the *Sunday Times* 'Rich List' of 2004, John Murphy is quoted as owning assets of £95 million, and his late brother was not far behind him. Nevertheless they were always helpful to the London Irish Centre and were at one time to be seen at its functions.

By September 1975, the running debt had been reduced to £4,702.[16] The omens looked positive. Bill Cagney felt passionately that a redevelopment would help meet the cultural, physical, spiritual and other needs of the Irish community.

Plans for Development
Although the money from the National Collection in 1971 had been directed towards the purchase of Hope House in

Kilburn, the budget for the first phase of the new development, which was to be next door at no. 50 Camden Square, was only £56,100, including £3,000 for a site investigation. This was a modest enterprise, focussing on the welfare service, which planned to combine a self-contained unit with a 24-hour operation, field work, counselling and accommodation for a residential social worker. Camden Council approved an application to pay for the new welfare offices.

There was unfortunately a problem of sitting tenants in the building that had to be resolved first, but Bill Cagney was confident he could manage it. The tenants and sub-tenants in these properties would have to be rehoused. He wrote to them individually to explain the position. *"Some time ago a suitable building was found in Kilburn (for increasing our hostel accommodation), so it was decided that the vacant site should be used for housing local homeless families. I have asked Community Housing Association to be the agency for this venture, which would include flats on the vacant garage site, with off-street parking and a children's play area. There is an opportunity to renovate the other properties on the site but nothing will be done to affect your tenancy without full consultation with you."*[17] It was felt by Camden Council's planners that any loss of housing here would be restored by the building of twenty-four flats in the new development.

Both the director and his architect Keith Roberts had, separately, knocked on the doors of the tenants in no. 50 Camden Square to try and explain their development plans, but these visits were unwelcome.

On the completion of this first phase, the development would be appraised, and further phases would be considered. Bill Cagney believed that the Centre was becoming too successful for its own good.

It was not designed well enough to carry out all its functions efficiently or effectively. More space for a hall was required, on the obvious site next door, behind the CHA land which had been bought for a bargain from British Rail.

One reason for his desire to build a new hall was that it was noticeable that larger Irish associations, such as the Limerick Association, which up until then had booked the function rooms for their events, were now turning elsewhere. The Kennedy Hall was continually booked. He knew that improvements were required, and he was determined to deliver facilities in which people felt at home.

He was a hands-on man. When the pressure was on in one of the bars Bill Cagney, unlike some other directors, was happy to pitch in. *"Cagney was never afraid to get in behind the bar and roll up his sleeves to do the washing of glasses."* Maeve Heath added, *"He never poured a drink, but he was very helpful whenever we were busy."*[18] Mossie O'Riordan said he also liked his pint.

The chairman of the administrative committee at the time was Tommy Dunne. A polite, considerate man and expert fundraiser with good business contacts in Dublin, he was also regarded as too soft. As far as the committee was concerned, Mossie O'Riordan,, who describes him as 'the Cag', says Bill Cagney was a "bulldozer" with them. The committee's confidence at that time was not robust, because it is said that other buildings were also offered to CHA. These included 12 Murray Street and the hostel at Hornsey Lane Gardens, but this proposal was not taken forward.

Local opposition also surfaced from some who felt that the Centre was being less than honest in the way it was dealing with the neighbouring tenants. The Camden Square Tenants' and Residents' Association supported the development for those in housing need, but petitioned the council to refuse planning consent until the residents in these houses were given some guarantee that they would not be evicted against their wishes. They also suspected that there was another agenda at work. This was that the arrangement with CHA was a smokescreen, and that a private developer, with more cash, would be sought. It was also rumoured that having received lucrative planning consent for flats here, Bill Cagney might use the sale to finance the development of the new hall at the rear.

John Cowley, chairman of the Association, was approached by anxious tenants. He predicted at a stormy public meeting at St Paul's church hall in the middle of the Square in July 1975 that even if the CHA agreement went ahead rents would be likely to rise. He alleged in a letter that Bill Cagney "*was trying to get rid of the working class in order to promote gentrification*".[19]

One tenant, Hilda Brock, was admitted into hospital with a nervous breakdown after she had been threatened with "*I hope you're going to take the next place we offer you. We could put all of your furniture out in the street.*" She was prepared to defy the council, and face a court hearing. Two days before the court date she was offered a property in Highgate Road.[20]

On the top floor of one of these houses Murphy's had set up a canteen or mess room for its men. Below them still lived a family. Although they had been on Camden's waiting list for seven years they had received no offer of a transfer until the day after the builders moved in. The view of the *Camden Tenant*, published on behalf of all the council's tenants, was that Bill Cagney and Bill Barnes, Camden's Director of Housing, had acted with indecent haste in ensuring that vacant possession for these properties was quickly

secured.[21] The Centre finally had to offer £15,000 to obtain vacant possession.[22] After some negotiation, the individual tenants were compensated or rehoused to their satisfaction, which enabled the welfare service finally to move into no. 50.

After some conversion, which was in fact funded by Peter Barry, the Minister for Foreign Affairs in the Irish government, the welfare office then proceeded to transfer next door. As Joan Moriarty said, "*We had great expectations for the place. We wanted to expand the office and also opened a little library upstairs. A lot of the books for that came from the Irish Embassy. They were very good to us. Then we wrote around to different companies. Lots of Irish companies gave us books for that.*"[23] She shared the new office with Anne-Marie O'Boyle. There was also room for an employment office, initially occupied by the Marian Employment Agency, which was managed first by Jim Casey and later by Austin Fields.

The London Irish Festival

All this, of course, also needed revenue funding. The annual concert at the Albert Hall had almost run its course because of falling income, but the other annual event, a festival organised with enthusiasm by the CICA on the first Sunday in July, was becoming more successful. This was an open-air festival of Irish music, sports and culture. On 13 July 1975, the London Irish Festival, as it became known, was held at Stamford Bridge, Chelsea's football ground. Promoted as a day out for the family, this was also the venue for the following year, after which it moved to Roundwood Park in Harlesden in Brent.

Entrance was by programme, which cost one pound, and thousands were bought at the gate. No one could guess at how many would turn up and customers were restrained by just a rope, which soon proved no deterrent, and a crowd invaded the pitch. Afterwards there was a feeling, expressed in a letter to the *Irish Post*, that the organisation had been poor, but also that the confines of a football stadium restricted the potential freedom or flexibility of such an occasion, where different events should be able to take place in different locations simultaneously. However, the county parades gave a sense of pride and identity, the entertainers entertained, the raffles were a success, and the majority of those who attended enjoyed themselves. As Johnny O'Boyle, the Master of Ceremonies, said, *"It will roll."*[24]

Again at Stamford Bridge, the second festival was said to be an improvement, but the venue presented the same restrictive problems. Letters to the *Irish Post* which complained that all the day offered was tug o' war and displays of Irish dancing did not reveal that the majority of those who attended had the time of their lives. However one letter emphasises the credit due to the comedian Joe Lynch for "keeping the show going". At the end of the day Joe Davis, who was in charge of the gate receipts, was left waiting for Securicor, who were to take the money to the bank. The company never turned up, but fortunately an official from Chelsea Football Club arrived, and together they found a shopping trolley and piled the money onto that. The takings remained in the club's safe for the rest of the weekend.

After considering Wormwood Scrubs as a venue for the third festival, it moved instead to Roundwood Park, Harlesden, which was supplied free of charge by Brent council provided that the event was properly insured. The view later expressed in letters to the press was that after the "fiasco" of the first year at Stamford Bridge, and the "boring event" of the second year at the same "hemmed in" venue, the expanse and freedom of a 30-acre park

was a happy contrast.

The receipts were also healthier. The third festival made £17,000 net profit for the Council of Irish County Associations, which was devoted to Irish welfare organisations in London, in particular to the London Irish Centre. Despite the presence of 50,000 visitors, they were all so well behaved that not a single penny had to be paid in compensation for any damage to structures or to trees and shrubs.

At its new venue the festival grew in scale and reputation. A pattern emerged. It commenced with a Mass at 10.00 am, and then a parade of the associations marching under their different county banners. The park was filled with stalls and exhibitions, and the day ended with a concert with bands and performers over from Ireland. Bringing their music over the years came Daniel O'Donnell, the Indians, Dana, the Larry Cunningham Band and others. Bill Aulsberry says, *"Roundwood for me was magic. Waterford had Gate B from seven in the morning to eight in the evening. It was a crazy, brilliant day."* He adds, *"Daniel O'Donnell saved it one year. The weather was not too good, and it had been waning in popularity. Daniel came to the rescue."*[25] In time, the traditional musicians were to play on another stage some sensible distance away.

Another festival attraction was Paschal Mooney, who was its Master of Ceremonies from 1979. Jim Butler, who was also from Leitrim, is effusive in his praise, *"He was an emigrant, he worked on the buses in London and then he came home and became a disc jockey. On RTE he played 'Country'. So when the festival came on, all he had to do was come after these groups to play in London. Also, the carriers like Aer Lingus and BEA carried them free. When he came over he cast an assurance that these people were coming, and he would MC for the whole day long himself. That's a contribution we*

The Irish Festival in London, 1984. (Joanne O'Brien)

could never ever assess."[26] Paschal Mooney is now a respected senator in Dublin.

Time to take stock

Towards the end of 1975 there came an opportunity for the Centre to pause briefly and consider its achievements. The 21st anniversary of its opening was celebrated on 17 September. Over the twenty-one years, from 1963 to 1975 a total of 23,596 people are recorded as having presented themselves at the Centre for the first time. The numbers varied year to year, from 776 in 1964 to 2,356 in 1975, and of all these cases, 6,693 returned later on for further assistance.

A celebration dinner was held at the top floor restaurant of Barker's store in Kensington High Street. The spirit of the occasion also reflected concern for the needs of the less fortunate emigrant, which was expressed in a speech by the Ambassador, Dr Donal O'Sullivan. To mark the event, a booklet called *Helping Hands* which traced the history of the first twenty-five years, was published.

The move of the welfare service into no. 50 Camden Square having been accomplished, attention now returned to the available land at the rear of the premises. At the meeting of the administrative committee on 6 October, discussion focussed on a new hall with a capacity for as many as 500 people at a dinner and dance. It would be built across the railway tunnels.

David Ashton-Hill, who was working at Keith Roberts' architectural practice, took on the specific brief for the hall. An earlier task had been to 're-face' the front of the

The architectural detail added to the façade of the London Irish Centre, by Keith Roberts Associates in 1975.

building with the cornices and decorations that had been removed over the years. He took casts from a house on the other side of the square.

He remembers that, with his surveyor John Tapley, he had to endure many administrative committee meetings. A feature was the long wait of up to two hours in the bar upstairs while the committee in another room came to a decision on the proposals he had previously put to it. Although differences had to be sorted out before they met him, David Ashton-Hill has said that any show of conflict was avoided. He believes that this was due to the skill of Tommy Dunne, whom he found *"a gentleman, who took the time to make you feel comfortable."*[27] Others would remark that Tommy Dunne could never say no to a priest.

Across the tunnels

Camden Council made enquiries about the type of construction proposed. The committee had already approached structural engineers and by mid-November had made a presentation to Camden planners for a hall designed by David Ashton-Hill spanning the tunnels. The committee recorded that, *"Although the new hall is considered a major change from the original plan, the architects are confident that outline planning permission will be granted.".*[28] This was after David Ashton-Hill and Keith Roberts had met the senior planner at Camden, Bruno Schlaffenberg, at a number of confrontational meetings over the exterior design of the hall. Schlaffenberg particularly wanted to see it 'articulated' like a terrace with a series of Georgian-style windows, but eventually it was agreed that the fenestration could be round-headed like the windows of a railway carriage. This was a reference to the rail traffic that passed beneath. There were practical complications also to be resolved, such as the loading on the tunnels and, once built, the issue of noise escaping from within the hall. Acoustic experts were engaged to deal with the latter.

In order to secure approval, the presentation to the council had apparently proposed that the extension would have various uses, including the one that all were agreed on, which was a new bar. There were those administrative committee members who actually wanted to see 'the longest bar in London' here, the length of the wall alongside Murray Mews. Guinness later offered to build it at its own expense, provided that it would be called the 'Guinness Bar'. David Ashton-Hill even suggested a colour scheme which included rich dark brown walls topped by a frothy cream strip below the ceiling. This most important decision was debated at length by the committee in the Kennedy Hall, while David Ashton-Hill again had to wait for a result in one of the Centre's other bars.

Nevertheless, Camden's planners now questioned the entire proposals, saying that they were over-development, and that the Centre should make better use of the existing building.[29] But despite their concerns, the planners in May finally recommended the granting of outline planning permission.[30]

There were further complications before permission was finally agreed. At a hearing, the Camden Square Neighbourhood Association was able to convince the council to agree that the Centre should itself implement facilities for the local community. Camden had previously proposed to build a youth club in the square, which had been unpopular with residents after a long history of neglect of the area. Unsurprisingly, residents had become exasperated. One of them, the actress Billie Whitelaw, collected a petition to ask the council to do something about the squalid play area. This had been a playground with swings and roundabouts which had just been condemned as unsafe. This equipment was later removed and replaced by an ugly container and a pond. Because of the obvious dangers of a pond, it then had to be drained and the container was ultimately replaced by a log cabin. For some reason the council said that the area would be open for only two mornings a week, and only for the use of Bangladeshi children.

Finally, a new youth club was proposed, regarded by surrounding residents as a potential source of nuisance.

The enquiry now instructed the Centre to provide a youth club on its own premises, with a door at the front of the building leading across the road to a new play area in the square. This meant that the council's own plans for a youth centre need not go ahead. Other conditions included proper sound-proofing for the future hall and a limit of 300 people using it at any one time.

It would be years before these conditions were met. In 1987 the Centre pro-

Laying the concrete beams across the railway tunnels in preparation for the weight of the new hall.

duced a scheme for a youth club downstairs with a day centre for the elderly, but the youth club was never built. Some years later, an air conditioning plant was installed on the roof of the new hall, which had never received planning permission or Conservation Area consent. This again did not improve relationships between the Centre and the local community.[31]

The projected costs shot up from £56,100 for the minor welfare extension works next door to £1 million for the entire project. This target did not daunt Bill Cagney, nothing did. Like other directors before him, he was irritated by the lack of willing on the part of the Irish government to assist the Centre financially. The committee decided to commit itself to raising the estimated £1 million required. The Bank of Ireland agreed to provide £420,000 to finance the first phase. An advisory panel was convened, which met in the Tara Hotel on 19 July 1977. Brendan Mac Lua, still editor of the *Irish Post*, was not convinced that there was any justification to spend such an amount, or whether such a large hall was actually needed. He asked how long the financial burden would continue and when would the Centre become self-financing. He had doubts as to whether the investment would be worth the effort, and was reminded of the follies or useless buildings built in Ireland during the Famine to keep people employed, and wondered whether this would become another one. Another sceptic was the former trustee, Jack Gleeson, the building contractor who had built the Kennedy Hall and the Douglas Hyde Lounge. He felt that Bill Cagney's ambitions were getting the better of him and resigned from the committee.

The Irish government says no

Father Cagney himself felt that it was a real irony that Irish emigrants in Britain were constantly being asked by Dublin to help the economy at home by buying Irish products and returning to Ireland for holidays, whereas initiatives in Britain such as the development of the London Irish Centre were receiving promises and blandishments from the government, but no cash.[32] "*I keep on saying it – and I will say it again – is there any member of the Irish government who cares about the Irish exiles?*", he demanded. "*Economically we are only asking for a very small percentage of what the Irish community in England has poured into the Irish economy, and we are asking the Irish government for that help only because we are in desperate need of it so that we can do much more for the exiles. Well, let me say that with or without the backing of the Irish government, we will go on with the £1 million extension of the Irish Centre for the benefit of the Irish community*

here in London."[33] Bill Cagney was certainly eloquent. Jim Butler, who had been a student colleague of his, recalled his "*great power in the pulpit. He had total domination of the congregation. He was a uniquely fluent preacher, a great debater*". In Australia he even had a radio show, on which he was often challenging his guests who doubted the existence of God. Bill Cagney enjoyed debate.

As if to support his opinion of the Irish government, a lengthy statement had been issued the previous year on behalf of the Commission for Emigrants by Bishop Eamonn Casey, in which it also slammed the government's refusal to give financial aid to Irish Centres in Britain: "*We have to report that the Irish government has refused to grant financial aid to Centres in Britain catering for the welfare of newly arrived Irish immigrants. We recommended that the government consider giving a capital grant to several centres in London and Birmingham labouring under a great financial strain to provide services for newly arrived Irish emigrants. We did so initially at a meeting nearly three years ago, to which we were invited by or government, and followed it up with a list of our proposals. In January of this year, after nearly two years of waiting for a decision from the government on this matter, we received from An Taoiseach a brief rejecting our recommendations, with no explanation for the decision whatsoever.*"[34]

Bishop Casey's statement also reminded its readers how the National Collection in parish churches of March 1971 had raised over £260,000, and how the bishops had urged the government to match this. Again and again there were approaches. In May 1973 the Attorney-General, Declan Costello, invited members of the commission to meet him. He suggested that they prepare a written submission. Eight months later, in January 1974, the then Minister for Foreign Affairs, Garret

Fitzgerald, and the Attorney-General met Bishop Casey. A further meeting, this time with the Taoiseach, Liam Cosgrave, took place in February. Any optimism was dashed when, two years later, the Commission received a rejection, which prompted the statement in 1976. Eamonn Casey was furious.

In spite of the misgivings of certain members of the administrative committee, and the reluctance of the Irish government to support it, Bill Cagney persevered. The appeal for £1 million was formally launched with some ceremony at the Centre in December 1977. Cardinal Basil Hume formally laid the first foundation stone and Archbishop Tomas O'Faich, Primate of All Ireland, followed carefully with the second. This was watched by members of the English and Irish clergy, by representatives from the Irish Embassy, and by councillors from Camden, Islington, Haringey and Brent councils. The local MP, Jock Stallard was also present, as were a number of people from Irish voluntary groups. *"Would it be too much to hope that, in this era when co-operation between the Irish government and the Northern Administration is being prompted in so many fields, the Irish Centre, which caters for the needs of exiles from both areas, might be accepted both north and south of the border as a deserving cause with a claim on the generosity of both administrations?"*[35] Whether it was a summary in the *Camden Journal* or not, Archbishop O'Faich's question was intriguing, but this was his first official visit to London since being installed as Archbishop in October. Little did he know that his brave words on joint funding

Archbishop Tomas O'Faich, Primate of All Ireland, in front of the architect's impression of the refurbished and extended London Irish Centre, with Fr Bill Cagney looking on.

would fall on stony ground, or the length of time that it would take for the money to be raised.

A few days later, on 13 December 1977, the Centre was visited by the Minister of State, David Andrews, who confirmed that a request had gone to the Department for Finance for either a £400,000 grant or a £1 million loan. He was the one member of the Irish government who seemed to respect Bill Cagney's ambitions.

There was now, however, a critical short-term cash-flow problem. Bill Cagney rang around all the Irish building contractors for help. As Mossie O'Riordan says *"There was a fellow in south west London, a big firm. I think he had his hopes pinned on that. That was the last straw, when that guy left him. He had promised him something"*. The banks were threatening to foreclose at the weekend if £48,000 interest was not deposited by the Friday morning. On the Tuesday he rang Mossie O'Riordan saying, *"We're in terrible trouble"*. They met, and he was asked to find £48,000. Mossie O'Riordan went to see Mr Foley, the manager of the Bank of Ireland in the Holloway Road, who also had the account for the Centre, and raised a £48,000 loan in his own name. The manager asked *"Was I sure?"* Mossie O'Riordan was described as *"a very brave man"* as he collected the money. This was deposited the next day which prevented the banks from pulling out.[36]

On the cover of the 1978 Annual Report was an architect's drawing, an aerial view which illustrated the ambitious redevelopment programme, showing a large, square hall beside Murray Mews. It was clear that with government support or without, Bill Cagney was determined to forge ahead. The budget for the project as a whole was now £1,349 million, with the hall alone costing £513,000. However Joe Davis and others on the social committee were irritated that there had been

so little consultation with the potential users. *"I think he thought at the time he would not have to pay for it"*, he said. *"He thought that it would be paid for by Murphy's."*[37] There was a tendency for Cagney's enthusiasm to be so consuming that consultation was forgotten.

Press distractions

There were other distractions. With a relatively high profile, the London Irish Centre intervened in a controversy which had been provoked by a sensationalist story in the *Daily Express* of 28 October 1976. This stated that Irish people in Britain were *"to the fore"* in a £200 million social security fiddle and that millions of pounds were being diverted to the IRA. The newspaper quoted an unnamed source in Scotland Yard as supporting its claim that, *"IRA sympathisers are milking the system of millions to pay for guns and bullets to kill British soldiers."*[38] The rebuttals came from different quarters. The Mayor of Camden, Cllr Brian Duggan, also protested and asked three north London MPs, Lena Jeger, Jock Stallard and Michael O'Halloran, to pursue the matter in the House of Commons. Cllr Duggan described the article as *"an incitement to racial hatred"*. The latter two MPs had connections with the Irish community, although from contrasting directions.

Jock Stallard, a Catholic Scot and Celtic supporter, was MP for the constituency of St Pancras North. Beforehand, as an apprentice aircraft engineer, he had achieved some local fame as an accomplished player of the piano and even of the spoons in a number of Irish pubs around Camden Town, such as The Victory and the Hawley Arms. From his home in Tottenham he used to walk to the Pride of Erin dance-hall near Warren Street to meet his girlfriend, Sheila, who was from Castleisland in Co. Kerry. Now his wife, they also visited the Buffalo. He has said that *"All the old hands were at the Buffalo', but we gradually moved over to the London Irish Centre."* He had been a local councillor, and in this position he says, *"I was invited to nearly all the events at the Centre"*. His Parliamentary career included a period as a Junior Whip which meant he could no longer take an independent stance on Irish issues. After his retirement from the House of Commons, Jock Stallard was ennobled in 1983 as Baron Stallard of St Pancras.[39]

He had always identified with the Irish, the largest ethnic minority in his constituency. In 1972 he had participated in the 'Bloody Sunday' march, alongside his constituent Sister Sarah Clarke, who later became known as the 'Joan of Arc of the prisons'. He now says *"There's not many like Sr Sarah"*. Supported by Sarah Clarke and Fr Brian Brady, he was active as a negotiator with the Home Secretary, Roy Jenkins, about sending back to Ireland the convicted Old Bailey bombers then on hunger strike. Lord Longford, still president of the Centre but also a Labour politician, assisted with this aim.

Michael O'Halloran was a very different person. He was an Irishman who, in his political stance, tried to deny it. Originally from Doonbeg, Co. Clare, he had been an agent for Murphy's on the early morning pick-ups, but was suddenly pitched into local politics with his election in 1968 as a Labour councillor for Station ward in Islington, a tiny ward of 3,000 voters where he was elected on a turnout of just 9%. There were some questions as to his motivation, and it was thought that his employment with Murphy's may have had something to do with it.

A year later the sitting MP for Islington North, Gerry Reynolds, died of a heart attack at the age of 41. Again, Michael O'Halloran was promoted for nomination

and won the seat. This was something of a surprise, because on that day there were five by-elections across the country, and with an unpopular mid-term Wilson government three of them were lost to Labour. However, in the months beforehand, a surprisingly large number of Irish people had joined the Islington Labour Party, and perhaps by voting early and, it is said, "often" they may have influenced this election. An enquiry was later held.

At this time both Islington and Haringey councils were funding the London Irish Centre, although not to the extent of Camden. Between 1979 and 1980 this funding was cut by Islington, because its Irish councillors disapproved of the Centre allowing political groups, such as the Anti-Internment League, meeting there. Michael O'Halloran encouraged his former colleagues in this action. It was said that he was terrified that he might be identified with the republican cause.

He later defected to the SDP, together with George Cunningham and John Grant, the other Labour MPs with Islington seats, but in his last election in 1983, with boundary changes reducing the three seats to two and seeing no nomination for himself, he defected in another direction, not back to the Labour Party but described himself as the 'The Labour Candidate' on the ballot paper, as opposed to 'The Labour Party Candidate', who was Jeremy Corbyn.[40]

It is not clear what influence, if any, the two MPs had in making a complaint to the *Daily Express*. On the other hand Frank Ryan, the chaplain, was defiant over the allegations. The Federation of Irish Societies also vigorously attacked them, and set up a committee to examine the case. On this was also Frank Ryan who made a formal complaint to the Race Relations sub-committee of the NUJ and to the Press Council. A series of letters was exchanged

The Press Council finally upheld the complaints against the paper, and Frank Ryan tenaciously demanded a public admission by the *Express* that the article was substantially wrong. *"We think there should be a public apology sought for the damage done to the good name of the Irish in Britain. We would like the Express to make a substantial donation to some charitable fund as compensation."*[41] With the continuing crisis over the hall, he may have had in mind to which particular charitable fund it should be directed. Unfortunately the newspaper had no further comment to make, but simply published the adjudication of the Press Council. Its Legal Manager ended his letter to Frank Ryan with a blunt, *"I do not feel able to assist you in your enquiries."*[42]

Arrivals at the doorstep

Distractions aside, the Centre still had its mainstream work. If there had been any decline in the mid-1970s in the numbers of those leaving Ireland, this was not reflected in the steady stream which arrived at the doors in Camden Square. Towards the end of the decade the numbers increased. Quite apart from the obvious need to find housing and earn a living, in January 1977 the IRA exploded several bombs in the West End, which resulted in Irish people being not altogether welcome.

The Centre was also receiving a higher number of deserted families, battered wives and psychiatric cases. These had to be referred on to the specialist social workers in the Social Services Department of Camden Council or elsewhere, as the Centre's priority has always been to give young people, if possible, a start in London which was trouble-free. As Bill Cagney said, there were not the staff or the expertise to deal with many tragic cases that appeared on the doorstep.[43]

However, there were also those who did not wish to remain in London, but were without the funds to take them home. Joan Moriarty tells a story.*"'Ah Sister', they'd say with tears dropping down their cheeks, 'my mother died last night. Sister, in the name of God can you give me my fare to go back for the funeral?' I'd say, 'Sit there now a minute and I'll see what I can do for you'. I'd go inside and ring the parish priest. 'Do you know Mrs So-and-so?' 'Indeed I do, Sister', he would say, 'For I was just talking to her half an hour ago up the street'. And I'd go back and say 'Now tell me the truth now, what do you want the money for, because your mother is hale and hearty?' 'Ah, sure sister, God forgive me Sister'. Ah, it was all roguery."*[44] She adds that they used to put bets on in the pub to see who could come down to the Centre and spin the best yarn to get the fare home.

For those who succeeded in convincing even her, the Centre had an arrangement with British Rail to provide vouchers for a return to Ireland. She would write a letter for the returning emigrant to take to British Rail and this would be exchanged for a voucher. It took a while for Joan Moriarty to realise that these vouchers could in fact be exchanged within three days for hard cash, and some of those she assumed had returned home perhaps never made it.

In June 1978 a new fund-raising deal was agreed between the Centre and British Rail Sealink. For every crossing above the total for the previous year the ferry company would set aside 8p towards the Irish Centre Fund. It is not known how far this increased the company's figures or whether the Centre gained much from this arrangement.

After eleven years service, in 1978 Anne-Marie O'Boyle left the welfare service to become a District Nurse in Kilburn. Tom McCabe says of her, *"She was the life and soul of the place, she made a great contribution, she was a very unusual person. She had been a nurse and she was wonderful in welfare, she had a great insight into it. She was really the driving force there."* Both Joan Moriarty and Anne-Marie had made it a part of their job to visit on a very regular basis the hostels in Kilburn and in Victoria. Anne-Marie has said that she also used to have an 'infirmary' at Hope House, for cuts and bruises and other injuries suffered by the young men on the building sites. She was replaced by Stacia Crickley, who is described as *"a very fluent and able person"* by Paddy Keegan.

Alongside this, the spiritual mission was not forgotten. Daily and Sunday Masses at the Centre regularly catered for as many as 400 to 500 people. The director and the chaplains also paid visits to the elderly and sick. The clerical staff included Frank Ryan and Patsy Carolan as chaplains, although Patsy Carolan had moved to take charge of Hope House. In June 1977 he was assigned to parish work in Bristol. Frank Ryan was then asked to take charge in Quex Road.

The women's hostel in Hornsey Lane Gardens also saw some changes. By then Thecla Cleary had been running the hostel with help from Sr Frances Morris. Unfortunately Sr Thecla had to retire after an illness in August 1977, and Sr Frances took over. She was later joined here by Sr Beatrice O'Callaghan.

Father Jim Butler

Another arrival was Father Jim Butler, who replaced Frank Ryan. A native of Drumshanbo in Co. Leitrim, he joined the staff of the Centre as a chaplain on 5 October 1977, to work with Bill Cagney. He had been a student with him and knew him fairly well.

After attending college at St Mel's, Co. Longford, he served as a parish priest in

Father Bill Cagney, at left, at the launch of the Sealink Scheme. Cllr Bill Budd, Mayor of Camden is to the right.

130

Wales for six years. He then alternated between Ireland, where he founded a parish in Darndale, within the larger parish of Coolock in north Dublin, and Britain. He also served in London. *"I hated it. I thought it was filthy dirty, the hustle and bustle. It wasn't aligned with my background. I was a country farmer."*[45]

It was later, during an eight year spell in Bristol, that he developed his enjoyment for cycling. Whenever he had the time he pedalled away from Bristol into the quiet countryside of Somerset, Gloucestershire or Wiltshire. *"It's marvellous down there"*, he recalled, *"glorious living history."*[46]

Jim Butler's cycling experience would later be put to good use in the saving of the Centre, but when he first arrived here it was the Jubilee year of the Queen's Coronation. He remembers that London, like much of the country, was 'done up' in celebration.

There was little to celebrate in Camden Square. He soon became aware of the enormous debt hanging around the neck of the Centre, and there was now a growing view that the redevelopment and linked expansion had perhaps been too ambitious. This was not helped by rising interest rates and a slow down in the British economy. Each year the many friends of the Centre and its committed volunteers had put in a tremendous amount of work to raise the necessary revenue to keep the Centre in operation, but this did little more than meet the rising interest payments.

When Jim Butler arrived the roof of the building was being renewed, and he and Frank Ryan had to move out of their rooms on the second floor and into no. 12 Murray Street opposite. The basement flat there was "heaven", says Jim Butler, because it was so quiet, but there was no heating. Another lengthy and expensive operation was the underpinning of no. 50 Camden Square, the home of the welfare staff. It had been discovered during the excavation work for the new hall that, *"The walls of that three storey building had begun to wobble. They had to tie in the walls with bars to keep them straight, and they investigated the foundations and found that they had no foundations at all, just dry rubble underneath the walls."*[47] Because the excavation was close to the railway tunnels, much of the work had to be done by hand rather than by heavy plant.

In another attempt to obtain funds, Bill Cagney now submitted a memorandum to the Irish government. This outlined how the Centre was catering more for destitute, urban emigrants, rather than the typical farm labourer of the 1950s. The memo emphasised how it would build a self-contained welfare unit for its staff with a multi-functional hall for reunions, benefits and charity functions. As if to refute Frank Aiken's, the Minister for Foreign Affairs, view that these services duplicated the statutory sector, Camden Council itself made the point in support, *"We are constantly providing welfare services and facilities which are not available to the Irish community in Britain, despite highly developed and sophisticated British welfare state structures. The welfare office of the Irish Centre is staffed by personnel whose ethos does not differ radically from that of the emigrant."*

This was seen to be helpful. The connections between Camden and the Centre were close. The Centre had affiliated to the Council for Social Services, the co-ordinating body for voluntary social services in Camden, at its foundation as long ago as in 1965. In 1978 a representative of the Centre was elected to its Executive Committee.

An important decision for the redevelopment was made on 13 June that year, when extra steelwork to support the struc-

The entrance in Murray Mews to the McNamara Hall during its construction in June 1979.

ture across the railway tunnels was agreed at £99,000. But in July there was bad news when it was learned that further work and money would be required to strengthen the foundations. Bill Cagney now travelled to Dublin to make a personal appeal. *"Where will the money come from is the question on all of our minds. It is my preoccupation 24 hours a day. Regretfully...our Irish government has not yet made a decision or replied to our pressing application."*[48] By now he was extremely anxious.

Although much attention was focussed on the incomplete hall, social and cultural activities flourished in the Kennedy Hall, the Douglas Hyde Lounge and the small bar upstairs. This was the heyday of the county associations, who organised their dinners, quizzes and other functions. As Mary Allen, the chairperson of the council later said, *"Some nights it was so crowded and busy you could hardly get up the stairs. People came in from all over London."*[49]

During this time a new chef called Jimmy McCluskey was appointed. He followed Larry Gosling, who had been discovered

by Frank Ryan dead in his bed one Saturday morning. McCluskey already had something of a reputation. *"No one could drink a pint of Guinness as fast as Jimmy McCluskey"*, says Maeve Heath. Nevertheless, he was a superb chef, specialising in simple Irish cooking. His collar-of-bacon and cabbage suppers were legendary. *"Jim done it the old-fashioned way, boiled the cabbage in the bacon water."*[50] This was usually followed by apple pie and cream. McCluskey was sometimes so tired after his efforts that he would fall asleep at the end of the evening and never make it home. Nevertheless, his culinary effort made a big difference and these suppers were useful fund-raisers, particularly when they were also accompanied by a live band and dancing.

Tommy Maguire

However, it was the traditional music that gained a deserved reputation. This was largely due to Tommy Maguire, who had first been invited to the Centre by Paddy Sheridan ten years before and had taken

One of the many children's bands at the London Irish Centre.

children's classes on weekday evenings and Saturday mornings.

In the 1970s the Centre was able to field as many as eleven different bands, with queues of young players waiting to join. *"The place was jumping"*, says Jim Myers, from Cork City, who had enrolled his son for lessons with Tommy Maguire. Nevertheless, he remembers him as a disciplinarian. *"If anybody slouched, he would shout at them. He was his own man, a difficult person to get on with."*[52] In spite of this, Tommy Maguire's reputation for carefully teaching the intricacies of traditional Irish music is acknowledged.

Sally Mulready recalls that, *"Every year Tommy entered numerous children for Fleadh Ceol National competitions. One year they went to Coventry by coach, which broke down on the way home. Tragically, a car ploughed into the back of the coach on the hard shoulder and one child died. She was* Marie McAuley, whose father was one of the outstanding Comhaltas leaders in London. Marie played the accordion and had just qualified to go to the All-Ireland, every young musician's dream. Tommy Maguire was also injured, and all the instruments in the back of the coach were destroyed.

"There was a huge memorial held for them. It was the largest event that I have ever been involved with here", she writes, *"We had to open up every hall in the Centre, and we relayed the Mass by loudspeaker out into the streets around the Centre. We also raised the money necessary to replace all the instruments, but the death of that young beautiful girl and the tragedy of it all was something Tommy never got over. He was never the same again."*

Tommy Maguire won the *Irish Post* award in recognition of his part in the development of music at the Centre. His legacy continues. As Sally Mulready, who has a family of accomplished musicians, writes, *"He taught hundreds of youngsters at the Centre, many like Eilish Byrne and Siobhan McDonnell went on to be All-Ireland champions. The very first lesson my own daughter had was given by Eilish Byrne who, with Siobhan, took Tommy's place after he died and continued to teach at the Centre. It's a service the Centre still provides now for third generation youngsters".*[52] One of those who provides it, Karen Ryan, was also a pupil of Maguire, and is now behind the successful 'Return to Camden Town' traditional music festival at the Centre each autumn. Meanwhile, Jim Myers himself has done a great deal to encourage traditional Irish music at the Centre through Comhaltas Ceoltori Eireann, the organising umbrella of traditional performance.

The Troubles intrude
The activities of the Council of Irish Counties were not only confined to bacon and cabbage dinners or days out for the family. The Troubles in northern Ireland were now making an impact on attitudes to the Irish community on the mainland. Although from its establishment the Centre had been determinedly non-sectarian and non-political, the council's AGM in 1980 unanimously called for a British withdrawal of troops. It also launched a campaign to 'Open the H Blocks' and called for an Anglo-Irish Conference to negotiate a conclusion to violence. This was as a result of the six northern Irish counties coming together in a joint action. The conspirators on the committee suspected that the recently admitted Armagh Association might have had other motives. A year later the council's committee sent *"telegram after telegram"* to the Prime Minister, Margaret Thatcher, during the hunger strike, *"imploring her to grant the hunger strikers special category status and*

save their lives." At times these telegrams would not receive a reply.[53]

IRA bombs in Oxford Street, and later in Camden High Street, brought the conflict much closer to the Irish community at the Centre. The police even warned the public to be suspicious of those with Irish accents. Joan Moriarty said: *"I haven't honestly felt any real repercussions, but at the same time it does create a dicey situation for us. Oxford Street stores like Debenhams hire a lot of Irish people because there is a constant turnover of staff in places like these. What sort of reaction am I now going to get if I ring up the canteen manager and say that I have some Irish people looking for jobs."*[54]

In November 1981, even the normally restrained Federation of Irish Societies complained about the Prevention of Terrorism Act to the British Home Secretary, William Whitelaw. The letter was read out at a meeting at the Centre by the chairman, Michael Hogan, who described remarks about the Irish by high-ranking police officers as *"tantamount to inciting racial hatred."* The National Council of Civil Liberties also condemned the PTA as *"neither justified nor an effective way of dealing with the bombing."* Its spokeswoman, Patricia Hewitt, now a senior Cabinet minister, described it as *"a major departure from normal legal standards"*, and that the Act had abolished the principle of Habeas Corpus and was by-passing Judge's Rules.

Demonstrations against the Act, including a torchlight procession in Camden High Street, were mounted across Britain. However much the directors of the Centre, and indeed other Irish priests, managed to retain their integrity, they were under constant suspicion. Bill Cagney maintained that he was tailed by the Special Branch for two weeks after the first IRA bomb in London. He claimed that all Irish community leaders in this city were now subject to police scrutiny. *"If they keep this up",* he said, *"They will be the subject of ridicule. They are just doing this to look as though they are doing something about the bombings."*[55] Like most leaders of the Irish community, however, he felt there were more important concerns for him.

In his introduction to the 1979, and 25th anniversary, Annual Report Bill Cagney wrote: *"The story of these twenty-five years shows how much can be achieved by marrying the tradition of voluntary effort with the public support needed to fund it, guide it and give it impetus. The driving force behind this success is the dedicated and totally unselfish work of our social workers over the years on whose initiative and energy the whole enterprise depends. The supportive element from so many understanding and generous Irish people, the consistent and sympathetic help from the London Borough of Camden, the Housing Corporation of the United Kingdom and latterly of the Irish government have made the past 25 years possible and sends us into the next quarter of a century with renewed dynamism and confidence."*[56] He needed this vote of confidence to push forward the fund-raising for the big scheme.

[1] Interview with Fr Jim Butler, October 2003.
[2] *Irish Weekly Examiner*, 22 February 1978.
[3] Interview Florrie Darcy, June 2004.
[4] *Irish Press*, February 1976.
[5] From *No Faith in the System* by Sr Sarah Clarke, Mercier Press 1995.
[6] Interview Fr Paddy Sheridan, October 2003.
[7] Interview Mossie O'Riordan, March 2004.
[8] The canal system of the 18th century was known as the 'Inland Navigation system'. The diggers of these canals were officially described as 'excavators', which became 'navigators' and then 'navvies'. From *The Men who built Britain* by Ultan Cowley, published by Wolfhound Press, 2001.
[9] Interview Joe McGarry, May 2004.
[10] Interview Christopher O'Brien, May 2004.
[11] *Ibid.*
[12] *Irish Post*, 14 August 1999, and thanks to Ultan Cowley.
[13] Interview Fr Jim Butler, October 2003.
[14] Interview Sr Joan Moriarty, March 2004.
[15] Interview Christopher O'Brien, May 2004.
[16] LIC minutes, 6 October 1975.
[17] CHA archives. Letter from Fr Cagney, 10 July 1975.
[18] Interview Maeve Heath, January 2004.
[19] Letter from John Cowley to CHA, 18 July 1975.
[20] Interview Iris Ryan, March 2004.
[21] *Camden Tenant*, February 1978.
[22] LIC Annual Report 1978.
[23] Interview Sr Joan, Moriarty, March 2004.
[24] Interview Bridie Shaw, May 2004.
[25] Interview Bill Aulsberry, May 2004.
[26] Interview Fr Jim Butler, October 2003.
[27] Interview David Ashton-Hill, March 2004.
[28] LIC minutes, 8 December 1975.
[29] *Ibid*, 2 February 1976.
[30] *Ibid*, 10 May 1976.
[31] Information from Bob Buchanan and Hugh Lake, June 2004.
[32] *Irish Times*, 20 July 1977.
[33] *Irish Weekly Examiner*, 6 July 1978.
[34] *Irish Post*, 1 May 1976.
[35] *Camden Journal*, 2 December 1977.
[36] Interview Mossie O'Riordan, March 2004.
[37] Interview Joe Davis, May 2004.
[38] *Daily Express*, 28 October 1976.
[39] Interview Lord Stallard, May 2004.
[40] Interview Valerie and Keith Veness, June 2004.
[41] *Irish Times*, 18 August 1977.
[42] Letter from Andrew Edwards, Legal Manager, *Daily Express*, 24 November 1976.
[43] *Irish Times*, 20 July 1977.
[44] Interview Sr Joan Moriarty, March 2004.
[45] *Ibid.*
[46] *Irish Post*, 25 August 1983.
[47] Interview Fr Jim Butler, October 2003.
[48] LIC Annual Report 1978.
[49] Interview Mary Allen, March 2004.
[50] Interview Maeve Heath, March 2004.
[51] Interview Jim Myers, 2004.
[52] Correspondence Sally Mulready, June 2004.
[53] Interview Bill Aulsberry, May 2004.
[54] Interview Sr Joan Moriarty, March 2004.
[55] *Evening Herald*, 30 October 1981.
[56] LIC welfare report 1979.

CHAPTER EIGHT

In the rapids of a gigantic river

Father Bill Cagney
Father Claude Malone

When in 1979 Paddy Sheridan returned to London from Irish Welfare in Birmingham, he joined Jim Butler as the other assistant chaplain. *"You saw a difference"*, he later said. *"Things were improving in Ireland, and I found that trying to go back to where you were when you grew up with something you were part of was not good. When you went back and tried to join the thing up again it didn't work.Different director, different attitudes, different people, it didn't work for me. My advice to anyone, no matter where you are, is never to go back."*[1] He also saw many changes at the Centre. The daily work of welfare advice and assistance continued, but much of the focus was now around the proposed hall.1977 had been described as 'a year of planning and decisions', while 1978 was 'a year of action'. Now, in 1979, everything tended to be secondary to the rising costs of the project.

Paddy Sheridan was aware that throughout the year there had been a hectic round of gala evenings, public appeals, race nights and darts tournaments. Organised by the accountant Tony Beatty, with the Waterford Association, a series of golfing classics took place to raise funds. Arsenal footballers David O'Leary and Pat Jennings, Watford captain Pat Rice and Ireland captain Tony Greelish all played golf on behalf of the Centre at Trent Park Golf Club on the northern edge of London. But even these activities were not enough to

Dancing a conga in Murray Street as part of a fund-raising event.

stem the crisis.

Bill Cagney had again lobbied the government, but Michael O'Kennedy, the Minster for Foreign Affairs, had now told the Dail that there could be no Irish government commitment until a study had been carried out.

The year began badly in January when the Irish Bishops decided not to organise another National Collection. Four days later the Bank of Ireland expressed its dissatisfaction with the fund-raising efforts of the Centre, but assigned Declan Quinn, a senior official, to advise and assist. Very soon he was insisting on structured repayments on the bank's loan.

Better news emerged when John Murphy and Sons re-quoted their costs at £461,000, which was helpfully below the previous £550,000, and Camden confirmed £14,000 towards the new welfare offices. Paddy Sheridan had a good word to say about Camden Council. *"If only for Camden Council we would have gone under. Camden Council, I thought it was the most Christian bunch I have ever come across. We got nothing only but great financial and moral support from Camden Council."*[2]

In spite of this support, the Centre appeared unable to reverse a lack of impetus in the fund-raising programme. People complained of fund-raising fatigue. Towards the end of the year the administrative committee decided to appoint professional fund-raisers for a fee of £1,000 a month with 12°% profit of whatever they raised.

Political change

In 1979 Jack Lynch retired as Taioseach. His succession was contested within Fianna Fail by Charles Haughey and George Colley. Haughey won and became the new Taoiseach in December 1979. He made Brian Lenihan the new Minister for Foreign Affairs and Michael O'Kennedy became Minister for Finance.

This political change had an impact in Camden Square. In April 1980, the Irish Lobby Group, a body which campaigned for Irish interests in Britain, managed to convince the new Irish cabinet to grant £300,000 to the Centre for the second phase of its expansion. The continuing efforts of Gerry Lawless, a journalist in London with the *Sunday World*, managed to achieve this, and it appears that Brian Lenihan was instrumental in the outcome.

This grant raised the total amount of contributions to £617,000, but the target had by now risen to £1.75 million as a result of the Centre falling behind in its interest repayments.

The news that at long last a government grant had been made was greeted with jubilation. Paddy Sheridan apparently danced with joy when he heard. *"Thank God and Charlie Haughey"*, he shouted down the phone. *"When Charlie was elected we crossed our fingers, saying it's now or never. It's great to think that the government at home realises the debt that it owes to the emigrants. When Ireland was poor, it was the money from the emigrants which helped to keep the economy ticking over."*[3]

It is said that three factors had made it possible for the new Taoiseach to break its twenty-five year tradition of parsimony towards emigrants. One was the amount the government had recently granted to an exhibition of Irish Art in London, which many had regarded as elitist, and it was felt that there should be some popular compensation for this. The second was the active support for the project offered by the new Ambassador, Eamonn Kennedy. The third was the result of a recent private enquiry which concluded that although the Oblates were involved with the Centre, it was run by its administrative committee on a strictly non-religious basis, putting welfare rather than religion first.

However the catch was that the £300,000 grant had to be matched, and Bill Cagney immediately began talking to the Hierarchy again about raising the additional sum by means of another National Collection. The expectation of the previous National Collection, in 1971, was that the government then would itself match the money that had been collected. This of course never took place. Now he hoped a Collection would match the proposed government grant.

The construction of the new hall while trains speed underneath to St Pancras Station.

His determination was afflicted first by further despair, then by farce and then, at last, by some success.

In the autumn there was no sign of the grant, and an enquiry learned that it was tied to the completion of the welfare offices at no. 50 Camden Square, which were still being built. This was compounded by the extraordinary confession in Dublin in November 1979 that its contribution had in fact been overlooked by the Irish government department because of staff shortages, and the Centre would have to apply once again. After its second application, however, Dublin was more efficient with its paperwork, and the £300,000 was granted by 9 December 1980.

The Centre then concentrated on building the hall and while the struggle to meet the debt continued, gangs of Murphy's men continued to work towards the aspiration.

This was a symbol of the credibility of Bill Cagney. It simply had to succeed. From the moment he had first walked through the door off Murray Street, having experienced splendid new ecclesiastical buildings in other parts of the world, he believed that this one deserved something to dignify it, to make it a venue of pride for the Irish in London. As he expressed it at his first AGM, *"It will not just be an imposing edifice, but will embody all that is best in our culture and tradition and will throb with the pulse of the Irish nation....."*. Stirring stuff.

A new hall at last

When the hall finally opened in November 1980 it exceeded expectations. Some anticipated that after all the effort it would be a disappointment. Instead there was a feeling of genuine pride in what had been achieved. Bill Cagney had his moment. However, there was one drawback. Extraordinarily, there had been no entrance designed from within the building, so people had to use the doors which opened onto Murray Mews. Yet it was spacious, and when empty of furniture looked vast

The completed McNamara Hall.

A stage was built in a corner.

However, the opening ceremony did not include a celebration in the McNamara Hall itself, because someone had forgotten to apply for a licence. Instead there was a lunch in the Kennedy Hall and a champagne reception in the upstairs bar. The distinguished guests included Cardinal Basil Hume, Archbishop of Westminster, Bishop Henderson of Southwark and also the current provincial Fr William McGonagle. Lord Longford, who was still president, also attended. He was now becoming increasingly forgetful. There is a story of him forgetting his overcoat as he was about to leave the Centre for home. When in the car he remembered, he described it as a "grey Crombie". Unfortunately, there were a number of grey Crombies on the rail in the cloak-room. When asked again for distinguishing features, he said that there was a jar of tablets in the pocket. The first pocket entered revealed a large hole, the second produced a jar of Cascara laxative tablets. Embarrassed, a member of the staff handed Lord Longford his overcoat.[4]

The first event in the McNamara Hall was a Mayo parish reunion, for which local Mayo priests came over to meet their emigrant flock. This brought together a large number of people, far more than expected and certainly far more than the council had allowed in its planning or licensing agreements. The first bacon and cabbage supper evening was one organised by the Waterford Association, which 470 people attended.

The expanse of the McNamara Hall.

It was certainly a popular venue. As a condition of planning permission, the council had insisted on a limit of 300 people, but this was frequently exceeded in the general enthusiasm. Warnings were issued, and Florrie Darcy sometimes had to explain herself to Camden Council officers.

On its first New Year's Eve there was a dinner and dance. Because it was impossible to hire staff without spending a fortune, all hands went to work. Bill Cagney and Frank Ryan pulled pints and washed up behind the bar. The chef, Jimmy McCluskey enjoyed cooking for large numbers, something that he was good at. He excelled himself.

If there was a collective sigh of relief that the hall had finally been built, there was still a certain apprehension about how it was to be paid for. Paddy Keegan reports a candid conversation with John Murphy, the builder, in which he was trying to explain the payment schedule. *"Ah, what does it matter"*, declared Mr Murphy, *"You're never going to pay it anyway!"*[5] In recent years he was heard to murmur that "the Irish Centre still owed him a fortune".

The debt again

Quietly, an advisory committee under the auspices of the Irish Department for Labour had been reconvened in October 1979. One of its members was Paschal Mooney, who was such a supporter of the Roundwood Park festivals. Even more quietly, in October 1980 it invited applications for grants from emigrant services to meet salaries of social and welfare workers. Eventually this committee was re-established with the mouthful title of the Advisory Committee to the Irish Government on the Irish Community in Britain, which later became better known as the Dion Committee.

Meanwhile the £1,000 a month contract with professional fund-raisers had resulted in only raising an extra £2,000 during the following year. One of their fund-raising events had been a dinner and dance, auctions and raffles at the Grosvenor House Hotel. As a money-raising enterprise it failed. Tommy Dunne said that *"The fund-raisers are a disaster, and we are back at square one."*[6] In November they were dismissed, but not before they had issued a writ for unpaid invoices. *"The Centre had to go to court to get them out. Something like £11,000 had to be paid to get rid of them"*, recalls Bridie Shaw.[7]

At the end of 1980 £891,407 was owed, plus £150,000 in interest and £25,459 additional interest on overdue interest. Moreover the Centre was committed to spending another £350,000 in the next phase for new welfare offices, which had been delayed while the hall was being built.

A second firm of professional fund-raisers was engaged. This proved to be a double disaster. This agency cost money but the debt rose instead by £114,153 to £960,318. When Bill Aulsberry raised the matter at a meeting of the administrative committee, he was told by the director that it was *"sub judice"*. As much as he respected him, Bill Aulsberry says that *"Cagney was a law unto himself."*[8]

The banks again drew notice to unpaid interest. There was another blow when the Irish Bishops formally refused the second request for a National Collection.

Although in January 1981 the Department of Labour renewed its grant for the welfare services, worth some £7,800, it made the comment that the service had deteriorated as a result of poor pay and staff recruitment. Bill Cagney refuted this. However, the welfare staff had begun to feel that with the concentration on the wider development they were not given adequate attention. The April meeting of the administrative committee even refused to allow them to see copies of the minutes

relating to their service.[9]

Although there had been a history of the bar and catering facilities helping to fund the welfare service, some staff thought that at times the income that the welfare service had been attracting might have been used to help fund the development of the hall. There was a debate whether the bar and catering should be self-financing, and that all the grant income should go to the welfare service. Of course, this was never enough. Ultimately the debt was the priority, and all unrestricted income had to be directed towards meeting this. The struggle for funds was aggravated by this conflict.

The welfare committee, which had been set up in the early days by Dr Larry Morton and others, was still functioning, but now with just two members, one of whom was an Irish councillor from Camden, Tom Devine, and Bill Cagney, the director himself.

Problems with Welfare
In May, the welfare staff were excluded from meetings of this committee. Anne-Marie O'Boyle says that the only discussion permitted had to with the director. Their feelings were not improved by the installation of a large water tank into one of the rooms that they used at the top of the building at no. 50. This led them to complain about their conditions and they submitted a list of grievances. Bill Cagney was said to be somewhat dismissive. Ironically, one intention of the development was to make things easier for the Welfare Department as a whole.

Joan Moriarty recounted to a newspaper the sort of routine cases that she had to deal with. The first was that of a young wife who was regularly beaten up by her husband. She had fled Ireland, leaving five young children at home. She needed time to get away and think her situation through, said Joan Moriarty to the *Cork*

Weekly Examiner. Next came a telephone call from a local hospital to say that a young Irish lad who had slashed his wrists the night before was being discharged into one of the lodging houses which accepts such vulnerable people.*"I asked what his age was, and they said twenty. I said for the love of the Lord will you send him down to see me. He turned out to be one of the nicest fellows you could meet, although very troubled and depressed. I got him sorted out, found him a nice place to stay and he agreed to a counselling session where he will get psychotherapy, if that is what he wants. I only make suggestions, he will have to make the move to help himself.* She was then confronted by two sixteen-year-old runaway girls she had to get back to Ireland. *"Runaway youngsters are the order of the day here, a lot of them come and pose at being much older. We rang the Gardai who told us they were both missing from home. The girls then disappeared. Before we found them again they had been hanging around Euston Station and the West End for four days. Can you imagine the kind of situation they could have found themselves in?"* On the same day Joan Moriarty visited a former employee of the Centre who was in hospital with a malignant liver tumour. Following that visit she left the Centre at the end of her day there, 5.00 pm, and visited Conway House in Kilburn. *"I stay at the hostel until 10 o'clock. While there, I see any boys who have problems with work, or who have personality problems, drink, marital problems or whatever."*[10]

In spite of internal difficulties, Joan Moriarty was a champion for the Centre. She appeared on Gay Byrne's *Late Late Show* for RTE in March 1981 to speak about the pressures on welfare facilities in Britain, following her annual report for the Centre in that year. She was later asked how effective that and the TV appearance had been. *"They're still com-*

ing over", she sighed, *"But now when they come to the Centre looking for help they say 'Oh I saw you on the telly back home'. It seems every day someone comes in here who has seen the Late Late Show and still left home. I had a lad here today looking for work who had seen me on television. 'No one believes that there is a work shortage in London', he told me, No matter what you do, they'll still come. At least he had bought a return ticket just in case, so part of the message must be getting across."*

Roundwood Park

Although the now traditional London Irish Festival each summer was organised by the Council of Irish Counties, there was usually a hefty donation made afterwards to the funds of the Centre. Parades, music and fun were some of the attractions in Roundwood Park, but the social opportunities were its great strength. Friends and families met for the first time in years to enjoy the day. In true Irish fashion there was plenty of music, and in later years two stages were erected in the park. The traditional and folk music, the ceilidhs and step dancing took place at one end, separated from the amplified music of the bands at the other.

Another tradition was the cakes that Jim Butler provided. He says, *"The festival was a dream, and my input was every year I would bake cakes. All from brown bread. They were sold off by the slice, with butter and honey and a beaker of tea."*. He baked them in the Centre's kitchen, once Jimmy McCluskey had finished for the evening. *"I would wait until he had gone, and then would attack the baking. The mixer that he had would make thirteen cakes at one time, so until one in the morning I sat baking. I was able to do four bakes through the night, and I'd be gone and tidied by the morning. That would go on night after night until I had five hundred cakes."* At first this was

Agnes O'Connell directing her pipe band during the procession at Roundwood Park.(Joanne O'Brien)

not such an easy operation. *"My first en- counter with that mixer bears reciting. I didn't realise there were three speeds on it, so on the first night I made my thirteen cakes with flour, salt, cream of tartar, all of the dry stuff that goes in, and then I decided to mix it dry before I wet it. I didn't realise the mixer was in top gear, and it blew the whole thirteen cakes around the kitchen. I spent the whole night long clearing. The flour got into every cup and saucer, it was a quarter of an inch deep across the floor. I was all night trying to clean up before Jimmy came in the morning. I was white from that myself."*[11]

A feature of the festivals was the car raffles. These began through the generosity of Mossie O'Riordan, who donated a new car for each of the early festivals. One year, by a stroke of luck, Tess Moroney won. For the sake of the Centre she did not claim her prize and offered it back into the raffle. It was then won by a parish priest.

The tradition was continued for as many as ten years by Jim and Mary Lehane of Killarney Motors in Neasden. The cars, which were usually Ford Fiestas and bought by them at cost price, were then decorated with bunting and parked on the top of the hill in the park on the day of the festival. During the previous weeks the particular car for that year's festival had been driven to the local churches before Sunday Mass, so that parishioners could see it and buy tickets. Members of the Council of Irish County Associations also visited local pubs to sell more tickets. At its height, as many as 18,000 tickets were sold for one car.[13]

In 1981 an estimated 80,000 people attended the festival, among them the Irish Ambassador, Dr Eamon Kennedy. Unfortunately, a melée developed near one of the beer tents in which ten policemen and six members of the public were injured.

It was said that young skinheads with National Front connections had been taunting Irishmen outside the tent. This was also a recurring problem at Conway House.

It is said that the incident was exaggerated in the press, particularly in the Irish press. Bridie Shaw was standing near Chief Inspector Aitchison at the time, who said to her *"Don't worry, Bridie, I often get worse on a Saturday night in the Kilburn High Road."*[14] Fortunately this event did not deter the Council of Irish County Associations from organising further festivals for many more years.

Inspection from Dublin

During the summer of 1981 the funding situation deteriorated further. In May, Irish government representatives who had visited the Centre to monitor their grant expressed their concern at the lack of progress with phase II, the new welfare offices.

Two members of the Dail also arrived from Dublin to see the progress at first hand. Paddy Sheridan was asked to take them out to lunch, which he was delighted to do with Anne-Marie O'Boyle as company. Driving one of the cars that the Centre then owned he took the party to an Italian restaurant he favoured in Marble Arch. However, because of parking restrictions he decided that they would wisely leave the car in Maida Vale and take a taxi to the restaurant.

They had a good meal, with Paddy Sheridan an impeccable, although tee-total host. When the bill arrived he emptied his pockets but found he did not have enough to meet it. Anne-Marie O'Boyle had not brought her bag. The two TDs, more amused than embarrassed, offered to pay the balance.

Without the taxi fare, it was then decided to return to the car by bus. They waited at the bus stop, but when one arrived Paddy Sheridan in his anxiety leapt

aboard. The bus was too full to take the others, and they watched him sailing off up the Edgware Road. The two TDs and Anne-Marie O'Boyle followed in the next bus, but noticed him walking back to where he had last seen them. They made it at last to the car, but waited a while until he turned up.[15] Nevertheless, it is assumed a positive report was returned to Dublin.

Paddy Sheridan's departure ...

Not long afterwards Paddy Sheridan was assigned to St Anne's parish in Birmingham. He says, *"I had no energy. I was dead and then of course sixteen months later I had this massive heart attack."* Fortunately he recovered. The pressure had been at times relentless. *"We'd have Mass every evening at seven, and then we'd have Mass every morning at nine. And eleven on Sunday"*, he recalls. *"I remember getting up to say the nine o'clock Mass, but I had not got to bed until six. I went to give a sermon, and then I stopped and said that I did not know*

Father Paddy Sheridan with friends at the London Irish Centre.

144

what I was talking about as I was absolutely cross-eyed with sleep, so I said you do not know what I'm talking about, I do not know what I'm talking about. I don't think He upstairs knows what I am talking about. We'll just say Mass and go."[16]

His years at the Centre were much appreciated. He was described by Bridie Shaw as,"a great worker. He kept those boys in order. If there was a fight going on, Paddy sorted them out. On one occasion a boy from the hostel said 'I can't hit you father, with your dog collar on', so Paddy ripped it off and said, 'OK, hit me now'."[17] He was a larger than life man, generous in his friendship.

It was a rule within the Oblate order that a priest would leave an obedience with whatever possessions he had brought and no more. If he had arrived with one suitcase containing some changes of clothes that is what he took away. However Paddy Sheridan was so popular when he left Camden Square on this, the second time, a collection was held, and he was presented with enough money to buy himself a small car. But before this precedent could be allowed, a special dispensation had to be granted by the provincial.

After Birmingham and then Tower Hill, he was assigned to Inisbofin, off Co. Mayo, and from 1998 to Tooreen near Ballyhaunis, Co. Mayo, where he now resides in the priest's house built for a previous resident, Father James Horan. Fr Horan had achieved an astonishing success in 1979 by inviting Pope John Paul to Knock for the centenary celebrations of the Knock shrine at which he also declared its church a basilica.

Tooreen is a very long way from the daily crises he dealt with in London and Birmingham. As Paddy Sheridan now laughs,"I'm only on loan here, as they haven't enough priests to go around. And the Oblates said, fair enough you can stay there for some time. They haven't told me to go,

not yet anyway."[18]

Meanwhile, back in Camden, Tommy Dunne reported in June 1981 that the interest payments were definitely not being met, and the Centre was facing an uphill struggle ahead. In July, it was facing certain defeat. "It would be difficult to make a case on behalf of the Centre, that widespread sympathy among the organised Irish (in London) is lacking ... allegations of a massive debt to build a white elephant have to be countered."[19]

... Bill Cagney's departure

At the end of September 1981 the committee learned that Bill Cagney was leaving. Jim Butler reveals that he was asked to succeed him. His response was that he would be willing, but for the full six years. He did not wish to step down after three."But having spent four years there to be followed by another six years, I thought it would be suicidal. It was extremely wearing on the system. Having done four years, I suggested that if they appointed somebody else I didn't mind staying on another two years to help somebody get into control."[20] It seems that he had some sway with the provincial at that time.

Bill Cagney departed on 13 October.

Father Claude Malone was formally welcomed into the post of director less than a month later on 10 November. His arrival must have been a relief to the administrative committee, chaired now by Martin Moroney, because following a visit the previous May from the Oblate provincial, Father Paschal Dillon, there had been some doubt as to whether the order would continue to maintain a presence at the Centre or even abandon it.

It is said that there had been some interference with the provincial's right to instruct priests. Prominent members of the administrative committee had different views. Donie Egan wanted Bill Cagney to stay, while Martin Moroney preferred Claude Malone. Both men were at various times chairmen. Fr Dillon was adamant that he would not take sides.

After seeing his hall finally built, Bill Cagney became curate of St Peter's in Leigh-on-Sea in Essex, and later returned to Australia. A man of determination he was known for his view that *"God is all-powerful, but He sometimes needs help from us down here."*[21] For all his idiosyncrasies, he is now remembered as a determined man, who was clear about what he wanted to achieve. He later told Mary Kenny that *"To wake up in the morning without a debt hanging over you is a wonderful place to be."* He died in Melbourne on 9 April 2000.

and Claude Malone's return ...
Claude Malone, ordained in 1971, had already some experience of England. He had been first, in 1966, a student priest at Quex Road and then from 1967 to 1970 a junior chaplain at the Centre under Paddy Hackett. After Camden Square he had been posted to the Oblate Novitiate Training College at Cahermoyle House. Thence he was based in Dublin for three years as director of vocations, visiting schools and colleges throughout Ireland. In 1976 he was asked to return to London once again, this time as curate at Quex Road where he remained until he was appointed in 1981 as director of London Irish Centre.

He once wrote of his first spell at the Centre: *"When I joined in the work at the London Irish Centre it was like being drawn along in the rapids of a gigantic river. I worked in the many departments of the Centre. Of them all I would opt for one that was seen as the first need, the hostels. They gave more than accommodation, they gave an invaluable opportunity of really getting to know the individual person. I used to go around the rooms of the men's hostel. It was around midnight when I knew that the boys would be in. The chat often went on to 1.00 am or 2.00 am. I feel that if I helped even one of the hundreds with whom I came in contact in this way it was worthwhile. The work at the Centre takes in practically every type of welfare case. There are 'inadequate persons', ex-prisoners, drug addicts, alcoholics, unmarried mothers, psychiatric cases, broken marriages, missing persons, and – unfortunately – juvenile emigrants."*[22] He has since added that there were also of course a number of very capable or talented people, who had left Ireland as a part of its brain drain.

There was something of a scandal in 1983. The Lord Mayor of Cork, John Dennehy, had suggested that the best place for the unemployed was England. Although long suspected as unofficial advice, this public remark created an uproar. In Camden Square, Joan Moriarty refuted the suggestion. Quite the reverse, her reply was, *"Don't do it. There are no good jobs to be found easily in London."* She admitted that many emigrants found living on the dole in London a better prospect than unemployment at home, *"but it looks very bad for people to be coming over here to pick up the dole in London."* The latest report of the Centre repeated the warning. *"In the current depression, the amount of education or qualifications attained is for the most part of little relevance in the job hunt. Surveyors are doing bar work, skilled tradesmen are glad to get labouring and labourers are fortunate if they are working at all. Apprenticeships are non-existent."*[23] Her words in the Irish press were not heeded as emigration rose. The compelling fact was that young Irish people could claim the dole in Britain at sixteen, two years earlier than at home.

The debt continued to be a headache for almost all of Bill Cagney's successors, including Claude Malone, but it was not until Father Jerry Kivlehan got to grips with it in the mid-1990s, by letting or subcontracting parts of the building to other users and by other means, was any radical attempt made to clear it. Joe Davis says, *"Father Jerry had to do the rescue job"*.[24]

As a curate in Kilburn, Claude Malone knew all about the debt at the Centre. It had assumed an almost mythological significance. He must have been singularly brave to take over at that time, and as he crossed the threshold in Murray Street once again he must have been fearful of being unable to manage it. His first challenge, as he told his colleagues, was to somehow reduce the weight of that burden. He was willing to listen to good advice, and he also had a 'can do' approach which helped to develop a more positive attitude among a potentially awkward administrative committee.

Regarded as "friendly, homely and well organised", Claude Malone was soon able to bring some stability to the committee in facing the debt and considering the long-term future of the Centre. This of course had nothing to do with his clerical work, but it reveals again that so many directors appointed to the Centre with such high expectations had no training, and must have floundered when trying to manage the complexities and tensions within the building.

Joan Moriarty, whose relationship with directors was not always productive, has said, *"The Oblates never trained anyone for anything. I said to Claude, 'Why does your congregation never train your men when they're younger?' Claude said 'Because they might leave'. I said 'That's no bad reason, because you then give them something to go out with'. I said 'Our community, the Vincentian Sisters, would continue to educate people. Even if they were half-way through UCD[25] we would continue to fund*

them until they had finished their degree. That was only fair and just'." In Claude Malone the committee was fortunate. He knew more than some of his predecessors about managing such a centre. He had also learned book-keeping during Paddy Hackett's time.

Meeting the debt

In January 1982 the committee learned that plans for the long-awaited welfare section had to be redrawn because of lack of funds. It was also said that the architects had overlooked the installation of toilets, but this may have been gossip. In March, the debt reached £816,000, with weekly repayments of £2,500 required. Claude Malone decided to call an extraordinary general meeting to deal with the crisis. The high interest rates, which had almost doubled since the scheme for the new hall had been launched by Bill Cagney in 1975 and the downturn in fund-raising during the economic crisis in Britain of that time, had pushed the deficit to its present level. So important was need to keep the debt

Fr Claude Malone after his parachute jump in Naas.

down, Malone would later recall how he and his colleagues would meet at eight o'clock on Monday mornings to count the bar takings after the weekend.

New fund-raising projects were always a priority. Ready to try anything himself, he later on went home to Naas to take part in a parachute jump with the Falcons Parachute Club to raise £70,000. His sponsors ranged from Aer Lingus to the local hairdresser, Charlie Byrne. He had never jumped before, and his first and only lesson took place just two hours before take-off. However, he landed safely and the debt was reduced.

All ideas to raise funds were considered. Sympathetic stories in the press were encouraged. An eminent supporter, the writer Maeve Binchy, wrote in her *Irish Times* column, *"If you're Irish and live in London, you'd be grateful to them* [the Centre] *a hundred times a day for the way they help your fellow Irish people"*. But support from people in Ireland, who perhaps had more urgent pre-occupations, was thin. *"There has never been a great tradition of Irish people back home sending us money"*, said Joan Moriarty. *"The Irish community here are most generous, they raise a lot of money for us. But no, back home I don't think people quite know what we need it for."*[26] The money obviously went towards the welfare of the existing Irish community, but support was also required for those with no family and few friends who had passed away.

Too often it had been remarked that some Irish people were dying alone, in poverty and sometimes even unidentified. In 1982 a woman from Donegal came into the Centre with a donation, as a result of the success of the Missing Persons' Bureau in finding a relative for her. With this money, plots were purchased in the Camden and Islington cemetery in Finchley, beside the North Circular Road.

Joan Moriarty takes up a story. *"Pat Ryan was always very good to me. Pat Ryan and daughter, they were undertakers. This guy we knew, he died under the arches in Holloway. God rest him. Paddy Ward. We got the limousine and four or five of the lads to where we were to have the Mass in Kentish Town. When we came out of the Mass there were the lads having a little top-up of the alcoholic intake. So I said, 'Come on, into the limousine'. Paddy was buried with all due honours. One jumped on the soil to make a speech about the virtues of Paddy's life. So I said, 'Come on now, we'll all go back'. We came down the Holloway Road until one of them says, 'Let us out here Sister'. Of course the pub was just there, and they were going to make sure that Paddy had a good send-off. It's very important for Irish people to have a dignified Catholic funeral."*[27]

The social life

The social life at the Centre continued alongside the welfare service. The bars were full, particularly at weekends. The McNamara Hall was spinning with dinners, dances, wedding receptions and ceilidhs. The Kennedy provided another venue. On some evenings different counties held functions in different halls. Another attraction was Sunday afternoon bingo, which Mary Kenny now organised in the Douglas Hyde Lounge, and was a great attraction for families. Unfortunately their parents would become so engrossed in the game that the children would occasionally cause havoc. However if Claude Malone was present he somehow charmed them into good behaviour.

As a new arrival, brought to Camden Square by his son's interest in music, Jim Myers immediately noticed Claude Malone's welcoming way. He began to become involved with the Centre. Although a jazz buff, through his son' musical interest as a student of Tommy

A concert in the Kennedy Hall.

Maguire, he also became active in Comhaltas Ceoltoiri Eireann.[28]

The dances at the Douglas Hyde were very popular. Joe Davis says that as the chairman of the social committee he sometimes had to ask people to stop dancing, because there were too many on the floor. This once annoyed one of the dancers who picked up a chair and attempted to strike Joe on the head with it. Fortunately, 'big' John Murphy, not the builder but now Life President of the Cork Association, noticed this and grabbed the man. Joe says that Murphy lifted him up, carried him down the stairs and threw him out into Murray Street. 'Strictly ballroom' had a different meaning in those days.

The burst of social activity, particularly that in the McNamara Hall, but with its only entrance in the relatively quiet Murray Mews, once again provoked objections from the neighbours. They objected to the Centre's weekday and Sunday music and dancing licence in 1984. Claude Malone was willing to meet them, and a number of measures were taken to control the noise, such as the installation of sound-limiting equipment. Unfortunately, although these mechanical devices may have made a difference, the behaviour of those leaving the premises in the early hours was less easy to control. Malone insisted that a member of staff was at the door, and musicians were asked to unload and load their equipment more quietly. It took a few more years of objection before another entrance from within the building was completed, and the Murray Mews entrance was discontinued except for emergencies.

Jimmy McCluskey was still the hard-working if somewhat erratic chef. He managed a team of as many as ten people in the kitchen, and was able to provide breakfast every morning for the staff, lunch for the welfare staff and priests and tea for whoever else was there. If a homeless or destitute person called at the door, he would happily make up a sandwich. At the same time he would be preparing a dinner for 500 people in the two halls that evening. His day did not end there, as Jim Butler recalled. He would be willing to serve chicken and chips at 1.30 am, and still be at work for breakfast.

There is a wonderful story from Maeve Heath that one evening he was cooking a roast turkey for a county dinner. A man wandered into the kitchen from one of the bars and, while Jimmy's back was turned, stole one of the cooked turkeys, stuffing it under his jumper. As soon as McCluskey noticed this, he dropped everything and chased after the turkey thief into Murray Street. Presumably realising that running up the road with a dripping hot turkey under his jumper was not particularly easy, the man stopped, pulled it out and threw it back at his pursuer, telling him what he thought of it. Jimmy picked it up off the pavement, and took it back to his kitchen where he washed it and re-heated it. Twenty minutes later it appeared on the table with all the trimmings as part of another enjoyable meal.[29]

The Troubles intrude

When the dinners and dances were over, it was never easy for Irish people to forget the troubled world outside the centre. The Federation of Irish Societies, which had been founded in 1973 as an umbrella body for Irish clubs and societies in Britain, held a conference in the Centre in March 1982, in order to re-assess the key points of its constitution. Later in the year, on a more political level it described the Prevention of Terrorism Act as "divisive and intimidating". Earl Jellicoe, who had been the 1973 government's Leader of the House of Lords, had been commissioned to carry out a review of the PTA, which much

public opinion felt was preventing free expression. The Federation stated that, *"The Act has stifled healthy political comment by the Irish community in Britain and has inhibited a vital and valuable contribution being made in discussion pertaining to Northern Ireland and Irish affairs in general. Innocent people have been arrested, frightened, stressed and stigmatised by the application of the Prevention of Terrorism Act. The vast majority of people detained have not been charged."* Although there had been a drop in figures held in custody in 1982, the total number detained since the introduction of the PTA in November 1974 had reached 5,501. Of these, just 96 people or less than 2% had been charged with offences under the Act.[30]

The IRA was now stepping up its mainland campaign. In July, two bombs exploded at Knightsbridge and Regent's Park in London, the first killing eight soldiers of a mounted detachment on their way to change the guard at Horse Guards' Parade. Two hours later a second bomb exploded under the bandstand in Regent's Park, killing six military bandsmen.

Irish priests in London were extremely wary of political involvement, yet they agreed that statements from their bishops calling on the IRA to cease fire had little effect. *"Their congregations have by now stopped looking for political leadership from the clergy. When Fr Claude Malone condemned the bombing in the Royal Parks an old man in the back of the chapel shouted 'Don't forget to pray for the bloody horses'. He does not resent the outburst, because it is a token of some interest 'whereas most Catholics feel powerless'. He is representative of those Irish priests who feel that they should return exclusively to spiritual duties."*

Irish Centre Community Services

Towards the end of 1982 Malone invited a high-powered contingent of clergy, diplomats and politicians to mark the formal opening of the new welfare department at no. 50 Camden Square, next door to the original building. They included Cardinal Basil Hume, the Archbishop of Westminster, Bishop Henderson of Southwark and Archbishop Cunnane of Tuam, who were followed by the Irish Ambassador, Dr Eamonn Kennedy and Cllr Tom Devine, the Mayor of Camden who was on the welfare committee. This extension of welfare provision separated those who came to the Centre because of their housing and other needs, from those who came for a social or other event. The guests were welcomed in Camden Square by the girls and boys of the London Irish Pipe Band.

The welfare service was formally renamed Irish Centre Community Services, the name it holds to this day. Under the management of Joan Moriarty, it included

Cardinal Basil Hume, Archbishop of Westminster, at the formal opening of the new welfare department at the London Irish Centre in 1982.

advice on work prospects, housing advice and support with Fr Kieron Kennedy. There was also family support, counselling and marriage guidance under Kay Bourke. Basic English classes were taught by Kay Leddy, and Irish language conversation classes by Siobhan Ui Neil. All the welfare staff were involved in issues of repatriation, referral, resettlement in Ireland, crisis intervention and domiciliary visits.

The occasion also celebrated the opening of a much-needed new entrance to the McNamara Hall, to which the £10,000 fund-raising achievements of the golfing maestro of the Waterford Association, Tony Beatty, and its membership had not only made a contribution but had also donated a chandelier of Waterford glass.

In his speech, Dr Kennedy said of the Centre, *"It was a dream come true, a beacon to countless people in need, a place of warmth and comfort, and a very necessary advice service which had been availed of by 2,000 new clients over the past two years. It was a magnificent functional building, which had the support of an Irish government grant of £300,000"*. He paid tribute to the interest showed by the Cardinal in the Irish community in London, to the work of the Oblate Fathers who had been involved at the Centre since 1967 and to Joan Moriarty, the chief welfare officer, and her volunteer helpers.

In contrast to that of the Ambassador, Cardinal Hume's speech was more saintly than secular, although he did urge the London Irish community *"To put the shoulder to the wheel"*, and voiced concern that Claude Malone and his chaplain, Jim Butler, were spending too much time in administration and fund-raising rather than *"Doing the primary work that they were sent here to do by the Order and myself – the work that God has called them to do in choosing them to be his priests."*[31] This was recognised by the director, but he was also acutely aware of the administrative burden placed on his shoulders.

In fact, Claude Malone was very keen to develop the welfare and advice side of the Centre's work, which had suffered under "the overpowering weight of responsibility" for the hall. He had felt that this aspect had hardly moved on since he remembered it as a priest here in the 1960s. The new, refurbished space next door now provided room for expansion, and he had now recruited more full-time staff. However, the debt, which had crept upwards to the psychologically important £1 million, still dominated, whatever the Cardinal may have said.

Now that the McNamara Hall had been completed, there was still the additional building development along Camden Square beyond the new welfare service, which needed negotiation and attention. These properties for the Community Housing Association were designed by another local architect, David Roberts, who was no relation to Keith. Although there had been some debate over the design between Camden and the CHA, they were nearing completion, and the name Hillier House had been chosen. This was after Dr Thomas Hillier who had been the first Medical Officer of Health of St Pancras, but coincidentally also after Maria Hillier, who had been a housemaid at no. 47 in the houses that were once here.[32]

By the end of 1982, Claude Malone had managed to reduce the debt to below the £1 million mark, with one creditor accepting a payment of £100,000 for a larger debt, and the Bank of Ireland also agreeing to a new arrangement. In these efforts he was assisted by Andy Rogers of the bank and Tony Beatty, the Centre's auditor. However, the Annual Report for 1983 recorded that "our new deal with the banks is conditional on repayment targets being set and reached".

Funding events

Neither the continuing support of the Council of Irish County Associations with its annual London Irish Festival at Roundwood Park, the annual and project grants from Camden Council, the National Collection at Irish Churches some years before, nor any sporadic payments from the Irish government seemed to make a sufficient impact on the sum needed. Different and sometimes innovative methods had been tried, from hiring professional fund-raisers during Bill Cagney's time which had failed, to a series of sponsorship initiatives such as walks around the Inner Circle of Regent's Park, and to persuading people to contribute the price of a pint or a packet of cigarettes a week. Yet the Centre always seemed defeated. The British economy had rising inflation and high interest rates. With payments overtaking income, there were times when the administrative committee of the Centre seemed to have lost control.

In spite of a series of different catering and bar managers, in itself a source of instability, the McNamara Hall now offered a potential for different bookings from the regular pattern of county association dinners. The bars and bingo sessions at the Kennedy Hall and the Douglas Hyde Lounge had been regarded as earners, but a wide programme of often surprising lettings at the McNamara itself was sought.

In February 1983 the celebrated Anna Scher Children's Theatre from Islington was invited by Doris Daly, a good friend of Jim Butler and stalwart of the Leitrim Association, to perform at the Centre in a new work written by 18-year-old Bernadette Burdis. Anna Scher herself was from Cork. Among the audience in the McNamara Hall were three London mayors, Ken Livingstone, leader of the GLC and the local St Pancras MP, Jock Stallard. On regular Thursday evenings there was

Anna Scher with Fr Claude Malone, 1983.

Karate at the Centre. The club was led by Eddie Batson who was a 1st Dan Black Belt. More successful was the amateur boxing, which had returned to the McNamara Hall on 31 March 1982. Converted into an arena, with a raised ring surrounded by seats, the hall comfortably accommodated these tournaments. They were usually junior championships staged by clubs from across London or by the Amateur Boxing Association. Parents and supporters would pack the hall, and the bar and chicken or sausage and chips would always be available. Occasionally there would be a 'dinner show', where the audience would dress in dinner jackets and suits.

The *"kids would fight toe to toe in the centre of the ring for their three rounds"*, a hard slog, and when the winner was announced the boy who had lost would sometimes burst into tears. Lee Morrish fought here at the age of 11, and went on to win the European Junior Championship.[33] Florrie Darcy says she enjoyed them. *"They were wonderful people. In at seven, bouts began at eight and they were all gone by ten."*[34] However, Claude Malone was never at ease with the boxing. It was allowed purely as an opportunity to earn money. As he later admitted, it was a mistake and prompted bad relationships with the neighbours.

Discos were also held on Saturday nights, also to the annoyance of local residents. They took place in the Kennedy Hall and in spite of the fact that only soft drinks were available, they were very popular. Some of the adults in other parts of the Centre could never understand why the young people appeared to be so drunk, and tried to observe if anything was smuggled in from the off-licence the other side of Murray Street. It was some time later when it was found that above the ceiling panels were hidden bottles of vodka, which the teenagers had discovered. The manager of the bar had been concealing his own stolen supply there.

In March 1984, it was decided that the discos would be discontinued because of disturbances and complaints from neighbours. At least one young man had already appeared in court. Claude Malone was verbally abused and threatened at one event before the police arrived in response to a call.

An altogether different sort of music was performed at other times. Irish traditional music had never left the building. Since the days of Tommy Maguire and his classes, many more young people had come to the Centre to learn the techniques of the fiddle or the tin whistle. Traditional sessions were a regular part of an evening's entertainment. In April, Brendan Mulkere, the leading traditional fiddle player who was tutor to some very established musicians, brought together some of his current pupils for a special concert.

Another crisis

Despite imaginative uses for the building, the overall financial position became worse throughout 1983. In May, the *Irish Post* published a banner headline proclaiming 'Cash Crisis in Camden'. Underneath, a strapline explained 'The Irish Centre is for Sale'. It continued in the same depressing theme, *"The mounting debts arise from the extensive redevelopment programme which was completed last year. The main creditors are the Bank of Ireland and the building contractors J. Murphy and Sons. There are also loans outstanding to three brewing companies. The Centre's auditors value the property at not more than £500,000, so that even if it was sold a financial problem will remain. The possibility now being pursued is a sale and lease-back deal. That would*

allow the Centre to continue functioning. The Centre's director, Fr. Claude Malone, told the administrative council that every possible solution is being investigated, 'but as the accounts show, time is not on our side'."

In the same issue, the *Post's* editorial made the point, *"The Camden Centre is two things under one roof: an invaluable welfare service and secondly a social venue whose essential purpose over the years was to raise the money to pay for the welfare operation. But it may well be that the two things no longer logically go hand in hand. Certainly it doesn't need a £1 million investment in real estate, with all the administration that it involves, to have an effective welfare bureau. Much better, three or four welfare operations positioned throughout London, and situated convenient to the areas of need, than the extensive apparatus required to run Camden."*[35] This argument must have also crossed other people's minds at the time, but it challenged the prevailing view of Bill Cagney, the Oblates and the Hierarchy. One of the few who was now privately considering broader options was the director, Claude Malone, himself.

At a committee meeting he made the provocative point when he said that perhaps it was time that the building was under lay management. In saying so he didn't intend to denigrate any of the priests who had administered the Centre over the years. *"But around the priests there has always been a labyrinth of councils, committees, patrons and lots more, stretching out to diverse places ranging from the office of the Archbishop of Westminster to the headquarters of the Oblate Order and the seat of the Irish Catholic Hierarchy"*. Since 1955, little had changed in terms of structure and constitution. Lord Longford was still the president and Cardinal Hume had joined the other bishops as a patron. The Centre would have to wait another ten years before this was properly tackled.

Another sceptic was Patsy Carolan, who believed that the interest in big functions had now passed, and the hall would never be viable. Larger county associations still tended to book rooms at hotels rather than the McNamara Hall, but this might have been more to do with the quality of the catering managers at the Centre. For some years they were continually being replaced. At the same time many Irishmen and women were enjoying alternative social venues such as the ballrooms of the Galtymore and the National in Cricklewood, and the pubs, big and small, which were dotted across London.

In the next issue of the *Irish Post* Claude Malone was typically robust.*"Make no mistake about it, we intend to survive. For over a year now I have been stressing at every opportunity our financial difficulties. Maybe your banner headline will drive home the point and people will listen."*[36] In a further letter he admitted, *"Yes we have a grave crisis on our hands. We are in urgent need of a 'survival kit', and that is why we are exploring every possibility but not the closure of the Centre. We need help and we need it urgently. Fr. Jim Butler's sponsored cycle ride of Ireland next month is no symbolic gesture. We desperately need the money he is endeavouring to raise. Time is definitely not on our side".* Sponsorship forms were published in the Irish press.

Although Jim Butler had been in training for his cycle ride, few people believed he would actually do it. It would be an extremely brave fund-raising effort. He says, *"I don't know what my foundation for this was, but I recall the financial committee spent six months trying to persuade me to do it. They had some information that I was a long distance cyclist. I didn't succumb for about six months, and wasn't obliging."*[37] In its bid to maximise income, lettings were important. In accordance with its constitution, the Centre offered a venue

Cllr Ken Livingstone speaking at the London Irish Centre.

where Irish groups and associations could meet.This inevitably included groups linked to the conflict in northern Ireland.

Meetings

The Troops Out Movement held a meeting here in April 1983. Later that month the second anniversary of hunger-striker and MP Bobby Sands' death was commemorated in London by a weekend of activities. It culminated in an evening of music, speeches and poetry on 5 May. Irene Ryan, a neighbour, remembers queues of people outside waiting to be admitted. Speakers included a member of the Ard Comhairle of Sinn Fein, Caoimhim O'Caolain, from Northern Ireland, Cllr Tom Devine, Mayor of Camden, and Ken Livingstone, who was seen briskly autographing on the back of the entrance tickets of well-wishers. As the *Irish Post* said about Livingstone, *"Standing in front of a series of banners in the McNamara Hall depicting* the hunger strikers, he told the packed meeting that 'the people responsible for the violence and deaths are the politicians here who refuse to raise the issue'. He added that the attacks to which he had been subjected by the press for speaking out on Ireland were intended 'as a warning to all others in Britain who dare put their heads above the parapet'."[38] Needless to say, he won a standing ovation.

Ken Livingstone had served as a councillor in Camden from 1978 to 1982, and with colleagues at Camden Town Hall must have watched with some apprehension the construction of the McNamara Hall. From 1973 to 1986 he was also elected to the Greater London Council, chairing its ethnic minorities committee from 1981 to 1986. Perhaps eyeing the Brent East parliamentary seat with its large Irish population which he was to win in 1987, he cleverly maintained a sympathetic attitude towards the Irish community in London, which also meant towards the aims of the Centre. Attempts were therefore made to obtain grants from the GLC, which at the time had a reputation for generosity if not profligacy.

However, these attempts were rejected. As Claude Malone said, "The Greater London Council has repeatedly turned down grant applications from Britain's best-known Irish Centre, because GLC officials mistakenly believe that it was owned and controlled by the Catholic Church". This misunderstanding had also been behind the initial reticence of the Irish government. The constitution stated that it was owned "by the Irish community", and administered by a lay committee. However, Claude Malone later admitted that if the church's contribution, first from Westminster and then from the Oblates, towards providing staff and supporting the work of the Centre and its fund-raising were withdrawn, its creditors would have become very nervous.

It was never clear why the GLC was so reluctant. The Irish Post reported, "In an attack on the GLC's Ethnic Minorities Unit, Fr Malone said, 'We haven't had a single grant from the GLC, and I honestly believe we have been discriminated against because they believe this Centre is totally controlled by the Catholic Church. That is totally false'. He accused Steve Brennan, Irish Liaison Officer at the GLC, of factionalising the Irish community and placing different groups in antagonistic relationships with each other. Last night Mr. Brennan, who has also come under attack from the Irish Commission for Culture and Education for his allegations towards this body, denied that the GLC had discriminated against the Centre. But Dublin-born (sic) Fr. Malone listed four grant applications made to the GLC by the Centre which would have provided help for the Irish community. They were for outreach workers for the elderly and unemployed, and women and to provide a Day Centre for the elderly. Each application had been turned down."[39]

A year later in 1984, an application to the GLC for £15,000 for eight computers to train people was successful. As Joan Moriarty says, "Upstairs we had a room at the very top of the house where we had got a lot of typewriters. We were going to start literacy classes. And we were given money by Ken Livingstone". As if in an about-turn, Michael Ward, Chairman of the GLC's Industry and Employment Committee praised the work of the Centre as a reason for making the award: "The Irish Centre is a good first base for new arrivals. We are very keen to encourage the Centre to extend its training activities and particularly to find ways of helping the very vulnerable young people who arrive with no money, no job and no skills". But for some reason the Centre never received the money, which would have benefited the young men in the hostel at Quex Road. The truth was, as Joan Moriarty adds, "We never claimed it. There was a bit of upheaval in the Centre *at that time. I want to forget all the negative things."*[40]

In due course she was to leave. Later, Paddy Sheridan remarked to her,*"Well you stuck it out anyway".*

The birth of Dion

However, the funding skies to the west were brightening. The Minister for Foreign Affairs of the Irish government, Peter Barry, made a series of visits to the Irish Centres in Britain to consider the services they provided. In June 1984 the Department for Labour set up the Dion Committee, which had developed out of the previous advisory committee. Named after the Irish word for 'protection' or 'shelter', it followed a government decision announced in its most recent budget to increase the resources for welfare services abroad.

The Dion Committee is now managed by the Irish Embassy, and continues to make grants to Irish organisations abroad. By 1987 the total grant was £250,000. From 1989 to 1996 this doubled to £500,000 a year. The committee is now also funding second-tier organisations, such as the Action Group for Irish Youth.

While the welfare services continued with their good work, Claude Malone's "rapids of a gigantic river" never abated. The pressures were relentless, and many people looked towards Jim Butler's impending cycle ride as one way to help reduce them.

[1] Interview Fr Paddy Sheridan, October 2003.
[2] *Ibid.*
[3] *Sunday World*, 27 April 1980.
[4] Interview Maeve Heath, March 2004.
[5] Interview Paddy Keegan, July 2004.
[6] LIC minutes, November 1980.
[7] Interview Bridie Shaw, May 2004.
[8] Interview Bill Aulsberry, June 2004.
[9] LIC minutes 7 April 1981.
[10] *Cork Weekly Examiner*, 16 April 1981.
[11] Interview Fr Jim Butler, October 2003.
[12] Correspondence with Tess Hutchinson, July 2004.
[13] Interview Jim Lehane, May 2004.
[14] Interview Bridie Shaw, May 2004.
[15] Interview Anne-Marie O'Boyle, July 2004.
[16] Interview Fr Paddy Sheridan, October 2003.
[17] Interview Bridie Shaw and Mary Allen, January 2004.
[18] Interview Fr Paddy Sheridan, October 2003.
[19] LIC minutes 7 July 1981.
[20] Interview Fr Jim Butler, October 2003.
[21] Interview David Ashton-Hill, March 2004.
[22] *Limerick Leader*, 13 March 1971.
[23] *Evening Herald*, 15 April 1983.
[24] Interview Joe Davis, May 2004.
[25] University College, Dublin.
[26] *Irish Times*, 1 May 1982.
[27] Interview Sr Joan Moriarty, March 2004.
[28] Interview Jim Myers, May 2004.
[29] Interview Maeve Heath, March 2004.
[30] *Irish Observer*, 4 September 1982.
[31] *Irish Observer*, 13 November 1982.
[32] Camden Square Neighbourhood Association Archives, 24 November 1982.
[33] Interview Ray Morrish, May 2004.
[34] Interview Florrie Darcy, July 2004.
[35] *Irish Post*, 4 June 1983.
[36] *Ibid*, 11 June 1983.
[37] Interview Fr Jim Butler, October 2003.
[38] *Irish Post*, 14 May 1983.
[39] *Ibid*, 28 May 1983.
[40] Interview Sr Joan Moriarty, March 2004.

CHAPTER NINE

The Irish cuckoo in the English nest

Father Claude Malone
Father Tom Scully

One of the legends surrounding the fifty-year history of the London Irish Centre is the brave or even foolhardy ride that Jim Butler was now considering. The committee pressed him into taking it seriously. As a colleague said, *"Now Father Butler is a man gifted with great perseverance. If any man worked with horses ploughing a field, he knows a horse goes up and down, up and down, and plods his way at a steady pace all the time. He may stop now and again to shake the harness, but he will keep going. That is the kind of steady worker that Father Butler is ... but he is a winner in the sense of a persevering man, and he has had this idea for years that he would like to do a sponsored cycle ride over 1,000 miles in Ireland and so he has been working in Ireland for the last months, and will be for the next two months, in organising the sponsorship and his route."*[1]

Jim Butler was a born fund-raiser. He ran football pool groups, and on his motorbike would visit as many as a hundred London pubs in a week to enquire about potential sources of employment and to collect the punters' stakes. At the age of fifty-eight he was no youngster, but had been in training for this ride since the previous December.

The list of those who were willing to be his sponsors was impressive. They ranged from bishops and businesses in London, to various reverend fathers, and a number of individuals and smaller businesses in

Ireland. He was sent a message of good wishes from the Cardinal Archbishop of Armagh, and given a rousing send-off by Claude Malone. *"The Lord said something about going two miles with him who asked that we go just one. What do we say of him who is willing to go 1,000 miles?"*, wrote Claude Malone in his address for the sponsored programme.

Describing his intention before he set off, Jim Butler said, *"We will be definable around the church and social centres around the towns we visit ... and we hope that we make it quite clear that we will be recognisable as a priest, and are in fact looking for funds for the Irish Centre. For the good of the Irish people, of course, who are in London and who come to us in need ... and if they are not in need there will always be an open door to anyone coming to London to the Irish Centre...."*[2]

Starting at Rosslare on 14 July 1983 and with the Mayor of Camden, Councillor Ron Heffernan, beside him to wave good-bye, this was to be a solo tour of a thousand miles across and around Ireland. Each year Camden's mayor was invited by Bill and Mary Allen to Waterford City for a civic visit as a guest of the Waterford Association. After his farewell to Jim Butler in Rosslare, Cllr Heffernan and his wife attended the various civic events which had been arranged in Waterford as guest of honour, and then continued to Mallow in Co. Cork, which was where Mrs

On the road during Jim Butler's 1,000-mile cycle ride in Ireland in 1983. From left to right are Martin Doyle, Father Butler's personal assistant and engineer, Mary Kenny, whose vehicle towed the caravan, Teresa Doyle, who looked after the banking of of the money collected, and Doris Daly, navigator, who also in charge of public relations and publicity.

Heffernan had once lived. A day or so later they caught up with Jim Butler pedalling hard on the road, and were then able to present to him a cheque from the Mayor of Waterford and the proceeds of a collection in the parish church in Mallow.[3]

This journey and its fund-raising purpose created a considerable logistical undertaking for a man on a bicycle. It required forward publicity, separate transport including a caravan for emergency accommodation, and at least four people to collect the money from bystanders or in the pubs en route, and then to bank it. This was not something that could be done from a saddle. But it was a major setback for Jim Butler when the Oblate students who were supposed to have helped him, *"let me down and had gone off working and forgotten all about the cycle ride"*.

He had to think fast. *"I explained this to Martin Doyle, and knowing the predicament I was in he said, sure, I'll be with you. Then Mrs Doyle immediately said she would come as well. And talking later in the hearing of Mary Kenny, Mary said she'd also come. I wanted a driver for the car and Mary was a driver"*. Mary Kenny was the only driver, but she had never towed a caravan before. *"It was a huge caravan and very hard to reverse"*, she says. *"We had to unhook it and then ask people to help push it around"*. It is not clear why there really was a need for a caravan, because no one slept in it, except perhaps, as Mary Kenny recalls, Jim Butler may have done so once. *"I hadn't a clue what was in the caravan. I never went into it"*, she says.

One day she broke down outside Ballinasloe in Galway. *"The Guardai helped us. I got away with it"*, says Mary. Fortunately Ballinasloe was her home town, and her family were able to offer rooms to the intrepid travellers. Mary Kenny still does not remember how she managed to tow the caravan into Carrick-on-Shannon.

Finding a fourth person who could give up the time was difficult. But Jim Butler was fortunate. *"Eventually Doris Daly heard me complaining and moaning, and she said she'd come as well. Doris was a wonderful person. She had gone to London to become a nurse, and she worked herself up to become an Area Health Inspector, and she was able to point out people that would be in financial need, and allow us access to these people so we could help them. Over five years we were able to distribute over £60,000 to support families who were financially in the red, and we were eternally grateful to Doris."*

Wearing T-shirts announcing 'Irish Centre, London – 1,000 mile Cycle Ride' as they accompanied him by car and caravan, this entourage was later described on RTE as "pensioners with hearts of gold".

With a sporting bicycle donated by Paddy Whelan, who owned a shop in Dolphin's Barn by Dublin's Grand Canal, Jim Butler pedalled away at seven each morning from his overnight address. *"Because I had to go to bed each night at nine o'clock this meant that I wasn't able to go in the pubs and do any collecting, but they didn't have to be up so early so they could afford to go in the pubs at night as a group. They collected an awful lot of money in the pubs while I was asleep."*[4]

The marathon involved nineteen overnight stops through Waterford, Cork, Tralee, Ennis and then up the west coast before completing the 1,000 miles at his native Drumshanbo in Leitrim. Local radio was fairly new in Ireland, but Jim Butler and his team took every advantage of the news-hungry stations to broadcast his message. As an Irish speaker he also did interviews in Irish at Spiddall in the Gaeltacht. He relied on his supporters from London to augment his fundraising efforts with their own.

It was Doris Daly and the Doyles who rattled tins around the pubs to add to the collection. *"They all went out collecting, and I was left in the car. It was Father Butler's car, and he had hired the caravan"*, says Mary Kenny.[5]

They were offered accommodation wherever they stopped overnight, with Jim Butler often staying in the local priest's house. Mary remembers how kind people were. One of the travellers enjoyed a bit of a social life, and although the others were very abstemious, an occasional drop of poteen was welcomed.

Jim Butler's determination was rewarded in a huge success. By the end of his journey he had raised £169,000, which was used to help wipe out the debt.[6] The Bank of Ireland generously gave him the exact money in pounds sterling without deducting any commission on the rate of exchange.

Beatty and Co. had been invited to become the auditors of the Centre. Although he had no wish to join a committee, Tony Beatty had learned of the problems there because he used to attend meetings, late at night, with the priests. He admired Claude Malone. Joan Moriarty remembers his role in helping to straighten up the systems. *"I think Tony saw through the set up. You know money was being stolen. There was a break-in here and a break-in there, and nobody ever knew anything. They went from crisis to crisis to crisis financially."*[7]

The rescue package

Tony Beatty first came over to this country from Waterford in 1955, working as an accountant. He later founded, with Brendan Mac Lua, the *Irish Post*. He was a passionate golfer, or as he says, *"played at golf."*[8] Through golf classics and his own personal donations he raised three instalments of £15,000, £25,000 and £13,000, along with £10,000 personally contributed for new work on the hallway of the building. A cheque was formally handed over to Claude Malone, alongside Noel Dorr, the new Irish Ambassador, a Mayoman, who had arrived in September 1983.

Tony Beatty was instrumental in reducing the debt. It is said that he took charge of the funds that Jim Butler had raised and invested them sensibly. With the help of people such as Andy Rogers, now Chair of the European Marketing Group, he successfully horse-traded between different creditors, anything to avoid bankruptcy. *"The Centre is now almost half a million pounds better off"*, he announced.*"What we need now are volunteers to undertake fund-raising to meet the new targets"*.

Details of the dramatic rescue package were disclosed at a meeting attended by 120 people. The opportunities had been made possible through the use of the more than £80,000 net raised by Jim Butler on his sponsored cycle ride. The first major creditor, which did not wish to be named but is said to be John Murphy and Sons, agreed a compromise settlement on 19 January 1984, subject to the agreement of the bank, but totally discharging the debt. Further help was provided by the second major creditor, the Bank of Ireland itself. The bank also agreed, in separate negotiations, to reschedule its loan to the Centre, freezing the £423,000 it was owed until the end of the following year. The help of Declan Quinn in this agreement was vital. Other deals were negotiated with the three breweries Courage, Whitbread and Charrington, who were together owed £170,000. Tony Beatty also organised proper stock-taking in the bar, found new staff and had them properly trained. These agreements with the breweries *"completely*

changed the profit and loss account of the Centre by reducing the annual interest charge to manageable proportions. The overall effect means that the Centre is now solvent."[9] Andy Rogers has said that *"With Tony Beatty, Declan Quinn and myself, a bruising series of debates and discussions took place."*[10]

This was good news indeed. As Jim Butler later said in the press, *"I would expect the Irish government to come to the rescue of the Irish Centre and pay off the debt, and let the priests, the committee and the staff get on with looking after the Irish people. After all, one million people have left Ireland, and many were helped by the Centre, and they in turn sent many millions back to help the Irish economy. It is now the duty of the government to help."*

The troubles of the Centre, although exacerbated by its building expansion, were not unique. Other hostels were also suffering financial crises, but perhaps for different reasons. Arlington House in Camden Town, whose relationship with the Centre was close, had ongoing industrial relations problems with its staff. A year before there had been a strike. Its viability, and that of the other Rowton Houses, looked doubtful.

Joan Moriarty shared reservations about Arlington House at that time. *"It was in those days we made several efforts to get into Arlington House and there was no way. If we wanted to see a man they would tell him and he would come down to us. The older Irish men, they went in there, and they stayed in there until they died."*[11]

Jim Butler's departure

Towards the end of the year there was some controversy in the Irish press about why Jim Butler was to be assigned elsewhere. It seemed that he was just settling in at the Centre after his triumphant cycle ride and there was plenty more to do, including raising more money, but the

Still cycling for funds having left the London Irish Centre, Fr Jim Butler receives a send-off from the Lord Mayor of Dublin at the start of another 1,000 mile ride.

provincial, Fr William McGonagle, had other ideas. The Leitrim Association protested at his transfer to a post in Dublin, as Doris Daly, a formidable champion, surmised, *"They're making him a storekeeper or some such. It's a punitive measure"*. But Jim Butler's vow of obedience ensured that he did indeed leave. The Council of Irish County Associations also intervened, but as the *Irish Post* hinted, *"It's said that letters are flying and Fr Butler isn't being universally referred to with affection."*[12]

This view was challenged by the scale of the tribute made by the Leitrim Association at a dinner and dance on 3 December. He was permitted to stay to enjoy this event as the hero of Leitrim, but he reluctantly left the service of the Centre shortly afterwards, on his motorbike. He rode away from Camden to the parish of Bluebell in south-east Dublin to become a curate, where his parish priest was his old friend Father Tom Scully.

Eleven years later, in 1994, Jim Butler was asked to return to Camden, but as he says in a recent letter, *"I had spent too much time laying foundations for the position I now hold to relinquish them and lose all the detailed effort."*[13] He is now living in Dublin, and spending much of his time fund-raising, something perhaps at which he is second to none.

Emigration increases

Another surge in Irish emigration during the 1980s tested the capacity of the existing services in London and elsewhere. The needs were now much more diverse, and often requiring specialist answers. It was the church which had once led the way, but from the end of the 1970s a largely professional Irish Voluntary Sector was accessing British, rather than Irish, public sector funds and starting to make an impact. Perhaps the first to become established was the Brent Irish Advisory Serv-

Hopeful emigrants leaving Dun Laoghaire. (Joanne O'Brien)

ice in 1978. It managed to deal with the cases in Brent and Willesden, which both lie across the Kilburn High Road. At first the London Irish Centre resented these groups whose policies and actions, particularly on issues such as advice on abortion, conflicted with its own, more traditional ethics.

The Action Group for Irish Youth was another. Founded by Joan Moriarty in 1984 and based in the Centre, it later adopted a more progressive position on many social attitudes, but Joan describes its origins in the Centre as *"the bare nucleus."* The AGIY reported the next year that unemployment in Ireland was causing hopelessness and defeat among young people, and was contributing to the latest wave of emigration to London. *"We have had 786 first-time callers at the Centre between January and June this year"*, she reported. She added that, *"The majority of the new callers were in the 16-25 age range, and estimated that the number of new arrivals who go to the Centre seeking help represented less than one tenth of the overall total of new arrivals. This suggested that about 16,000 young people arrive in London in 1984 – equivalent to the entire population of a town the size of Kilkenny."*[14]

It was estimated that the numbers emigrating had doubled in the year. A 70% increase was reported as arriving at Camden Square, with many seeking help with employment and housing. The arrivals came from both the south and the north of Ireland, where sectarian conflict had driven many people out. Many were under twenty-five and unskilled. Jobs in Ireland were now scarce. If they could not be housed by the London Irish Centre or the other agencies, they were forced to sleep rough or in squats. However, even if they were unable to find work in London, the housing and welfare payments they were entitled to in Britain were still more generous than those at home. The Associated Press Agency, picked up by many newspapers, repeated the theme in December 1985. *"The Irish are on the move again, flocking by the thousands to Britain, to escape recession, unemployment and high taxes. Some Irish commentators are speaking of 'the curse returned', portraying Ireland as a country again losing some of its finest to foreign shores. Irish government assurances that it is a mere trickle are not believed."*[15]

A few Conservative MPs leapt into the debate feet first, to make political capital out of the figures of Irish emigration. They called on the government to request that the Dublin authorities stop the flow of young Irish people coming to Britain to seek work. One of them, Terry Dicks, MP, said, *"We have our own problems over unemployment, and we cannot afford to pick up other people's problems. The sooner the British Government realises that, the better. Immigration should stop completely. We should not have any special relationship with the Republic of Ireland. They wanted to be an independent state and their relationship with us should be the same as with other countries."*[16]

In spite of the internal problems of debt and attacks from outside, the Centre continued with its programme of welfare and other advice, and also provided in its two halls and the Douglas Hyde Lounge, an attractive place for people to meet and socialise. The day-to-day needs still had to be faced. In 1986 Claude Malone was quoted, *"As I open up the place each morning I see a few men waiting, straight from Euston. More and more I notice that it is young married men, often with a young family back home. Sometimes they break into tears. A social worker here might be the first person that they have unburdened themselves to. Many simply don't know what to do ... leaving was an act of desperation."*[17]

However the 31,000 who emigrated in the year to April 1986 also included white collar workers, which Charles Haughey, then leader of Fianna Fail, described as a brain drain. He called upon the Fine Gael Taoiseach, Dr Garret Fitzgerald, to resign, saying that the clear implication was that many of those who were leaving were educated young people, who should be at the forefront of economic development in Ireland. This would be a major issue in the forthcoming elections.

Party politics in Dublin aside, as requests at the Centre for assistance reached unprecedented levels Claude Malone told the *Irish Times* that it had put the Centre under *"tremendous pressure"*.[18]

The Troubles return

England, and particularly London, was now a potent battlefield in the IRA's campaign. During the aftermath of the bombs at Harrod's and Brighton, Claude Malone was called upon constantly by the media in Britain and Ireland for interviews. He was reported as saying in the *Nationalist and Leinster Times*, published in Carlow, Laois and his native Kildare, *"Every time there is bombing or a killing we just cringe. Invariably we are the first to suffer any backlash. Some Irish people will avoid work for a day or two, until things quieten down. We get threats here at the Centre and I have often been put under police protection. The Centre is an obvious target."*[19] Many nights, in the early hours, the Centre received false alarms. Fire engines and police would arrive after having received a 999 call. The director lived over the shop, and as a key-holder was often disturbed at night while the Centre was searched for bombs or for an elusive outbreak of fire.

Towards the end of the 1980s, the perceptions of the Irish by ordinary British people were slowly beginning to change. Various reasons have been ascribed for this. It may simply have been that after a period of negativity, people were beginning to question their beliefs, as if thinking there must be something serious behind the IRA struggle, even if its methods were abhorrent. This was aided by a growing understanding of an Irish history that had been excluded from most English school-books. The TV programmes of Robert Kee and others not only broadcast this history, but also set northern Ireland in a wider, British and also Irish, context. Another influence was in the public impression of Taoiseach Garret Fitzgerald, who was seen to be a sensible politician, someone with whom Margaret Thatcher, as she said of Gorbachev, could

do business with.

In December 1985 the Anglo-Irish Agreement was signed. It was welcomed by the Federation of Irish Societies, whose chairman, Seamus McGarry, said *"Over the years the Irish question was presented to the British people as nothing more than a series of atrocities and disasters. Here for the first time constitutional politicians are actually discussing the whole Irish question in a positive way. That has removed from the British people the fear of talking about it. It is no longer a terrorist thing. It is a political thing."*[20] The Federation welcomed the Agreement as *"a quest for peace, stability and justice which we hope will ultimately lead to reunification."*

Departures and arrivals

It was a loss to the Centre when Joan Moriarty, who had been in the welfare office since 1974, first with Anne-Marie O'Boyle and then with Stacia Crickley, was appointed to the provincial assembly of her community, the Vincentian Sisters. She left at the end of September 1984, although she continued to work part-time in lieu of her notice and to fill the gap until her successors were appointed. Bridie Rooney, who was the secretary, assisted with the administration until new staff arrived. Eventually Sr Breda O'Reilly joined the welfare staff followed by an "intellectual young man" called Seamus Taylor.

From Carrick-on-Shannon, Seamus Taylor very soon became familiar with the myth held by some applicants at the Centre that *"you can have a really cushy life here on the Welfare State"*. He said in the press, *"the reality is different. The dole will pay £48 a week for eight weeks' worth of B & B, a sum you never see, and you get £31 a week for yourself. You have to survive in London on that. After eight weeks you're out on the street."*[21]

Breda O'Reilly later retired from her order because she decided to marry, and returned to teaching. In 1987 Seamus Taylor took over the directorship of the Action Group for Irish Youth, and expanded its work from premises in the Salusbury Road, and from there joined the Irish Community Liaison Unit of Haringey Council. After a senior position as Director of Strategy at the Commission for Racial Equality, he is now Director of Equalities and Diversity at the Crown Prosecution Service.

Confident about the five years he had spent at the Centre, in 1986 Claude Malone was appointed as director at the Barrett Cheshire Home in Dublin. At the time he left Camden Square, the debt had fallen from a peak of nearly £1 million to a more manageable £475,000. He pays tribute to Tony Beatty, *"whose renegotiating skills were hugely influential in the successful outcome."*[22]

Later, he left the priesthood in order to marry Orla O'Hanrahan, a Third Secretary at the Irish Embassy whom he had met in London, and who was described as *"the attractive face of the Irish Embassy."*[23] Joan Moriarty remembers that she would sometimes ring to find out how things were at the Centre. The reply was, *"Oh, they would be a lot better now if you could help me find Claude occasionally. I knew the romance was in fair bloom at that stage."*[24] The truth was that he had indeed fallen in love, and the other truth was that Roman Catholic priests were not allowed to marry. Claude Malone resigned the priesthood.

Many at Camden Square admired him for his difficult but honest decision, and he was missed after he had left. Unfortunately it was said by some begrudgers that a few people tried to forget him, because he had done *"such a terrible thing."*[25]

A year after the birth of their first child in 1989 Claude Malone's wife Orla was appointed to the Irish Embassy in Paris where she served for five years. In 1995 they returned to Ireland. The next posting was to Boston, USA, where she served as Ireland's Consul-General until the family's return to Dublin in 2002 where they now live.

Throughout this time, the directors of the Centre were also directors of Irish Centre Hostels. This was largely based on two hostels, that for young and older men at Conway House in Quex Road, Kilburn, which was being very ably managed by Frank Ryan, and that for women at St Louise in Medway Street, Victoria. Although matters relating to these hostels were occasionally on agendas of the administrative committee, they were almost separate entities and perhaps wisely avoided too close a connection to the internal problems of the Centre.

Father Tom Scully

Father Tom Scully, Jim Butler's colleague in Bluebell, was the next director to be assigned. Soon after his arrival one Saturday morning he was entering the building to say Mass when he spotted five young men sitting on duffel bags outside the door. *"Off to a match lads?"* he asked. *"No, we've just arrived"*, was their reply, *"Do ye get people jobs here?"*

Tom Scully had just written an open letter to *The Kingdom*, which was widely republished. Headed 'Emigration Crisis', he opened it with *"It is now beyond dispute that emigration from Ireland is now occurring on a scale unprecedented in recent times. We are convinced that a certain amount of careful thought and planning before deciding to leave Ireland for London would help avoid the necessity to call on agencies such as ours."* He helpfully offered the following tips: *"1. If you are one of the few already working at home, then evaluate your presen*

Tom Scully with key members of the Council of the Irish County Association, including on the left Bridie Shaw and on the right Mary Allen.

job in terms of security compared with what you hope to find in London. 2. There is a very big shortage of accommodation in London, and that which is available tends to be very expensive. Securing accommodation is likely to be your greatest problem in London. 3. Bring money for at least two weeks for your accommodation and food, plus fares to travel to job interviews. We suggest that you bring a minimum of £200. 4. You must bring your Birth Certificate and/or your Passport. Do not bring a baptismal certificate because this is not acceptable as identification. 5. Bring references from employers or schools. If you are a tradesman bring your tools. 6. Do not arrive on a Friday or over the weekend. On these days businesses and agencies are closed".

"We are not saying 'Do Not Come'", Tom Scully concluded, "We have no right to say that. But we are convinced that too many people are arriving here unaware of the facts until they find themselves homeless and destitute. And secondly we feel we have some

obligation to give you these facts. Our final piece of information is do not come to London with the address of a welfare agency or Irish Centre in your pocket and turn up to the door in the hope that they may sort you out. We cannot do that anymore. Our service is stretched to its very limits."[26]

While he had been at St Anne's in Birmingham, Tom Scully was appointed the local representative of the Catholic Housing Aid Society. It had recently joined other Housing Associations to form a Housing Advice Liaison Group. He became its director from 1971 to 1975, and during this time built 700 new homes. It was this challenge which had persuaded him to decline an offer to go to the London Irish Centre in 1981. This was at the departure of Bill Cagney, when Jim Butler was also approached. Instead Tom Scully was assigned to Bluebell parish which was also served by the Oblates.

When Claude Malone was due to leave the Centre, Tom Scully was again asked by the provincial, Fr William McGonagle, to take over. He arrived in September 1986, reluctantly because he felt he had not completed his time in Birmingham.[27]

It was an inauspicious start. When he came with his suitcase he found the building locked, and he had to sit outside for half an hour before someone opened it up for him. In fact Bridie Shaw, then treasurer of the Council of Irish Counties, who had raised a considerable sum to buy chairs for the McNamara Hall, was at the back of the building waiting for them to be delivered. She had hit upon the idea to 'sell' the chairs in order to raise funds by saying *"When you come to dinner at the Irish Centre, wouldn't you like to sit in your own chair?"* She spotted the disconsolate figure of Tom Scully in Murray Street, and welcomed him to his new assignment by saying *"Take off your jacket, Father, and give us a hand with these chairs."*[28]

Although as a young man Tom Scully had studied accountancy, he had also trained as a teacher, and enjoyed an interesting period as a mathematics teacher in the late 1950s at Belcamp, the Oblate college near Malahide north of Dublin. He was also a proud Offaly man from Tullamore, and was President of the Offaly Association in 1968. He coached its Gaelic Football team the following year, winning the All-Ireland in 1971 when they defeated Galway. For this achievement he was voted Sportsman of the Year in 1972. As if this were not enough, he was named as Offaly Person of the Year twelve years later in 1989. Gaelic football had occupied much of Tom Scully's time, having coached teams in Lancashire, Birmingham and Warwickshire. Mossie O'Riordan says, *"He was a fine man, he liked his GAA anyhow"*. He certainly did, and had little time for those who did not.

After he had settled in the Centre, he joined the Offaly team in a quiz with Roscommon. One question was "What wood is a hurling stick or hurley made from?".The answer, of course is native ash.[29] When someone answered "sycamore", Tom Scully crossed himself and was heard to mutter "Glory be to God". He was regarded as direct, straight to the point, and "not to be messed with".

Some Centre activities

He found himself the first months at the Centre extremely lonely.The 1986 Annual Report did not make happy reading. The administrative committee under the leadership of Tommy Dunne did its best to reduce the pressures on the new director. However, the huge increase in emigration in the 1980s had put a heavier burden on the welfare or Community Services Department, as it was now known. The Welfare Report of 1986 recorded 2,443 new callers, an increase of 14% on the previous year. Among them was a big increase in the number of women, many of whom were pregnant or lone parents. About 500 arrived at the Centre in that year, with nowhere else to go. Many of the younger women were referred to the Crusade of Rescue at St Louise hostel in Victoria, run for the Centre by Sr Anthony. There was also some good news in the report. The accounts showed that the debt was reducing, with grants of £37,122 from Camden and of £42,812 from the Irish government. Donations in the year totalled £53,402, including £25,000 from the London Irish Festival.

The report also described some of the services offered. Volunteer Brian Duggan, who ran the Missing Persons' Bureau every Monday and Thursday afternoon on the first floor of the Centre, had received 107 requests from the distraught relatives of

Brian Duggan in his office at the London Irish Centre.

people who were missing. Thirty-six cases were carried over from 1985 and a further seventy-one had been added. He had managed to locate thirty-two people or 25%, while another seventeen had managed to return to their homes of their own accord. Others were contacted by letter, which gave the Centre a success rate of approximately 50%. Later, in 1990 Brian Duggan was given the underworld-sounding name, 'the Finder'. At times the Gardai in Ireland have contacted him for help.

For the *London Evening Standard* he explained his work.*"There are a multitude of reasons why people have 'disappeared'"*, he said. *"It may even be a consequence of them not writing home. Many people write to their mothers after they have left home. But when their mother dies, the home interest often dies with her. Others prefer to be anonymous due to family pressures or their own feelings at having to succeed as though they have to prove something to their loved ones. Many lose contact because they are ashamed of the circumstances that they find themselves in. Many Irish working in the construction industry use false identities to avoid being tracked by the DSS. If they are killed on site, as has happened in Finsbury Park seven years ago, they cannot be identified, particularly when they have also used a false address."* It is almost impossible to find and account for the majority of those on Brian Duggan's caseload. *"A lot of them think that the streets of London are paved with gold. But when they get here they end up sleeping on the same streets."*[30]

The Department of Social Security later threatened withdrawal of its co-operation in 1992 because it was thought that the Missing Persons' Bureau belonged to no valid or recognised organisation. A campaign led by Denis Cormican, who was then chaplain at the Centre, included an approach to the Minister, Nicholas Scott MP, in which it was pointed out that that

they were not just members of the general public but were in fact part of a voluntary organisation supported by Camden Council and the Irish government through its Dion Committee. The British government duly reversed its decision.

The Centre was a place full of diverse moods. In one room families cried in their despair, in another there was laughter in a bar, and in a third there was music and dance. Irish cultural activities, in particular traditional music which included lessons in tin whistles, fiddles and Uillean pipes, took place most nights of the week. There was also Ceilidh Dancing with the John Maguire Ceilidh Band. The traditional music was promoted by Comhaltas Ceoltoiri Eireann under the enthusiastic direction of Jim Myers. The performance of traditional Irish music, and also the opportunity to participate in the GAA, offered young Irish people a point of contact with their background, and although they played for fun, *"It is the music of their people."*[31] Jim Myers was also the Comhaltas representative on the administrative committee, which brought the financial troubles of the Centre into sharp focus for him.

At about this time, set dancing commenced at the Centre. Developed from the European quadrille, it became very popular in Ireland during the nineteenth century where it was danced at crossroads in the country or in shebeens in the towns and villages.[32] There had been set dancing workshops in Cecil Sharp House, home of the English Folk Dance and Song Society in Camden Town, which had interested Geoff Holland, a Cornishman, and these workshops had encouraged him to arrange set dancing classes at the Centre where they became equally popular. *"The Centre has always aimed to provide the real McCoy"*, he says, *"and to preserve the integrity of the tradition."*[33]

A fiddle class at the London Irish Centre. (Joanne O'Brien)

Despite the sometimes hostile climate caused by IRA activities, few felt prevented from enjoying the Centre's facilities. The popular entrance used to be through a door in Murray Mews. Mary Kenny sat, on guard, in the reception area, scrutinising all who ventured in, with or without a fiddle in a case. The Centre provided some warm reassurance for many Irish people at a difficult time.

In spite of all the cultural and social activity, Tom Scully was of course aware that the Centre was still reeling from the debts incurred by the construction of the McNamara Hall. It still owed £460,000. *"That was an awful lot of money, the interest rates at that time were very high, and most of the money was borrowed at over 3%* *base rate. So we were paying 21% interest rates. Paddy Keegan, who was our manager (sic) was able to buy off the breweries and to borrow some money to be able to pay off some of our debts and to get a better rate."*[34] He was also aware that within the organisation there was a continuing conflict among sections of the staff who believed that there was a loss of focus.

Welfare tensions

The relationship between the welfare service and the director had become strained during the time of Bill Cagney, and this tension had lingered through the directorship of Claude Malone.[35] It was said that Bill Cagney had treated the social work staff "with animosity, aloofness and

170

indifference", and that he had even banned the social workers from using the kitchen. *"We were never allowed into the management meetings, except when asked. We had to fight our corner when we had to give a report"*, says Joan Moriarty.[36] During Bill Cagney's time a huge investment in time and resources had been directed towards the hall, which caused some resentment. Claude Malone, who followed Bill Cagney, found his own time taken up with paying the bills. Just before Tom Scully arrived, the welfare staff had just managed to persuade Claude Malone that they should retain their own committee, under the administrative committee led by Tommy Dunne, but with their own budget, their right to deal with media enquiries and to have parity with the social workers in Camden Council. Tom Scully, however, was not convinced. His immediate priority was to deal with the debt, and one budget had to suffice for the moment. Feeling sidelined, the entire committee resigned in 1987. Some said that the welfare staff had been regarded as too political in trying to subvert the policy-making role of the administrative committee.

It appears that the referendum in Ireland in June 1986 on the constitutional prohibition of divorce was the catalyst. The welfare staff found that significant numbers who came for assistance were suffering from the breakdown of their marriages. The view was that *"Ireland needed to deal with it at home, rather than export it to us"*, and that *"The Centre was not there to mop up the failure to deal with it in Ireland"*.[37] This position caused great friction. An emergency committee was convened to debate it. Fr Bobby Gilmore, who was on the committee, surprised most people by supporting the position of the welfare staff, who were regarded as trouble-makers by others.

In July 1987, Tom Scully found himself running the welfare and advice service almost single-handed. However he resolutely rebuilt it, appointing a more broad-based welfare committee, which included professionals in the field of social work. Nicky Murray was later recruited, followed by Paul Murphy.

In retrospect it was felt that the welfare staff had made a valid point. The service had its own separate budget until 1986, but when this became subsumed into the general account it disappeared, even to offset the loss in bar trading. There was no wonder that they felt aggrieved. The running of four bars at the Centre, which were supposed to be making a profit, had become too much of a priority. It was a circle of suspicion, illustrated by monthly rows between Tom Scully as director and the catering manager, which was only broken by the intervention of Touche Ross and the Charity Commission.

Tom Scully had called in these auditors to regularise the Centre's position with the tax authorities. Alternative accounting systems were badly needed. Another reason was that different procedures supported by new software were now required, and the traditional systems had to be changed. Tim Brennan, who had loyally served as an accountant, was asked to enrol in a two-week course to learn the new systems, but decided that he could not do so. For the same reason Tony Beatty, who had been so helpful to the Centre, found his audit no longer accepted.

As chairman and volunteer accountant respectively, Tommy Dunne and Paddy Keegan went to Touche Ross, the financial advisers, for help. It was learned that because the Centre was a charity the auditor had assumed that there was no tax to be paid on profits earned at the bar and through catering. The advice of Touche Ross in 1989 was that there must be a clear separation between trading and non-trading services, and charitable and other activities. This meant that the welfare service should indeed have its own budget.

To help meet the debt, the Oblates at their headquarters in Dublin provided a loan of £300,000 at 11%, later reduced to 7° % – well below the base rate – to buy out one large slice of the debt. Tom Scully also tried to persuade the Centre to take a more businesslike approach to contracts, beating one tender down from £26,000 to £9,000.

The neighbours

In addition to these challenges, the McNamara Hall was creating some problems externally. The neighbours around the Centre, in Camden Square to the front and in Murray Mews at the rear, had for years been complaining of noise disturbance. This was not only the noise of excavation, piling and construction while the hall was being built, but also the noise produced by music and social activities. It would spill out onto the street at night-time. Another complaint was of taxi and other engines running in the street in the early hours of the morning while they were waiting to take people home. The residents were not amused.

Since its inception in the early 1970s, the minutes of the Camden Square Neighbourhood Association have recorded complaints from its members, coupled with reassurances from whichever director was there at the time. Privately, Tom Scully would have liked to point out that the Centre had been operating in Camden Square and Murray Street since before many of these residents had arrived. This may have been true for some, but certainly not for all.

In 1987 he assured the CSNA that staff were doing their best to keep the noise down, and those leaving the building would be controlled, but the problem recurred again and again. In June that year the Centre's alcohol licence was due for renewal, and members of the CSNA decided that they should object. Patricia Herbert of Camden Square, whose parents attended Mass in the Centre's chapel, led a deputation to the magistrates' court, and although they made a strong case the licence was granted. She also led deputations to Camden Council when the public entertainment licence was to be renewed. It was said that *"she could run rings around the council."*[38]

Residents were furious that the Centre had its licence renewed. Mr Murfit, a postal worker living in Murray Street, said *"It's a blooming nuisance. I have to be at work by six and I am woken up at 1.30 am."*[39] The licence was granted on condition that that the noise would be controlled inside the building and when guests were leaving.

The evening or night-time activities of the Centre continued to rankle with local residents for years. On 13 March 1990 the licensing subcommittee of the council rejected the Centre's application for a dance and drinks licence for the Kennedy Hall. A number of local residents had objected to the proposal on the grounds of the annoyance that the Centre and its users had caused. On 13 March it was accused of doing nothing for the local community, and of instead being a place of drunkenness, noise and fighting. A local barrister living in Murray Mews, Graeme Williams, spoke of *"The Irish cuckoo in the English nest"*. This was a night in which racial prejudice surfaced in the Town Hall, which had spent so much of its resources in raising awareness of race issues.[40] In October of that year a petition was collected of objectors to a licensing extension to one in the morning, on Friday and Saturday, but the extension was agreed.

The day centre and the youth club

Meanwhile, the need to expand further in order to alleviate the welfare problems that were an increasing part of the service was encouraging the administrative committee to bring new spaces into use. It was decided to convert a part of the ground floor, which had been unused for years since the hostel had transferred to Conway House, as a youth club and a day centre for the elderly.*"It's for older people, the men who came over here to build the roads in the 1940s"*, Tom Scully said.[41]

The youth club had been part of a promise given by the Centre to the council long before, in return for the planning permission for the McNamara Hall. This community facility for all young people would open onto the square, on which would be the play space to be managed by the Centre itself. It had been thought by residents that this would obviate the need for the council to build a separate young people's play area in the Square.

In order to carry out the conversion, Tom Scully persuaded AnCO, the Industrial Training Authority in Ireland, to run an employment training scheme in the Centre in which eight apprentices, who came from the FAS training centre in Athlone, worked. In effect this enabled the labour costs to be paid for by an outside agency. Work started in July 1987. Camden Council made a grant of £120,000, the Allied Irish Bank made another and the Council of Irish County Associations also presented the project with a cheque for £20,000, which was part of the proceeds from the London Irish Festival.

The day centre was opened on 25 May

Young apprentices from Ireland commencing the work on the day centre, 1987.

1988 by the Minister for Labour in the Fianna Fail government, Bertie Ahern, TD. Also present was Ambassador Andrew O'Rourke and Cllr Bill Budd, the Mayor of Camden. It offered subsidised lunches from Monday to Friday for up to seventy-five people at a time, with other activities such as ILEA-funded crafts classes and outings to the seaside. Very soon up to a hundred people were using it each week. Brian Duggan became chairman of the new day centre.

The youth club was never opened. Nor was this situation ever enforced by the council.

Later in the year it became clear that young Irish people, who had benefited from Irish state training courses run by FAS, AnCo and Manpower at home, found that these qualifications were not recognised when they arrived in Britain and looked for work. Father Denis Cormican, who was an assistant chaplain, said *"It is one of the most depressing situations we face – young intelligent people who have no recognition of their skills."*[42] After going to Dublin to lobby Toyota Ireland, with an introduction to some of Tommy Dunne's business connections, he obtained a £75,000 sponsorship deal to assist these young people to train for British qualifications. The Centre was then able to work to establish stronger links between the Irish and British youth training schemes. It was later intended to secure further financial assistance from the European Social Fund.

By 1987 the British economy had picked up and was rising fast, leaving an Irish economy in recession. *"Between June and September we had 7,500 young Irish people coming through the door"*, Tom Scully said.[43] During this year the Centre dealt with 13,500 new arrivals. Although job prospects in London were indeed better, it did not induce some to arrive better prepared.

In fact the pattern continued of *"many innocent people arriving at the door at 7.00 am, with all of 50p in their pockets. One Sunday morning we met five people with just £10 between them, and all their possessions in a few plastic bags"*, said Tom Scully.

The 'Repatriation' debate

The problem for the emigrant was that the cost of renting even the most meagre accommodation could be prohibitive. Rents of £45 a week for a single room were common. Most places required one month's rent in advance and a deposit. Tom Scully said in the press that at least £1,000 was needed to set someone up in any flat. Social welfare payments were able to help, but they had been considerably reduced.

Faced with severe cutbacks and increasing pressure on housing resources, some local authorities chose to initiate a policy of returning home those Irish families who were seeking accommodation in London by issuing travel warrants. *"The bill for housing the homeless"*, said Cllr Gareth Smyth, Chairman of Camden's Housing Committee *"is £20 million a year, a tenth of the council's total budget."* This policy was allegedly justifiable under the Housing and Planning Act 1986, in which a council must first establish that an Irish local authority has a specific empty property of minimum standard which it is prepared to offer that family. Camden council defended the policy, saying that it had been brought about by a chronic lack of resources, and denied that it was racist.

It was stated that such warrants were only offered in specific circumstances. The council's housing officers would check first that a family had any connection with another local authority in Britain, but if there were none it then investigated whether there was "safe and suitable"

THE IRISH CUCKOO IN THE ENGLISH NEST

accommodation available to them in Ireland. Council Leader Tony Dykes denied this, saying that Camden *"has never and will never return people anywhere. Such distortions cause great damage."*[44]

It was the unions in Camden's Homeless Person's Unit which had alerted some councillors to the fact that this policy was being implemented. At this time the Labour Group of the council was deeply divided along political lines, and eleven members had been opposing cutbacks from 1986.[45]

There was a call by this grouping for the resignation of Councillor Gareth Smyth, and the council itself came in for severe criticism for pursuing this policy, with accusations of pushing a racist, anti-Irish approach, and effectively forcing the repatriation of homeless families to Ireland by offering travel warrants.

However, Cllr Smyth said that thirty-one travel warrants had been issued since the council had adopted this policy in 1986. They had all, without exception, been issued to Irish families. The reason is that these families had made themselves "intentionally homeless" by leaving suitable housing in Ireland, and were therefore ineligible for re-housing in Camden.[46]

The *Guardian* revealed that council officers had advised council members of a report by the Race Relations Committee as far back as April that this policy would be racially discriminatory. It would be unlikely to be upheld if challenged in the European Court. Camden's Labour Group, which was not exactly cohesive during this period, was on the verge of a split over the issue. Cllr Satnam Gill, who was Chair of Policy and Resources, said *"The families should not have been sent back."* Gareth Smyth said he was unaware of the Race Relations Committee report.[47]

Many of the homeless families on Camden's register also came from other countries than Ireland. However, a council officer explained that language and cultural links made it easier to telephone and check whether alternative accommodation existed in Ireland.

It was this ease of checking up on details that concerned Tom Scully. Telephone calls were simply not enough, he told the *Catholic Herald.* "A telephone call to a housing authority in Ireland regarding the possibility of available accommodation is not in our opinion a guarantee that suitable accommodation will be provided. The family at least must have confirmation in writing of the type and quality of the housing available. We at the Irish Centre have had the experience of only a few families who have been offered travel warrants, but have no direct evidence that these have been accepted. A family that fulfils the criteria is not obliged to accept a travel warrant."*[48]

Council officers re-stated that the financial position in Camden was such that the authority could only offer a basic service to emergency homeless people, and could not cater for anyone for whom there was a suggestion of accommodation available elsewhere.

"The problem is how different local authorities interpret the legislation regarding a family making themselves intentionally homeless", said Tom Scully. *The real problem is the shortage of housing in Britain, particularly in London. Where jobs are available accommodation is very scarce and the only solution is for the government to supply finance to local authorities to provide housing in areas of greatest need. Over the years Camden have made significant efforts to provide accommodation for homeless families, as can be seen from the amount of money they have spent. But we feel that all councils should face their legal responsibility as laid down by the 1987 Housing Act."*[49]

Inevitably those with more militant views intervened. The Irish in Britain

Representation Group had already challenged Camden over this issue, and managed to convince Brent not to follow the same course.

In May 1988 Camden was slammed by a report from Matthew Warburton of the Association of London Authorities. The Homeless Person's Unit was closed yet again, and people were forced to sleep rough on the streets and in the parks and railway stations of London. The report urged the council to reopen the Unit, and said that travel warrants should only be issued to applicants who were not intentionally homeless and who were willing to accept them.

The allegations returned a year or so later when it was disclosed that a teenager, Susan Twomey, had been repatriated to Cork. She had come into Camden's care after local police had issued a place of safety order, and she had been placed in several homes from which she ran away. A review of her circumstances led the council to place her in 'secure accommodation'. Her case was due for consideration under a 28-day care order from Camden Juvenile Court, but she was flown back to Ireland the day before it was to be heard. Contact had already been established with her mother. Cllrs Angie Birtill and Kate Allen, on the left of the council, called for an independent enquiry, and accused their council of using "racist" policies of repatriation against Irish people needing help.[50]

With council rates capped for a third successive year, the crippling financial crisis for many local authorities continued, and the voluntary sector again became an easy target for cuts. In January Camden announced cuts to a number of groups, which included a 10% cut in its £35,000 grant to the Centre, reducing it from £38,606 to £34,746. The *Irish Post* headlined it 'Camden Aid for Irish

Slashed'. Tom Scully called it *"an awful burden."*[51] The biggest loser was the Irish in Britain Representation Group which would lose £53,471. The organisation asserted that this was due to its criticism of Camden over the deportations of homeless Irish families. Soon after the announcement, Pat Reynolds of the IBRG spoke at the Centre at a meeting on housing and Camden's responsibilities.

The matter was finally resolved by the Association of London Authorities which introduced better monitoring of such policies.

New legislation

In his introduction to the Annual Report of 1988, Tom Scully said that the proposed Local Government Finance Act and proposed housing legislation would increase the cost of accommodation without offering any compensatory increase in Housing Benefit. Changes in housing and social welfare legislation were also creating an increasingly difficult environment for new Irish arrivals.

In April 1988 Dr Michael Woods, the Minister of Social Welfare, paid a visit to London to be briefed by Social Security officials on forthcoming British legislation. Measures to be introduced by the government on 11 April 1988 would hit the youngest applicants, those from 16 to 18 years of age. Unemployment benefits were to be replaced by Income Support, and paid fortnightly in arrears. Supplementary Benefit was to be abolished. The other major change, to be introduced some months later, in September, would be the withdrawal of direct welfare payments from young people under 18 years until they have taken up a place on a youth training scheme. Dr Woods believed that there could be delays of between six weeks and three months before a young person could be placed on such a scheme.

He came to the Irish Centre to talk with members of the welfare staff. Denis Cormican, who met him, said that the estimated 20,000 Irish emigrants at that time receiving Supplementary Benefit would receive no income for two weeks from April, when the new regulations came into effect.He addressed the Irish press, *"I would urge all those planning to emigrate to leave home prepared. Life is not going to be easy here."*[52]

This legislation caused an impact on the numbers of the young Irish who were resident in hostels in England. Their numbers dropped sharply. This was partly because they no longer had the subsistence payments to meet the hostel fees, and so they slipped 'underground', by rough sleeping or by disappearing into squats. Earlier in 1988 Conway House had only thirty-five residents in the under-18 age group, but by the end of the year the number had dwindled to three. *"The really dangerous thing is that the youngsters are ending up in squats, where they have no protection. They are becoming invisible, they are not on any register and nobody knows where they are"*, said one of the workers at Conway House, John McHugh.[53] The Brent Irish Advisory Centre estimated that there were over 1,000 squatters in the Kilburn and Cricklewood area, the majority of them Irish.

When his colleague Dr Woods visited England, Brian Lenihan, the Minister for Foreign Affairs, asked in Dublin for the situation to be investigated and also examined the possibility of providing emigrants with financial assistance. However there were reservations about such a scheme, in that it might encourage young people to emigrate.

Paul Murphy, then co-ordinator of Community Services at the Centre, had already warned that *"Unless you have money, a ticket to London is just a ticket to*

two weeks' starvation and sleeping in DHSS hostels, if you're lucky. The British government seems only too happy to cut back on the social welfare system, so all the safety nets that emigrants used to have are all gone. There's no longer a legal obligation to help you."[54]

Even during times of crisis, the extremes of life swirled around the Centre. In September 1988, the London Irish Society, established a year before by a group of young professional Irish people in London, held a ball at the Grosvenor House Hotel to raise funds for its services. At £35 a ticket,*"The cream of Irish society gathered under the chandeliers. Elegant gowns feathered elegant ladies. Some gentlemen looked resplendent in their monkey suits as others were heard to express the wish to change into their jeans. Everybody, except the hungry, was impressed. So miniscule were the portions that a robin would definitely seek out another means of filling its stomach. Fr Tom Scully did not stand on ceremony as he spoke of the Irish Centre, which in many circles is being termed, genially, as 'Tom's Place'."* This was the tongue-in-cheek report in the *Irish World.*[55] Gina Mackay, the celebrated Irish harpist, performed, and the evening raised £15,000 clear profit.

By this time the Irish Bookfair at the Camden Centre in Bidborough Street was an annual feature. This followed a tradition of book fairs which had been held at the Festival Hall, and at which there was always a strong Irish section. The programme over the March weekend in 1988 included the launch of *The London Irish* by Tom Connor, which was the first broad-based research into the condition of the London Irish for over 25 years. Written for the GLC's London Strategic Policy Unit's Irish section, it concluded that the marginalisation of the Irish ethnic minority was as a result of "its lack of success in attracting adequate resources from

Fr Tom Scully and photographer Mel McNally enjoying a joke at a London Irish Centre function.

statutory agencies or its development and survival." The event, established a year before by a group of young professional Irish people in London, was officially opened by Dr Noel Browne, who had been Health Minister during the coalition government of 1950, and he took the opportunity to promote his autobiography, *Against the Tide*. A more popular Irish author, Maeve Binchy, attended and discussed her writing with an audience.

The conflict in northern Ireland continued to have an impact on the services at Camden Square. People from both Catholic and Protestant communities were arriving at the door having been bombed out of their homes or with threats hanging over their heads if they had decided to remain in the six counties. London was seen as more anonymous than the Republic. Within the Irish communities of London people could hide with some assurance of safety. The Centre's welfare service managed with these clients as best as it could.

Associated with the conflict, cases of miscarriage of justice in Britain were never far from the front pages. Campaign meetings were often held in the Centre – the Guildford Four, the Birmingham Six and Judith Ward were among the better known causes, but with far less publicity there were many other people arrested and taken into custody. The Guildford Four of course had a connection with the Centre, from their familiarity with Camden and with Gerry Conlon and Paul Hill as residents of Conway House when the bombs exploded.

Controversy at Roundwood Park

The harassment felt by the Irish community prompted some sections of it to react, but others to comply. In a reversal of previous policy, the organising committee of the London Irish Festival in 1988 refused to allow the Birmingham Six and the Guildford Four campaign groups, and also the Irish in Britain Representation Group, to set up stalls in Roundwood Park. No detailed reason was given for the refusal, but the GAA also pulled out in support. Paul May, the co-ordinator of the London campaign for the release of the Birmingham Six, said he was mystified by the decision. *"It's this kind of attitude which leads to innocent people becoming imprisoned – the keep your head down attitude. How would any information on the Birmingham Six conflict with the aims of the Festival?"*, he asked. *"We see it very much in welfare terms. There is no more important welfare task than securing the release of innocent prisoners."*[56]

The irony was that the MC of the festival, Leitrim-born Senator Paschal Mooney, was one of the few Irish politicians who had actively campaigned for the release of both the Birmingham Six and the Guildford Four, and had attended the six men's appeal the previous January. Perhaps as some mitigation, it is said that the Council of Irish Counties made a

178

donation to the campaign fund of £5,000.

The conflict was later defused by a compromise which confirmed the ban in 1988, but which said that, for the following year's festival, the campaigns would again be allocated stalls. Fr Bobby Gilmore of the Irish Chaplaincy Scheme, who was abroad when the refusal was made, said *"I am sure that space could be found if organisers showed just a little more concern. I would not like to think how those in prison view what is going on"*. Bobby Gilmore was closely associated with the campaigns to expose the miscarriages of justice, often in the face of opposition from the Hierarchy.

The following year's festival, on 2 July, signalled its demise a year or two later. A policy had been introduced to prohibit the sale of alcohol in the park. Predictably, some people arrived having had more than enough in nearby pubs and carrying their personal supplies. In due course the police were pelted with bottles and cans, which resulted in fifty-five arrests. Seamus Troy, the Chairman of the Council of Irish Counties, was said to have found it difficult to hold back his tears. Tom Scully announced that this was the first instance of such trouble in fifteen years.

The disturbance was swiftly prevented from becoming more serious by the arrival of mounted police and the Territorial Support Group. This was seen as an over-reaction by some, including Frank Ryan. He was quoted in the *Kilburn Times* as saying *"The spark could be the law's treatment of those arrested. The resentment that local Irish youths are feeling towards the police and British society in general will boil over."*[57] Frank Ryan, working on the front line at Conway House, would have been well placed to make this comment. He must not have been short of another comment on the news just three months later.

The release of the Guildford Four

The Guildford Four were finally released on October 19, 1989. As the *Guardian* reported, *"The Guildford case broke the dam. Month after month wrongful convictions were set aside: the Birmingham Six, the Broadwater Farm Three; the Cardiff Three; the Swansea Two; the East Ham Two; Judith Ward; Stefan Kisko and the Taylor Sisters. All had been convicted of murder, and all were, in the proper sense, victims of miscarriages of justice – they didn't do it."*[58] For some reason this remarkable list did not include the Maguire Seven, of whom Giuseppe Conlon died in prison in 1980. If published a few years later it might have added the Bridgewater Four, of whom Patrick Molloy died in prison in 1981.

The release of the Guildford Four was made in two stages. Gerry Conlon, Paddy Armstrong and Carole Richardson were discharged from the Old Bailey together, but Paul Hill was taken to Belfast pending a hearing on his conviction for another offence. The remaining three were taken away by ITN to the Holiday Inn at Swiss Cottage, from where Gerry Conlon had to call Gareth Peirce, his solicitor, to rescue him.

There was therefore no spontaneous party at the Centre, as there would be in eighteen months' time for some of the Birmingham Six. However there was a gathering here later on, organised by Paul May and the campaign group. It was arranged at short notice, and someone had to run down to Sainsbury's to buy food.

After some busy and controversial years, dominated by external matters as much as the internal questions of the debt, in September 1990 Tom Scully was assigned to parish duties at Leigh-on-Sea, near Southend. This was the parish to which Bill Cagney had been assigned before him. Maeve Heath, who worked behind the bar at the Centre, remembers that by the smell of his pipe tobacco she could always tell when Tom Scully was nearby. *"He enjoyed his pipe but he never touched a drink. A good old fashioned priest"*, she now says, *"A great man to visit the sick."*[59] Given the issues that prevailed over his four years as director, it is surprising that he had time for much in the way of pastoral duties.

Denis Cormican was away on a course at Stillorgan, near Dublin, which still had a month or two to run, but he finally took over as director on 20 December 1990.

The debt had been reduced to £250,000. The place was now in better shape than when Tom Scully arrived in September 1986. As he says, even now, *"There was a good committee there, and it was going well. The bank and the council and everybody weren't after us for money."*[60]

1   Interview with unknown colleague for RTE, June 1983.
2   *Ibid.*
3   Interview Ron Heffernan, June 2004.
4   Interview Fr Jim Butler, January 2004.
5   Interview Mary Kenny, May 2004.
6   Some final figures, eg in the LIC Annual Report for 1983, quote £81,778, once costs were deducted. In one sense the precise amount does not matter because of the positive publicity and self esteem that the physical effort gave to the Centre at a difficult time. And of course, the begrudgers derided the effort as 'Buttons'.
7   Interview Sr Joan Moriarty, March 2004.
8   Interview Tony Beatty, March 2004.
9   From LIC Financial Statement, 31 December 1982.
10 Correspondence Andy Rogers, June 2004.
11 Interview Sr Joan Moriarty, April 2004.
12 *Irish Post*, 19 November 1983.
13 Correspondence Fr Jim Butler, December 2003.
14 *Irish Post*, 28 July 1984.
15 Associated Press, December 1985.
16 *Irish Times*, 9 September 1985.
17 *Irish Independent*, 25 July 1986.
18 *Irish Times*, 25 July 1986.
19 *Nationalist and Leinster Times*, 11 October 1985.
20 *Irish Times*, 27 December 1985.
21 *Irish Press*, 26 January 1987.
22 Correspondence Claude Malone, April 2004.
23 *Irish Post*, 7 May 1983.
24 Interview Sr Joan Moriarty, April 2004.
25 Interview Maeve Heath, January 2004.
26 *The Kingdom*, 24 March 1987.
27 Interview Tim Scully, October 2003.
28 Interview Bridie Shaw, January 2004.
29 The sport of hurling is often described as 'the clash of the ash'.
30 *London Evening Standard*, 19 August 1985.
31 Interview Jim Myers, June 2004.
32 Although interest died in the 19th century the quadrille was revived in the 1980s, and now is danced 'wherever green is worn', as Tim Pat Coogan might say. In fact there are two distinct types of such dancing, one known as Set dancing and one as Ceilidh dancing. They are both partner dances but the standard hold in sets is that the partners face each other as if in a waltz, whereas in Ceilidh dancing the standard hold is side by side.
33 Interview Geoff Holland, June 2004.
34 Interview Tom Scully, October 2003.
35 Administrative Committee minutes, 11 February 1986.
36 Interview Sr Joan Moriarty, April 2004.
37 Interview Seamus Taylor, July 2004.
38 Interview Iris Ryan, March 2004.
39 *Hampstead Advertiser*, 25 June 1987.
40 *Camden Tenant*, March 1990.
41 *Irish Times*, 26 September 1988.
42 *Irish Post*, 8 August 1988.
43 Interview Fr Tom Scully, October 2003.
44 *Guardian*, 13 November 1987.
45 Information from Angie Birtill, June 2004.
46 *Catholic Herald*, 27 November 1987.
47 *Guardian*, 14 November 1987.
48 *Catholic Herald*, 13 November 1987.
49 *Irish Post*, 21 November 1987.
50 *Ibid*, 6 August 1988.
51 *Ibid*, 30 January 1988.
52 *Ibid*, 8 April 1988.
53 *London Irish News*, 24 December 1988.
54 *Irish Press*, 29 March 1988.
55 *Irish World*, 30 September 1988.
56 *London Irish News*, 28 May 1988.
57 *Kilburn Times*, 27 July 1989.
58 *Guardian*, 4 July 1994.
59 Interview Maeve Heath, January 2004.
60 Interview Tom Scully, October 2003.

CHAPTER TEN

A safety-valve in times of trouble

Irish Centre Housing

Throughout the history of the Centre the provision of housing for the emigrant Irishman and woman arriving in London was seen as an important function. This had been taken up with enthusiasm by George Groves and Tom McNamara, who must have had something of the entrepreneur about them. They acquired buildings that they converted into hostels in Tollington Park and Hornsey Lane Gardens. The former, for men, operated from 1953 to 1969. In 1968, its last full year, there were 290 men staying there.[1] The latter, a hostel for girls, was opened in 1954. From McNamara's time as director of the London Irish Centre, this was run by Miss Harrington who was from Cork, but when she became ill she was replaced by Sr Thecla Cleary. After Tom McNamara had been appointed the hostels were administered by the Centre. In fact they were leased, such was George Groves' business sense. The girl's hostel in Hornsey Lane Gardens closed in 1975, when its replacement, St Louise, was acquired.

The Centre's administrative committee decided in 1969, that it would be helpful to register as a housing association which could then apply for grants. As a result, Irish Centre Hostels Ltd was formed in July 1969 as a separate legal entity but within the London Irish Centre itself, although there was an overlap among the members of the management commit-

tees. In 1995 this association became Irish Centre Housing Ltd, because it provided more than just hostel accommodation.

The third hostel, which opened in August 1955, was of course the men's hostel in Murray Street, in the hastily renovated upstairs rooms of the Centre itself. This catered for younger men, while older ones continued to make the journey to Tollington Park. Occupation rates for these three hostels during the first twenty-one years has been estimated at 95%. This was not only an achievement, but also demonstrated the continuing need.

For some years there had been the possibility of an extension to the Centre along the Camden Square frontage which would have consisted of additional hostel accommodation. Perhaps wisely it was decided that, with the help of the National Collection of 1971, the acquisition of a building in Quex Road, in the heart of Irish Kilburn, was a better choice. The frontage along Camden Square did become housing, but as flats managed by Community Housing Association.

When they heard from the Holy Family Sisters of Bordeaux that Hope House could be up for sale, the director Paddy Mee, Tom McCabe and Paddy Sheridan hastened over to Kilburn to meet the Mother Provincial. This was the same order to which the welfare officer Anne-Marie O'Boyle belonged. The Sisters knew that at £150,000 they were offering it at well below market value, but this was an expression of their generosity towards a charity. The purchase price was shared between the National Collection and Camden Council, which was willing to contribute a mortgage of £87,249. If it had been offered to a commercial agent or client as private housing, the price would have been very much higher. The Sisters' gesture was a service to the Irish community.

The National Collection
The portion of the purchase price that was finally to come from the National Collection was only £75,000. There had been issues around the delay in its distribution, and also finally of the unexpectedly low allocation. These did not improve relations between the Centre and the Irish bishops who were administering the grants. There was a belief among them, it seems, that with its bars and its bacon and cabbage suppers, it was not short of revenue. The Centre, however, resented the prospect that other, newer London organisations should be receiving equivalent funds. Frank Ryan, who was later a director of Hope House, says that, *"There were a lot of hard feelings about this. No one knew where the rest of it went. At one time we were told that it was capital spending only, then that it was for anything other than capital spending. The Collection did much less than it should have."*[2]

The final allocation of the money appears to have been as follows: London Irish Centre – £75,000; Irish Welfare, Birmingham – £75,000; Hammersmith Irish Centre – £45,000; Oxford – £12,000; Benburb Base – £45,000.[3] Nor were any of these amounts matched by the Irish government, as had once been hoped.

Conceived as an imaginative way to raise funds for Irish emigrants, the National Collection was therefore something of a disappointment in Camden Square. As the first centre of its kind, the London Irish Centre had, arrogantly, tended to take things for granted. Other Irish welfare institutions had spotted the chance to apply for funding and had made their own bids. However, at the Centre, no feasibility studies had been carried out, the tendering process was poor, and its agreements were always verbal.

This dissatisfaction surfaced at the formal opening ceremony of Hope House by Archbishop William John Conway in March 1974. Bishop Eamonn Casey arrived late, which created further irritation. In a speech which perhaps could have first thanked the Irish Bishops' Committee for its generosity, Paddy Mee questioned Bishop Casey on the paucity of the allocation. It has since been reported that the bishop riposted by saying that, in his view, none of the money should have gone to Hope House, or indeed to the London Irish Centre. His relationship with Paddy Mee was not cordial.

In spite of Bill Cagney's efforts to persuade the bishops' committee to arrange another, no further National Collections took place until one on St Patrick's Day in 1996, which raised money for the Irish Episcopal Commission for Emigrants on behalf of the Irish Chaplaincy. Since then, individual dioceses have raised money for the chaplaincy through collections in their parish churches.

In due course, the younger men left in Camden Square were transferred to Hope House when it had been refurbished. The name was soon unpopular with the unemployed residents who had to endure the gibes of staff in benefit offices who described it as 'No Hope House'.

Conway House
It was renamed Conway House, after the Cardinal who had opened it, and was designated as a hostel for up to a hundred

The rear extension to Conway House, showing the Telefon box from Dublin.

men between the ages of sixteen and twenty-three. Patsy Carolan, its first manager, was fortunate with the firm of contractors, Finnegan's, who were friends of Paddy Mee and involved in building works in the Centre itself. They converted the rooms of the former nursing-home into smaller units and fitted extra toilets. It was also important that the building conformed to current local authority and Housing Corporation standards. For this and all the repair work,*"they hardly charged the Centre anything at all. I was paying the men exactly the week's wages that they were getting and that was all. The boss really was making no money at all."*[4] Teams of volunteers such Pat Hegarty, Luke Kennedy, Martin Moroney and Martin Doyle, with able support from Bridie Shaw and others, would go up to Quex Road with pots of paint and decorating equipment to make the place ready for the first residents.

Reflecting his commitment to housing, the first chairman to be appointed to the hostel management committee was Martin Moroney.

The exterior was not neglected. Hope House became identifiable from the outside by an old-fashioned green Irish telephone call box on the corner. When the wooden Telefon boxes in Dublin were being removed in the 1980s to be replaced by modern ones, the nostalgic Frank Ryan applied for one of the old ones and this was shipped over to Kilburn by Telecom Eireann. Irish street signs were also erected on the walls of the building.

Unlike the usual perception of hostels, this was a relatively light, airy building, with a TV lounge and a garden. Rents were then around £10 a week, and for that residents had their bed and two meals a day. It was described as a 'lean and mean' organisation. As Patsy Carolan said, *"If the*

183

chef didn't show, it was me who had to cook all the breakfasts."[5] The place was run on a shoestring, with volunteer help. As Frank Ryan says, *"The volunteers did a great deal of work, and I cannot speak highly enough of them. We were competing with landlords and landladies and trying to maintain a high level of service. A lot of our guys were being paid cash, and we wanted to be affordable."*[6] When it opened, three of the Sisters of the Holy family, its original owners, continued to work there.

If it housed less than seventy-seven residents Conway House was uneconomic, so it was important to keep it as fully occupied as possible. In 1976, average occupancy was ninety-eight, and there were 427 new users. The rooms were fitted out as single rooms or doubles, but some had as many as six beds in them. Those beds were sought from hospitals, and the bed covers came from the Royal Navy. The bedside lockers were flimsy and most men did not lock theirs because it would draw attention to what may have been placed inside. Heating was from electric fires powered by pay meters, which were vulnerable to burglary.

The hostel closed its doors at 12.30 am. Residents could obtain late keys, but many who had not done so would attempt to enter through a window. Two of the better-known residents, Paul Hill and Gerry Conlon, at one time shared a ground floor room. Paul Hill writes, *"This was a popular way to enter the place, and when we were in bed asleep other lads used to come in, fumbling and stumbling in the darkness and crashing into the beds. This used to provoke some high words between Gerry and the late arrivals."*[7] 'Better-known' is perhaps not the best description for Hill and Conlon, who, if it had not been for a disgraceful miscarriage of justice, might have been just another two unemployed lads from Belfast who had made their way to Kilburn in search of work.

The intention, at least in the early days, was not to take too many people from one Irish county because this could set up divisions. This was particularly the case with northern Ireland. As Patsy Carolan has said, *"The Troubles were raging, so we were careful to keep the balance of the house, for management purposes."* Frank Ryan puts it another way, *"We had some old and some young people. We had English people and some people from northern Ireland but mostly from the south. I don't mean that you would be playing one off against the other, but a mix kind of gave a balance. You always had the problem of alcohol. A lot of those wet the bed and spoiled the mattresses. I got Murphy's to send a big lorry to take the mattresses away. I said to some of these fellows, 'What woman would want to sleep with a fellow that wets the bed? For God's sake, you know you can't'. You were always trying to get the guys to sober up."*[8]

Patsy Carolan, who returned some years later for a second term with Irish Centre Housing, said, *"There were an awful lot of old people that had come and had worked under wrong names on the lump, and were living in terrible conditions. I tried to change the vision. Later we began to build some flats for the older people."*

Finding the younger men work was not difficult. There was a woman called Mrs Byrne, *"She was an agent of O. C. Summers. She took everybody I had. It didn't matter if they could work with a spade or only sweep or make tea, she would find them a position where they could do that. There was never a problem getting work for them, and at that time we did make them work. We didn't allow them not to work. After three days they had to be working."*[9]

184

St Louise

There were also significant changes in the hostel accommodation for girls and women at that time. The relative remoteness of Hornsey Lane Gardens, and the fear of danger on a late night walk up from the bus stop, helped persuade Paddy Mee that a hostel in the centre of London would be preferable.

St Louise Hostel at 33 Medway Street, near Victoria in Westminster, was regarded as an ideal replacement. Joan Moriarty was a persuasive voice in its acquisition. *"Medway Street belonged to us, the Daughters of Charity. And it was for closure. So I went to Father Mee and said 'Father Mee, buy it'. He said he hadn't the money but I said 'Just go, go and buy it, you'll find the money. So he went and he negotiated with the community. It was only chicken feed by comparison to the market value."*[10] It was in fact Bill Cagney, who followed Paddy Mee a few months later, who formally made the decision to replace Hornsey Lane Gardens in favour of St Louise.

The building had been run for thirty years by the Daughters of Charity of St Vincent De Paul, providing accommodation for 300 girls, of whom over half were Irish. An important aspect of the Sisters' work had been to meet the trains at Euston on which they arrived. Sr Catherine, a former manager, said, *"There were always the improvident ones who arrived without making arrangements, and with nothing but a small case and a few belongings. These always had to be looked after and catered for, as the risks and responsibility for not doing so were grave."*[11] By the 1970s the Sisters had seen their membership decreasing, and so decided to dispose of their hostel. They were, however, content to remain as managers of the building.

Because they had been determined to encourage full occupancy by keeping rents down, St Louise was seriously under-

St Louise Hostel in Medway Street, Westminster.

funded and required major repairs and renovations. After the purchase, a housing consultant was hired by Irish Centre Hostels for this purpose.

In January the hostel began operating under the new management, but by the end of the year it was partially closed for refurbishment, in particular to make it safer if ever there was a flood, at a cost of £747,000. Its boiler and other equipment was below the water-line if the Thames ever breached its normal levels. The Housing Corporation offered a generous grant of £730,000.

As manager of Conway House, Patsy Carolan was critical of how St Louise had been managed. He felt that it was too much like a convent. He was able to use his influence to change this by reconfiguring the single rooms into clusters of small flats, each with a television and some cooking and ironing facilities. There was a canteen in the building for meals, instead of the traditional dining hall with its institutional food that had once been there. With a long list of detailed specifications, it took six years to make the hostel totally available for accommodation. Midway through the process, the building contractor went into receivership, and work came to a halt but not before materials already on site had been secured. This caused major delays.

At its re-opening ceremony on 5 May 1981, Cardinal Basil Hume described St Louise Hostel as *"a symbol of love and care which is the true measure of Christianity which we serve."* With accommodation now organised for 130 girls and women, it was one of the most comfortable hostels of its sort in England, offering security and high standards.

St Louise became a very popular for those coming over from Ireland during the 1980s, with many booking accommodation before they left home. As Sr Anthony has pointed out, *"Girls are more able to look after themselves than boys".* Unlike the rule in the men's hostels, they were allowed to stay here for longer periods and some remained for months. *"I don't believe in short-stay hostels",* Sr Anthony who was in charge, has said. *"It might take a year to get a girl on her feet. A few weeks wouldn't give her any stability of mind."*[12] Its convenience to central London was seen as an asset. It was also closely connected to sources of employment through agencies and the hotel trade. Rents were kept affordable, because women's pay was generally lower than that of men, but this was seen to be a disincentive to moving on.

Some girls just turned up. St Louise took them in, registered them with the DHSS if they had no job, and looked after them until their money came through. For a girl who had arrived from a small Irish town, the DHSS procedures in London were daunting. Often dirty or drunk and occasionally violent, the people queuing inside the offices could be intimidating. *"I tell the girls to take a book so they don't have to listen to the boys' taunts",* was the advice of Sr Anthony.[13] Arranging the registration and benefits could take several weeks, during which time the girls were often without money.

As patterns of emigration changed, St Louise became less attractive to Irish girls, and its rooms were filled instead with those from Italy and Spain. Nowadays the former level of social support required is reduced, and mainly consists of welfare rights, immigration advice and health or mental health counselling.

Its early years were a time of expansion for the new housing association. It did not go unnoticed in 1988 that while the British government and its agencies were supporting Irish Centre Hostels and other voluntary Irish organisations to an amount of £2,350,000, the Irish government remained extremely parsimonious.[14]

From the beginning, the aim had been to house people on a short-term basis, so that once work was found they could move on along the route of local landladies or into council housing. This would keep a constant turnover of residents, assisting new arrivals who needed temporary accommodation. However, during the 1980s many young people left Ireland disturbed by family relationships or because of anti-social behaviour. Many others left northern Ireland under threats. There were also others, already here, who had been abused or abandoned by the Irish or British social security systems. For those suffering in this way, finding work and accommodation was not so easy.

Police curiosity

Conway House was seen to be one place which offered a haven, in particular for those escaping from the Troubles whether they had been threatened by paramilitaries, suffered punishment beatings, had been dealing in drugs or had a record of joy-riding. A bed and a welcome were offered. No questions were asked.

During the IRA bombing campaign on the mainland the Metropolitan Police assumed that Conway House in Kilburn was some sort of IRA staging-post. Incredibly, they thought that its membership would willingly put their names to hostel registers, be content to visit DHSS offices, sign benefit forms, swagger around the streets and get drunk in local pubs. In truth IRA volunteers were often from the south of Ireland rather than from the north, and kept quiet under false names in safe houses. They rarely mixed with the general Irish population.

Patsy Carolan says. *"They had cameras opposite, seeing who was coming in and out. I was very clear in my mind about it all."* This is endorsed by Frank Ryan. *"There were a lot of fellows who had nothing better to do than look out the windows. They saw the movements in the house opposite, so they waved. There was a whole lot of things about them watching us watching them, there was all this stuff going, and the phones being tapped."* In addition to photographing those who came and went, undercover police also penetrated the hostels. *"There were always police in the house. I caught a couple of them and asked them to leave. They would be asking a lot of questions. They would be a little more sophisticated that the ordinary run-of-the-mill fellow, we would question them and tell them to leave."*[15] Ironically, Patsy Carolan was also on the Camden Community Relations Board at that time. At one local meeting a senior policeman from Hampstead told him that

they had all the information they needed. Nevertheless, Conway House seemed under siege from the Special Branch. Raids or hoax bomb threats were common.

Two victims of police action were, of course, Paul Hill and Gerry Conlon. Patsy Carolan remembers them arriving at the hostel on 20 September 1974, after having being directed there. *"Everyone directed you to Quex Road or to Murray Street, they were the two places you were geared towards"*, says Paul Hill. *"Not only did you get a bed, you would get a start or an indication of where you'd get a job. Even more importantly, you'd get a chance to meet people who came from the same part of Ireland as yourself. You had a bond and you felt you belonged."*[16] Although they had known each other in Belfast, Hill and Conlon had met again by chance in Southampton.

Gerry Conlon has further memories. *"Fr Carolan, I discovered later, was very reluctant to take us in, because he knew nothing about us. We could produce no letter from our parish priest back home... and we had no other kind of refer.ence. But when he saw us looking like half-drowned rats from the rain he did the right Christian thing and said he'd let us in."*[17] Patsy Carolan said that he took pity on them. *"They were wet, and they had no money. I still remember the room I put them in."* They were allocated to St Louis room, on the ground floor just four feet from his own bedroom.

They were typical of most residents, working on building sites and enjoying the *craic* around Kilburn. While Conlon spent time in local betting-shops, Hill visited the Carousel, which was the new name for the Buffalo in Camden High Street, where he enjoyed the Irish showbands. He also visited the London Irish Centre. *"I went for the music, and also I think the drink was subsidised and you could get a cheap drink there. You could linger around a little bit, and also get a late drink before they pulled the shutters down. It was likely if there was a band on, you weren't breaking any curfews and you could kind of mingle, become a member of the Roscommon Association or somewhere, a place where you'd never been."*[18] He remembers with admiration the Centre's work.

The Guildford bombings

At about 9.00 pm on Saturday 5 October 1974, bombs exploded in two Guildford public houses, killing five people and injuring fifty.

After a few pints with Conlon in Kilburn that morning, Paul Hill had travelled to Southampton to see his girlfriend Gina, whom he used to visit at weekends. He first learned about the bombings from the front page of the *Sunday Mirror* the next morning. That afternoon he returned to London by train, which coincidentally had been diverted through Guildford because of works to the track, and travelled onwards to Conway House. He went to his job on a building site the following morning.

Gerry Conlon, however, remained in Kilburn on 5 October, weaving between pubs and betting-shops.*"By four o'clock I leave Paddy (Carey) in the bookie's and go back to the café beside the Memphis Belle and then go back to the hostel. I've had at least six or seven pints by this time, so I just collapse on my bed and fall asleep. At some point Paddy Carey comes in and hands me a bag of cassette tapes and a player that belong to his bird ... Around the same time 'Paul the greengrocer' comes in from work ... I'm still half-pissed from the afternoon. Later I go in the TV room ... About nine I go to the phone in the hostel and dial the number of the Engineers' Club in Belfast"* where he hoped to speak to his father... *"I go back into the TV room until about half past ten and then to bed."*[19] In fact he was described as being in the TV lounge, drunk and causing a nuisance, just as a newsflash on the television announced the bombings.

Sr Sarah Clarke writes of *"The cast-iron alibi which the police knew perfectly well. Ten people at the Quex Road hostel had seen him that night. They remembered him being there – ten people including a nun and a priest. That night they were watching the news and the flash came on about them. Gerry was fooling around and annoyed them, so someone hit him and they put him out of the room. He went to the room that he was sharing with another young man."*[20] This was Paddy Carey. Two weeks later, on 19 October, Conlon returned to Belfast to visit his father who was unwell.

On 28 November Paul Hill was arrested. As if on cue, the following day the Prevention of Terrorism Act was rushed through Parliament. Its provisions, including exclusion orders, gave enormous practical and social difficulties for thousands of Irish people. While some managed to keep their heads down and get on with their lives, others were harassed or even arrested under its draconian powers. By the evening of this day, Hill had falsely confessed to eight murders. Under brutal interrogation, he had given names, most of them extremely improbable.

One name was that of Patsy Carolan, the well-intentioned manager of the hostel. Two detectives from Guildford arrived at Quex Road, and said that they wanted information. They would return in the morning to take him to Guildford for questioning. Patsy Carolan was worried and informed his superiors. *"When they brought me into the police station they knew that I wasn't involved. But one policeman gave me a rough time. I was in for a day. They brought me out for lunch in fact and showed me around the pubs that were bombed. They then questioned me further and brought me back to London."*[21] In Guildford he was told that Hill's statement had implicated him throughout. He denied it all.*"When the questioning was over I told one of the detectives that he was the greatest bastard I had ever met."*[22] Fortunately, he was able to produce the stub of the airline ticket, which proved that he had returned home over the days of the bombing.

A week later the police asked Frank Ryan if he would help them with their enquiries. He mentioned that if Conlon had really been guilty and a member of the IRA, he was surprised that he did not even have the money to leave London.[23] As Frank Ryan says, *"I wouldn't normally give him money for a newspaper, because he'd never come back. Let alone give him a bomb."*[24] He had borrowed £5 from Frank Ryan towards the cost of his return to Belfast on 18 October, about a fortnight after the Guildford explosions. He was planning to hitch-hike to Stranraer for the crossing, wearing a ridiculously long Afghan sheepskin coat. Gerry Conlon later admitted to being on LSD, but to Frank Ryan it seemed that he also had mental health problems.

Anne-Marie O'Boyle was also questioned by the police, who put it to her that, with a name like hers, she must be in league with the IRA. She had to point out that she was in fact from Leeds and half-English. She now admits that at the time she had slightly suspected that Hill and Conlon might have been guilty, and although she saw them on the day of the bombing she had no idea how far away Guildford was, or whether Conlon could have travelled there, bombed the pubs and returned the distance to Kilburn within the alleged span of time. She was genuinely shocked that, as possibly guilty men, they appeared to be behaving so innocently during the days afterwards.

Although he himself was away, Patsy Carolan remembered that *"On the night the bomb went off Frank Ryan and Sr Anne-Marie were looking after the place"*. He himself was visiting his mother in Ireland. *"Conlon was in the house, and he could never have got back from Guildford to Conway House in the 45 minutes that the police say he could have. No one ever came to see me about that. No solicitor, no defence ever came to us to talk about that, which was a very strange thing."*[25] No efforts were made to seek alibis. Nevertheless it now seems strange that they did not immediately volunteer their information to the authorities.

Soon afterwards, Anne-Marie O'Boyle left the employment of Irish Centre Housing, and worked in Kilburn as a District Nurse for seven years. In 1984 she went to the Philippines as a missionary. During a leave, she was interviewed again by the Special Branch, who were able to tell her every word of a correspondence she had with a former resident of Hope House who had ended up in Long Kesh.

The trial opened at the Old Bailey in September 1975, eleven months after the bombings. *"It always stood out. We were always convinced that they were not the pair"*, adds Patsy Carolan. During the trial the prosecuting lawyer, Sir Michael Havers, QC, who five years later was to become Attorney General in Margaret Thatcher's first cabinet, said that no alibi witnesses had come forward for Conlon. However it had been discovered later *"That there were statements in custody from two police witnesses, both taken in January 1975, who in fact provided him with an alibi. Gerry Conlon always maintained he was fast asleep at the time, and unbeknown to him he had been seen asleep by a witness whose name was known to certain police officers."*[26] This was Paddy Carey, who had been flown over from Belfast especially to give evidence for the defence, and was then informed by one of the defence team that he would not be required until the following day. When he was told that he would have to find his own accommodation, and was expected to do so with no money, he promptly used his return ticket to fly home. The next day the court was told that he had not turned up.[27]

The London Irish Centre played a part in the protests and campaigns against the sentences by providing a venue for meetings. Paul Hill's aunt, Theresa Smalley, and her husband Errol had formed the Guildford Four Campaign, which met in its various rooms. They asked Sr Sarah Clarke to join them. Unwilling to join any committee, she instead recommended two solicitors, Mike Fisher for Hill and Gareth Peirce for Conlon. Gerry Conlon accurately described Sr Sarah as *"This wee Irish nun, who is a kind of mighty atom. She looks like a saint but she has a withering tongue that would strip paint if she set her mind to it."*[28]

Why the Oblates at first raised no more than a cursory question about these arrests has never been adequately explained. Perhaps they felt, as Irishmen, that this was essentially a matter for the British authorities. Perhaps they felt, as priests, that the due process of the law would eventually release the innocent. Or perhaps they also felt that even although they may have provided evidence that was not used, they had done their best. *"I did my bit to get Conlon and Hill released alright"*, says Patsy Carolan later. *"I met Gerry Conlon a few times afterwards. There was a lot done for those, maybe they felt we didn't do enough. There was a lot of work done behind the scenes for them. Anne-Marie had a very big influence. When the police came to interview us, Frank and me, we refused to see them unless they interviewed Anne-Marie, because she was the one who knew that Conlon was in the house that night. We later went to the Cardinal and the Cardinal was onto us to keep quiet, especially Frank Ryan, because we were stirring too much."*[29]

The slow route to freedom

Cardinal Basil Hume became interested in the condition of Gerry Conlon's father in the summer of 1978 after a letter from Conlon's mother, Sarah. Her husband Giuseppe had been arrested in the Maguire Seven 'bomb factory' case. The Cardinal visited him in Wormwood Scrubs in December 1978, and what he learned had a profound effect on him. He wrote to the Home Secretary, Merlyn Rees, in March 1979. Then followed a series of letters and meetings with the succeeding Home Secretaries, William Whitelaw and Douglas Hurd and letters to Prime Minister Margaret Thatcher.

Frank Ryan began receiving threats. *"There were guys who wanted to offer protection. 'You know what, Father? You're going to get killed'."* He thought they may have been common criminals, but it persuaded him to contact Cardinal Basil Hume. *"I managed to explain this to Cardinal Hume, and was invited to meet him. He sat in a rickety old chair, and made me very welcome and listened to what I had happened. I think I was the first person to have an eyeball-to-eyeball with Hume. Maybe I planted in him the impression of doubt."*[30]

Eventually Cardinal Hume's interest led to the formation in January 1987 of what became known as 'the Deputation'. This was a heavyweight body that also included the two Law Lords, Scarman and Devlin, and two former Home Secretaries, Roy Jenkins and Merlyn Rees. They were assisted by the writer Robert Kee, whose book *Trial and Error* about the case had already created a stir, and by some of the defence team. In turn the campaign to reopen the case was strengthened by other books and television programmes, all pointing to grave miscarriages of justice, not only in the case of the Guildford Four but also in that of the Maguire Seven. It was these elements of the campaign and the weight of the Deputation which met Douglas Hurd on 23 July 1987 that finally led the Home Secretary to re-examine the case.

The Avon and Somerset Police were appointed in August 1987 to investigate fresh evidence. They later filled a warehouse near their headquarters in Bristol with papers relating to the case, including the Guildford police files. In January 1989 Hurd agreed to refer the case back, which allowed Gareth Peirce to make a search of the warehouse. She uncovered key inaccuracies and contradictions in police evidence, but more importantly she found witness statements that had never been revealed at the trial at the Old Bailey.

Most shocking was a statement from 'Paul the greengrocer', Conlon's friend at Conway House, whose real name was Charlie Burke and who worked at a fruit and vegetable shop in Neasden Lane. In his statement, dated 18 January 1975 he mentions the presence in Conlon's room of *"Pat the labourer from northern Ireland"*, who was Paddy Carey. There is another key passage. *"I got back to Quex Road about 7.00 pm, because we take stock Saturday night. I packed my gear, and Gerry was in his bed. He was the only other person in St Louis Room. He said he was broke and asked to borrow a quid, but I never let him have it. About 7.30 pm I caught a taxi and left Quex Road for the last time. When I left he was still in bed."*[31] Burke's statement, if it had been used, might have demolished the case against Conlon. However, the file had been marked by the police 'Not to be shown to the Defence'. This revelation was a scandal.

Another factor was the confiscation by the police of records from Conway House in December 1974, after Paul Hill had been arrested. They were never available to the defence in preparing for the trial in September 1975 or the appeal in Oc

tober 1977. In early 1988, knowing that the Avon and Somerset police enquiry was under way, Frank Ryan arranged for Irish Centre Housing solicitors to threaten legal action over the return of the records.

After they had been finally handed back, albeit with some details missing, *"I got in a computer and looked for dates by winding the clock back to whatever date it was, and we would recreate the events of that day. What the weather was doing. What bands were playing. Who was in our hostel. Where they came from. What rooms were they in. I began to build up information as to who was there."* The hostel residents contributed 10p a week fro their rents for five months to buy the computer. Frank Ryan then painstakingly wrote to a large number of the residents of the hostel at the time of the bombing, asking them if they could recollect Hill or Conlon. A man called Michael Kennedy responded from Galway to say he could remember Conlon in the TV Lounge when the newsflash came onto the television screen. *"We traced him. So we passed the information to Hume, and Hume, if you like, fired a torpedo into the trial."*[32] Cardinal Hume passed the evidence to Douglas Hurd.

Michael Kennedy had left England a week after the bombings, as a result of the anti-Irish feeling he had experienced. He read about Conlon in the press, *"but I felt that if I went up in court I would end up by being charged for murder myself. You could tell the truth in those courts, and they would show you they were telling lies."*

Having been instrumental in discovering information that helped clear them, Frank Ryan was elated at the freedom of the Guildford Four. *"I have felt personally incarcerated for the last fifteen years as though I wouldn't be free until they were. But I also feel angry. This system seems geared to making this kind of tragic mistake and now there are other cases to be looked into."*[33]

Paddy Hill, at left, greeting Gerry Conlon of the Guildford Four after his own release as one of the Birmingham Six, 1991.

Paul Hill of the Guildford Four after his acquittal in 1989.

The arrival of Frank Ryan

In 1977 Patsy Carolan had been assigned to Kingswood in Bristol as a parish priest. He was followed into Quex Road for a brief period by Christy Dunne, of whom Frank Ryan later said, *"It wasn't his kettle of fish."* Then in 1978 Frank Ryan himself, who had been working as a chaplain at Camden Square, was assigned as manager of Conway House. Like Patsy Carolan before him, before he arrived he spent some time visiting other hostels, trying to learn about good practice.

In a relatively long history, Irish Centre Hostels or Housing has only appointed two separate directors. Although the individual hostels had managers for many years, the director of Irish Centre Housing was not separately appointed until Patsy Carolan returned, in 1990, for another seven years. Antonia Watson, the current chief executive, took over in 1998. However, key to the sustainability of Irish Centre Housing were the staff and volunteers, and also the dedicated time offered by Oblate brothers and students gaining work experience.

With Tom Scully as director the Centre managed to survive the episode of the Guildford Four, and continued to concern itself with its prime interest, the welfare needs and housing of emigrants.

Soon after he arrived at Quex Road, Frank Ryan purchased no. 18 next door from John Best, who was a major land-owner in Kilburn. The Sisters of the Holy Family had previously sold him the site, although they had in fact originally bought it, and the house on it, from him some years before, and had demolished the house to extend their nursing home. When they later realised that their time in Kilburn was coming to an end they decided not to rebuild. With surprisingly good business sense, they sold it back to John Best, as an empty plot, for £45,000. Frank Ryan bought it with money from the Housing Corporation, and built on it housing units for the elderly. Although the hostel for older men continued for some years in Tollington Park, this was the first time that Irish Centre Housing moved away from the policy of providing accommodation only for younger Irish people.

Managing Conway House

As unemployment increased during the Thatcher years, work in primary industries such as construction, became more difficult to find. These and other factors meant that residents stayed longer in the hostels. One of Frank Ryan's accomplishments was the ease and fluency with which he could write. *"Conway House was not only a hostel, but also a welfare centre in its own right. We have given hope to those in despair, accommodation to the homeless, we have fed the hungry, we have given a wash and clothing to those who were smelling, we've nursed the sick, we have found jobs for some of the employed, and above all we have cared for those who have been rejected."* He continued, *"Some young people were visibly relieved to have left home, even though they had nothing and their future was insecure. Some left conditions of abuse, hostility, poverty and exploitation. They arrived as broken people. They needed time to recover from their experiences, time to think and freedom from pressure. We have in particular been of help to those affected by the troubles of northern Ireland. We have been a safety valve in times of trouble."*[34]

Hostel services came under further strain in the late 1980s when young emigrants living in London found conditions increasingly tough. The lack of jobs was a major problem. Changes in social security legislation meant that benefits were also far more difficult to obtain. They were weeks in arrears, and benefits to those under eighteen were withdrawn. In addition, urgent needs payments had been abolished. Locally, the Homeless Persons' Unit of Camden Council closed.

Above all, in 1989 the Community Charge, or poll tax as it was more colloquially called, hit the country. Hostels such as Conway House did not escape. Managers were made personally responsible for the collection of the tax from their homeless and often unemployed residents.

The Camden Irish Forum, which had been established by Cllr Angie Birtill and others, campaigned for exemptions to hostels. Frank Ryan applied to Camden for an exemption but was refused. He organised a test case, which was publicised by meetings and also by press articles which predicted his likely prison sentence. Eventually an officer from the council arrived to inform him that he had been granted an exemption. The officer apparently muttered that Conway House *"had caused more trouble than it was worth."*.

The hostel, known for its vigorous Irish presence, became the focus of local difficulties. Apart from particular problems of discipline and demonstrations inside, which included a 'dirty campaign', and an incident when four young men barricaded themselves in a room and hung a banner out of a window, the place was regarded by some outside as a provocation. The hostel's residents had sometimes been involved in local anti-social activity, including confrontations with the police. Attacks on the hostel were then made, usually in the early morning, when sometimes as many as thirty people hammered on the door and threw stones at the windows.

There were various reasons for this. Frank Ryan ventured one explanation. *"Our lads can, in a sense, raise the temperature around here. They're very active young fellows and that puts pressure on the local girls. This can cause problems. Local people have taken out their frustrations on this place here, as result."* There were also much more serious, even racist reasons. The attacks could become extremely violent. It was feared that petrol bombs might be used, so the hostel stocked up with fire extinguishers. In spite of Frank Ryan's view, that of the priests in charge was that these attacks were motivated by the National Front with local support, as a response to what was happening in northern Ireland. A similar anti-Irish incident took place at the festival at Roundwood Park at about the same time.

In 1989, of Conway House's 1,311 users, 312 or 24% were from northern Ireland.[35] It had offered a home to many who had been ordered out of the six counties by unionist and republican paramilitaries, *"The Royal Ulster Constabulary was probably glad to see the last of them"*, said Ryan. He believed that many found peace here for the first time in their lives.

After some years' service, in 1989 Frank Ryan was assigned by the provincial to his original first ministry, Leith in Scotland. After Leith he was moved back to London, to West Kilburn where he worked in a desolate landscape of poorly designed tower blocks and high rates of crime. In 1996 he moved again, to the Irish Welfare Centre in Birmingham.

The return of Patsy Carolan

Having returned from his own parochial duties in Bristol and then Leigh-on-Sea, Patsy Carolan resumed charge as director of Irish Centre Housing. Paul Hill knew both priests. *"I kind of found Fr Carolan a bit deeper, more into himself, where Fr Ryan would say what he was feeling. He would make it loud and clear to people what he thought of them, getting in late or whatever."*[36] Paul Hill said that he retained an innate suspicion of the priesthood, because as a child he remembered the parish priest reporting his misdeeds to his parents.

Patsy Carolan's second period with Irish Centre Housing was marked by bold acquisition and expansion, and at the same time he developed an abrasive but respected relationship with the Housing Corporation. He was also now the director of Irish Centre Housing, a change that

Denis Cormican, the director of the Centre itself, had introduced to share the responsibilities more equally.

Patsy Carolan first believed that he had to make some changes to the existing housing stock. He had been disappointed with the situation he found at Conway House, where most residents were without work and suffering from problems of drug or alcohol abuse. The geographical balance had also been disturbed, with people from northern Ireland now more dominant. He put up the rents from £80 to £112 a week, still relatively cheap.

He subdivided the building, with twenty-four beds on one side. Here he transferred those who were working and charged them £47 a week, so that they would be able to afford to go to work rather than exist on benefits. *"Of course the Corporation came down on me over that too, and said that we cannot have differential rents in the same premises, which I thought was crazy"*. So he decided that this section be renamed Mee House to circumvent the problem, but this was eventually changed. For this new accommodation he arranged for this section to be converted, with a kitchen on every floor to serve six or seven rooms.

Moving away from the idea of the traditional large hostel, he felt that smaller units were more appropriate. The first building acquired after his return was one in Highgate Road, which was bought for £300,000 from Fitzpatrick's, the building contractors, and arranged for twenty residents. This had been designated by the Housing Corporation for rough sleepers but Patsy Carolan was not convinced that he should fill all its units with people from the streets, because he wanted to bring in *"a few decent people into it and create a mix which I did. Of course I got into trouble with the Housing Corporation over that. They told me that they would not give me money again, as I had not followed out their procedures. They were right in a sense, but I think from a management point of view we were right. We took quite a few off the streets, and the project went very well. We had good management there."*[37] This difficulty with the Corporation brought him into trouble with members of his committee, although he says that the chairman, solicitor John McCormack, was very supportive.

The acquisitions continued. Another house, which had been a former bank, was bought in Queen's Crescent in Kentish Town. With flats here for nine younger people who shared facilities, this was rented more cheaply. It was later adapted, like Mee House, to a hostel for working men.

Job Powerhouse

Irish Centre Housing had always tried to offer its hostel residents more than just a bed and meals. Following the tradition of the Marian Employment Agency, another agency with a snazzier title, Job Powerhouse, was set up in 1994. As Patsy Carolan said, *"We had all these young Irish people coming down who didn't know what to do with life, they had no ambition, they didn't know what they wanted to do, no training, no skills, so we were talking about what we should be doing for them. We started off some type of training, and the priest in charge of the Irish Chaplaincy here at the time said there was a young man who had done some work for the bishops in the west of Ireland. He would be suitable, his name was Derek Hanway. So we hired him to set this up, which he did. He made a success of it, and had great contacts and marketed it to other parts of London."* At first developed with European funding, its purpose was to provide vocational guidance and training to over three hundred people a year. Based in Camden Square, it provided outreach or satellite services to all Irish Centre Housing hostels, as well as working with

travellers' sites. *"The St Pancras Housing Association backed us financially. We needed partners, because it was very expensive. Irish Centre Housing was putting £15,000 a year into that, and we got some grants. I convinced my committee to give me that £15,000 which was a lot of money."*[38] In the six months between January and July 1999, Job Powerhouse facilitated 173 people, of whom less than a third were Irish. It now operates from new premises inside Irish Centre Housing's offices in Holmes Road, Kentish Town.

Irish Elders

Meanwhile, the range of housing services to specific groups, such as offenders, travellers and the elderly also increased. In any recent study of the condition of the Irish emigrant in Britain, and there have been many, the statistics illustrate that older Irish emigrants are now the single most deprived ethnic community in London.[39] They have poorer health, die earlier and have experienced higher rates of unemployment than the British average. They also suffer from high levels of discrimination, alcoholism, suicide and inadequate housing. Irish women form the largest section of the Irish community in Britain, but due to the prominence of negative stereotypes in the media and in British culture, their relative *"Invisibility does not protect Irish women in Britain from racism. Indeed they are more often more exposed since their productive and reproductive roles connect more firmly to British society"*.[40]

Most of the elderly tenants of Irish Centre Housing have spent a lifetime working and contributing to the development of Britain's and Ireland's respective economies through their labour, their tax payments and their postal order remittances to their families at home. Their cause has been taken up by Sally Mulready and the London Irish Elders' Forum, which has an office in the Centre, and which campaigns for recognition of the contribution of elderly Irish.

Dunne Mews, off Leighton Road, was later acquired as a home for people who were too old to work. Some had been heavy drinkers, but they were now delighted to be placed in self-contained flats of their own.

More premises

Irish Centre Housing was then offered premises with eighteen units near Camden Town, known as Caulfield Court, as accommodation under the 'Rough Sleepers' Initiative'. Patsy Carolan tells a story of how he and the architects had a meeting with the planners in Camden Town Hall. *"They were very strict on parking. We wanted twenty-six flats and they said you only have parking for twenty-two, so I remember that the lady, she was a German lady with a hell of a reputation, she said Father, you won't get twenty-six flats on this but you will get twenty-two. I said that's what we will have, and the meeting finished. The fellows with me were amazed at this. No negotiation."* Somehow eighteen units emerged.

President Mary Robinson, who visited the Centre in 1995, also formally opened Dunne Mews and Caulfield Court. The Housing Corporation had at first insisted that the latter take in all rough sleepers, not just those who were Irish. Patsy Carolan agreed, as long as he could hold interviews as to their suitability. However, when he refused a number of people he was strongly challenged by Camden Council, which asserted it had nomination rights. This led him to decide that he could probably continue by financing Irish Centre Housing from rentals and by borrowing alone, rather than rely on grants from Camden or the Housing Corporation. The council now has no nomination rights here.

Patsy Carolan is a man who knows what he wants. *"Our policy was that if anybody came, and we had a vacancy, they were taken in. We didn't want the house just full of refugees. We could have done it, and it would have been easier to manage. The Irish were far more difficult. Like getting them to go to work. We were always insisting that they went to work, that was always the aim. It gave them stability, dignity and a pound in their pocket."*[41] Later, he gave an interview to the *Irish Post* in which he said that the Irish housing associations, which were connected through the Irish Housing Forum, were not receiving their fair quota of support from local authorities such as Camden, compared to other ethnic minority housing associations.[42] It had also been recognised by members of the council with Irish interests in 1994 that Camden did not appear to be supporting the Irish community as powerfully as it did other ethnic minorities in the borough.

Nomination rights were a contentious issue. In order to claim Housing Corporation funding, the association had to agree that the local authority had a right to nominate people from its waiting list to a proportion, which is rarely less than 75%, of the vacancies in the property. As a result, any Irish association was now housing fewer and fewer Irish people, who were not regarded as an ethnic minority. By contrast, black housing associations were able to operate a system which allowed black people, recognised as ethnic minorities, into their housing. It took some years before the Irish were recognised as an ethnic minority for housing purposes.

This view was explored in a report commissioned by the four housing associations in the Irish Housing Forum, which concluded that *"More Irish people endure poor housing than the rest of the population. They encounter particular difficulties in finding housing and suffer worse housing conditions when they do. They are over*

President Mary Robinson of Ireland at the London Irish Centre, 1995

represented among the homeless in the capital. Housing needs are compounded by the fact that many Irish people suffer from poorer health and have a shorter life expectancy than the rest of the population. The needs of young migrants and the elderly require particular attention ... While more boroughs and housing associations are aware of the needs of the Irish community there is much to be done. The Irish dimension is absent from policy-making, and 'invisibility' remains an issue. It is therefore unsurprising that lettings of local authority housing to households of declared Irish origin are low, even in the boroughs where the [Irish] population is at its highest."[43] The belief of the Irish Housing Forum, which is now defunct, is that this report should remain conspicuously on the desks of every senior local authority housing officer in London.

Arás na nGael

In 1996 Patsy Carolan wanted to acquire Aras na nGael, the Brent Irish Centre building in Salusbury Road, near Queen's Park, in north-west London. It was in receivership. *"That got me into serious trouble"*, he says. *"It was an unbelievable site at an unbelievable price. The big problem was that it had a handball alley. There were vested interests in that. Ken Livingstone, who was then the local MP, got the money or part of the money."* Handball is an Irish game, and this was the only court in Europe outside Ireland itself. *"The court was beautiful. I knew that the club and the 27 units of housing attached to it would go hand in hand, but that we couldn't get rid of the bar."*[44] The place had also suffered from financial problems, and there were deeply conflicting arguments about its sale and purchase.

A housing advice worker at the London Irish Centre, 1980s. (Joanne O'Brien)

Patsy Carolan finally clinched the purchase for £550,000, despite being outbid by an Arab property company.[45] It was planned that the Irish Centre's function room and lounge would be refurbished, with offices rented out to Safe Start, an Irish voluntary body, and to the Brent Irish Advisory Service. The remainder of the building would be converted into sheltered accommodation. This eventually became St Eugene Court, with twenty-six units for older people, predominantly Irish, who are supported by a warden

It was ironic that Irish Centre Housing was then trading more successfully as a non-profit organisation than the London Irish Centre itself. Patsy Carolan's entrepreneurial sense challenged the wisdom of those more traditional members of his management committee. As he said, *"They made life so difficult for me. Even when I had them convinced that we should go ahead and house old people here, I was asked 'have you done any survey that is needed?' It was so obvious that it was needed. I had done it,* *and they condemned it."* John McCormack supported Patsy Carolan in his initiatives but the committee thought he was pushing forward too fast. *"Meeting after meeting was very angry."*[46] He and the new chairman were not the best of friends.

The contention at Salusbury Road was that the committee insisted that the tendering process should be above board, and that the entire site should be retained for Irish Centre Housing, rather than a part left to become a bar. Irish Centre Housing wanted the acquisition done correctly, whereas it was thought that Patsy Carolan was cutting corners, which would mean another fight with the Housing Corporation.

As a result of rules introduced by the Corporation, the relationship between the Irish Centre Housing and Camden's Housing Department became strained.

With skills that had a particular individual style, Patsy Carolan's desire was for expansion while there was still a need. He had made the decision to invest in new buildings, and did not want funds to languish in the bank. He wanted to spend, particularly at a time when properties were relatively cheap. *"We should be buying and moving ahead"*, he says. *"The staggering thing is we never had to borrow money. We were financially very viable. We had an excellent accountant in Paddy Keegan."*[47] When Patsy Carolan left in 1997 for Dublin, there were indeed no debts and £400,000 was in the bank. Meanwhile the Centre's debt at Camden Square was looking unassailable.

The arrival of Antonia Watson

After his departure, there was no suitable Oblate to take his place. Antonia Watson was appointed to replace him in April 1998, although consultants had bridged the gap of a few months before she could take up the job. Her experience beforehand had been with other housing organisations such as the Novas-Ouvertures Group and Look Ahead Housing. This appointment marked a couple of firsts. She was the first woman to become a director of Irish Centre Housing and the first who was not a Catholic.

When she arrived, she felt that although *"its heart was in the right place"* Irish Centre Housing was not a particularly professional organisation. There was a small staff team, but little or no revenue funding was coming in except through housing benefits. Soon after she arrived she was able to obtain revenue support for Conway House and St Louise. Nevertheless, she has said that she found that the Housing Corporation regarded Irish Centre Housing relatively well. There was certainly no criticism of Carolan's time, but a lot of attention was paid after he had left. It was *"admitted to be a difficult task to monitor an ordained priest, but after he had gone there were no adverse reports."*[48]

Antonia Watson's arrival may have sig

nalled a decided move towards secularisation. Although there was a chapel at St Louise, the one in Hope House had never been used during the time of Irish Centre Hostels. It later became a useful boardroom. No questions about religion are asked of applicants. But at one time, presumably looking at the numbers from the north of Ireland, Frank Ryan had jokingly suggested a need for a hostel for Protestants.

There was a mixture of people at Conway House in 1998, about 60% of whom were Irish. The hostel was at full occupancy and although most residents were young, there was no trouble between different age groups. Among them there were still people with drink problems, ex-offenders and those running away from trouble. Very few residents were working. At St Louise, which now has 130 bedrooms, there are even fewer Irish residents, with most of its residents now African from places such as Somalia.

Through Job Powerhouse and more directly, staff still give advice on welfare benefits and employment, and continue to help residents who need it to find more permanent accommodation. All the hostels provide a 24-hour support.

Using the language of a housing professional, in contrast to those who were in the job before her, Antonia Watson has outlined her vision. *"Irish Centre Housing aims to be responsive to the needs of all its residents and potential residents. It expects to develop accommodation and support services for Irish people with alcohol and/or mental health difficulties, as well as extend its work with rough sleepers. A number of our older residents and elders in the communities have expressed a wish to return home. (We) intend to investigate the opportunities, through partnership working in the Republic of Ireland, to respond to this need."*[49] Increasingly the possibility of assisting elders

Antonia Watson, Director of Irish Centre Housing.

scheduled as general housing, but was later renovated to accommodate seven people who had been dependent on alcohol and had since been through detox and rehabilitation before returning to independent living. After it had been renovated, it was named Hackett House, after Father Paddy Hackett, the first Oblate director of the Centre, and was opened in December 2001.

The recent list is impressive: Forde House, Highgate Road, Dunne Mews, Caulfield Court, St Eugene Court, and in Antonia Watson's time, Bethany House, a former YWCA hostel and Anglican convent with 94 beds in Islington, and Townsend House, which has 18 beds in Borehamwood, Hertfordshire. Some of these developments were achieved with housing association partners.

Jerry Kivlehan, the director of the Centre until August 2004, restated some of the difficulties that Patsy Carolan and others encountered. *"Most of Irish Centre Housing's development has been from its own resources, but as an Irish housing association we have to work three times as hard than anybody else to get statutory and local authority support for developments."*[50]

Although local authorities now nominate residents to almost all the Irish Centre Housing premises, and provide 'move on accommodation' to one bed flats, people still arrive looking for accommodation from the welfare service at the Irish Centre at Camden Square, as they have been doing for fifty years.

to return home, with understanding and care, has risen up the agenda.

Although perhaps in a less dogged way, Antonia Watson has followed Patsy Carolan's desire for expansion while the housing need remains. He had re-established Conway House and refurbished St Louise, which were followed by acquisitions and developments at An Caisleen, a home for the elderly which was opened in May 1990 by the Minister for Social Security, Nicholas Scott, and Cardinal Hume. Soon after, a building in Kingsgate Road, in Kilburn, was bought from Camden for £77,500. Initially this was

1   LIC 14th Annual Report
2   Interview Fr Frank Ryan, October 2003.
3   These figures are based on notes by the Irish Department of Labour, Committee on Emigrant Services, 1979. It is possible, but un-likely, that some other services received funding of which the committee was unaware.
4   Interview with the author, **(GH: author of what?)** October 2003.
5   Interview Fr Patsy Carolan, October 2003.
6   Interview Fr Frank Ryan, October 2003.
7   *Stolen Years*, by Paul Hill, Doubleday 1990.
8   Interview Fr Frank Ryan, October 2003.
9   Interview Fr Patsy Carolan, October 2003.
10 Interview Sr Joan Moriarty, March 2004.
11 *Our Histories, our Futures*. Interview with Sr Catherine, June 1999.
12 *Sunday Telegraph*, 12 April 1987.
13 *Ibid.*
14 Report from Conway House, 1988.
15 Interview Fr Patsy Carolan, October 2003.
16 Interview Paul Hill, April 2004.
17 *Proved Innocent*, by Gerry Conlon, Hamish Hamilton 1990. This book was later adapted as a film called *In the Name of the Father*.
18 Interview Paul Hill, April 2004.
19 *Proved Innocent, ibid.*
20 *No faith in the System, ibid.*
21 Interview Fr Patsy Carolan, October 2003.
22 From Fr Patsy Carolan's statement to the Deputation, written 14 November 1986.
23 From Fr Frank Ryan's statement to the Deputation, written 14 November 1986.
24 Interview Fr Frank Ryan, October 2003.
25 Interview Fr Patsy Carolan, October 2003.
26 From the Court proceedings, quoted in *Stolen Years ibid.*
27 *Proved Innocent ibid.*
28 *Ibid.*
29 Interview Fr Patsy Carolan, October 2003.
30 Interview Fr Frank Ryan, October 2003.
31 Statement of Charles Joseph Burke taken at Guildford Police Station, 18 January 1975.
32 Interview Fr Frank Ryan, October 2003.
33 *Kilburn and Willesden Recorder*, 25 October 1989.
34 *Being of Help in the Turbulent Years* by Fr Frank Ryan, 1988.
35 *Irish Post*, 14 April 1990.
36 Interview Paul Hill, April 2004.
37 Interview Fr Patsy Carolan, October 2003.
38 Interview Fr Patsy Carolan, October 2003.
39 *Emigration and Services for Irish Emigrants*, by Brian Harvey. Published by the Irish Episcopal Commission for Emigrants (IECE) and the Irish Commission for Prisoners Overseas, 1999. This publication does concede that a significant number of Irish emigrants have done well eco-nomically.
40 *Discrimination and the Irish Community in Britain*, by Dr Mary Hickman and Dr Bronwen Walter. Published by the Commission for Racial Equality, 1999.
41 Interview Fr Patsy Carolan, October 2003.
42 *Irish Post*, 25 March 1995.
43 *Still beyond the Pale* by Helen Cope, com-missioned by the Cara Irish Housing Associa-tion, An Teach Irish Housing Association, Irish Centre Housing and Innisfree Housing Associa-tion, July 2001.
44 Interview Fr Patsy Carolan, October 2003.
45 *Irish Post*, 13 April 1996.
46 Interview Fr Patsy Carolan, October 2003.
47 *Ibid.*
48 Interview Antonia Watson, May 2004.
49 *Our Histories, Our Futures*, by Colm Power for Irish Centre Housing, 1999.
50 *Ibid.*

CHAPTER ELEVEN

Signed, sealed and delivered

Father Denis Cormican

Described as a modest and humble man, Father Denis Cormican already had experience of the London Irish Centre as a student in 1967 with Paddy Hackett and then as a chaplain from 1987 to 1990 under Tom Scully. He took over the directorship from Tom Scully in December 1990, although he arrived in early 1991.

Tom Scully was posted to Leigh-on-Sea, near Southend, while Denis Cormican was still in Stillorgan on a management course to prepare him for the Centre. There was therefore a gap of a few weeks before he was available to move into Camden Square and with justifiable concern, Jim Myers, a member of the administrative committee, telephoned Tom Scully to say that he did not believe that this arrangement was fair on Denis Cormican. He felt that there should be a proper hand-over, but was reassured that everything was in order.

Denis Cormican became the ninth director of the Centre, but was the first from Northern Ireland. From Glenavy in Co. Antrim, he went straight into the Oblates after school and then worked on the mission staff and also taught in the vocational education school in Emmet Road, Inchicore, in south-west Dublin. He came to Kilburn as a student in 1967, but was quickly reassigned to the London Irish Centre hostel.

He worked with the young men of the hostel during the earlier part of the mornings, because they had to be out by

Fr Denis Cormican with an intrepid fund-raiser.

9.30 am and it was less busy afterwards. He then spent time with the Missing Persons' Bureau. Cormican had some success at this, and was able to reunite a mother in Ireland with her daughter in England in a record two hours with three well-placed phone calls. They had not seen each other for five years.

After this period as a student, he was sent home to northern Ireland, to the Royal Victoria Hospital in Belfast. This was at the beginning of the Troubles, but by 1972 he was a chaplain in the military wing of Musgrave Park Hospital, in the unit which looked after wounded IRA men. He then worked in Liverpool, and back in Bluebell parish in Dublin, before the provincial, William McGonagle, assigned him to join Tom Scully in Camden Square. It was the current provincial, Paul Byrne, who asked him to take over.

He had a lucky start. On his first day, an employer rang the Centre to ask for forty fit men to work immediately in the Isle of Dogs. Denis Cormican was pleased to be able to provide them. Jobs were plentiful at that time, and gangs of labourers who had just arrived from Ireland and were hungry for work could be almost entirely recruited from Conway House.

It had been a policy that the Centre should always present a positive image of the Irish in Britain, which it was hoped would transcend the inevitable difficult times. When in February 1991 the IRA fired mortar bombs at 10 Downing Street, very narrowly missing John Major's cabinet in session, Denis Cormican was invited onto BBC television to comment, and drew attention to how such attacks had made the Irish community so vulnerable to abuse and hatred. The anonymous hate phone calls that the Centre had been receiving immediately ceased.

A day for freedom

Soon after, the Centre hit the headlines of the national press with a celebration. On Thursday, 14 March 1991, the Birmingham Six, who had spent sixteen years in various prisons as Britain's biggest mass murderers, were freed by the Court of Appeal. Campaigning for this eventual victory had been taking place across the country, inside and outside the Irish community, and supporters' meetings had taken place in the Centre. Family, well-wishers and campaigners gathered at the Old Bailey to hear the news. Emotions ran high. When, at 3.30 pm, Lord Justice Lloyd announced that *"in the light of fresh evidence which has been made available since the last hearing in this court, your appeal will be allowed and you are free to go"*, relatives and friends in the public gallery leapt in the air. When word reached the street there was uproar. Unfortunately some supporters outside missed the moment of the occasion. Not expecting such an early decision, Paul Hill of the Guildford Four was said to be among those who were in the bookie's opposite the court, watching the Cheltenham Gold Cup.

Outside the Old Bailey, Billy Power, one of the Birmingham Six, shouted above the noise of the crowd that while they had just been released, Judith Ward was still in prison. Hoarse with joy, he added that the Tottenham Three and the Bridgewater Four were still locked up. Nevertheless, Irish pride began to reassert itself in the streets of Britain, although the IRA campaign was by no means over.

A reception was hastily arranged at the London Irish Centre, where the Kennedy Hall was made available. The six men were driven away from the crowds outside the court in three Daimlers and with a police escort. As the convoy headed north through the streets of Holborn, three minibuses packed with supporters peeled off to frustrate the reporters who were following in taxis. They were taken first to the Columban Fathers' Missionary Hostel in Hampstead for a quieter reunion with their families, which had been arranged by Fr Bobby Gilmore of the Irish Chaplaincy. Fr Gilmore had been brave enough at one stage to defy the Hierarchy in Ireland in his steady support of the Birmingham Six. The only paper allowed into the Hampstead house was the *Irish Post*, because *"Their coverage of our plight and the editor's unshakeable belief in our innocence gave a great boost to our families years before the rest of the press took up the torch."*[1] Then four of the six were whisked away by the *World in Action* team of Granada Television to a hotel in Berkshire, while the other two, Paddy Joe Hill and Billy Power, were brought to the Centre. As Sally Mulready has said, they felt they had a duty to the Centre, which had been the venue of so many campaign meetings. She also remembers Billy Power, once so familiar with the Irish community in Birmingham, asking her what the London Irish Centre would be like.

The celebrations resumed here, interrupted by more speeches. Billy Power said he didn't want to criticise anyone, *"This is a time for joy and rejoicing"*, he said. However he did add that that for the first ten or twelve years of their imprisonment the Irish government had not been interested in their case.[2] As the bar was closing, another man walked in to be told that he was too late for a drink. When he announced, *"I've been inside for 16 years, and now I can't even get a pint of Guinness"*, faces fell. This was Johnnie Walker, another of the six who had left the Granada party and caught a taxi back to London. Unsurprisingly, the bar remained open, indefinitely.[3]

This freedom party was followed by another three days later, on St Patrick's Day. This also took place in the Kennedy Hall and included Billy Power and Hugh Callaghan. It was the first opportunity they had to buy a pint, and they simply could not manage it. They had forgotten basic practices, and were flabbergasted by the prices, even in a subsidised Irish Centre bar. There was of course music, and Hugh Callaghan joined in the singing. At one point he left the celebrations and entered the small bar upstairs. He asked Maeve Heath, who was serving, if he could sit there, because it was all too much for him. Someone in the bar asked him for a song. Callaghan began, quietly and falteringly, the first verse of *Danny Boy*. Irish faces looked into their glasses with tears in their eyes.[4]

Following the releases of the Guildford Four in 1989 and the Birmingham Six in 1991, the Centre became a venue for celebration whenever miscarriage of justice cases had been won. Often a small room was set aside for the released prisoner first to meet his family. This tradition has continued even when the released prisoners were not all Irish, and included the Bridgewater Three in 1997.

Billy Power soon joined other campaigns based at the Centre. *"He set up the campaign for the release of Frank Johnson, his friend from Wormwood Scrubs who was also innocent"*, says Sally Mulready.[5] Frank Johnson was released in August 2001, twenty-six years after he had been imprisoned for alleged murder. Having engaged Gareth Peirce as his solicitor on Billy Power's recommendation, he spent his first night of freedom as Billy Power's guest.

With the release of the Birmingham Six, the Centre was now in the headlines for reasons that Irish people could take pride in, and Denis Cormican was confident of his future. Twice before he had declined the offer of a post here as director, but now he looked forward to his assignment. The days of crowded bars were in the past, but both the Kennedy and the McNamara Hall were open for business. Anti-drink driving laws, parking restrictions and the competition from other venues had pushed the numbers down. Surprisingly, however, as pubs found that entertainment licensing laws now deterred them from engaging live musicians, the traditional Irish players returned to places such as the Centre, and brought with them their audiences.

Catering for souls or other appetites

Denis Cormican was described as a *"good pastoral priest, but not a businessman"*. He was much more interested in the welfare office and in the care of the many people who used its services. Each Christmas he organised the dispatch and delivery of hampers to the needy. He was also committed to the success of the Centre as a haven for those who sought security or peace. His clerical status was forgotten whenever he lent a practical hand. It was not unknown for him to be seen cleaning the Centre's toilets with a mop. But as he often emphasised, he was not ordained to run a bar, and was uncomfortable as a social figurehead.

There had been a history of mismanagement on the bars and catering side for some years. Takings were not properly checked and money disappeared. A night cleaner was responsible for boxes of stock being removed through the back door.[6] The bars were allegedly earning £500,000 a year, but operating at a loss. Managers came and went. Not only was there a recurring loss of stock, but there was also 'shrinkage'. Jim Myers commented that *"The place was robbed blind for a period."*[7] On one isolated occasion, the agency staff who were serving at the bar of the upstairs Douglas Hyde Lounge made off at the end of the evening with the drawer from within the till.[8]

In time the pressures of a building with four bars within it, and indirectly the hostels associated outside it, took their toll on Denis Cormican's health, and he proposed to the administrative committee that Patsy Carolan, who had now returned to Irish Centre Hostels, should be appointed its overall director, rather than only the manager of Conway House.

For respite, he enjoyed a card game of 'twenty-fives' and a plate of sandwiches with some of the older members on a Thursday evening. He drank orange juice. But the stress was such that he would often light up a second cigarette, forgetting that there was one already alight in the ash-tray.[9]

Administrative changes

The meetings with the administrative committee, held in the Kennedy Hall, were often a nightmare. During Claude Malone's time the chairman had been Martin Moroney, whom Joe Davis described as *"The great father figure. When you went to him for advice, he was always so calm."*[10] He was succeeded by Donie Egan, from Tullamore in Offaly, who was followed by Tommy Dunne.

Tommy Dunne's address to the 1991 AGM was typically eclectic, but perhaps ignored some of the realities beneath his optimistic surface. He welcomed Lord Longford, who was still president, to the meeting, and thanked the Oblates for their commitment and support. He also thanked Tom Scully for his continued interest. The Dion Committee grant was £84,220 and that from Camden was £37,947. However, he said that the recession was causing hardship, which had been exacerbated by unspecified problems in Camden Social Services. There was now an increased workload on the desks of the Centre's welfare staff. The Luncheon Club and Day Centre were catering for thirty to forty people a day. Irish language classes were flourishing. The Marie Halpin School of Dancing had recently performed in Lourdes. The chapel had transferred from the top floor to the ground floor. And the meeting heard a talk on the formation of a limited company given by someone from Touche Ross. This was the sort of stuff the administrative committee liked to hear.

It was also clear that important changes were on the way.

A supporter of the Centre but who was

not a member of the committee, Monsignor George Stack, could see problems ahead. He had been a parish priest in Kentish Town at Our Lady Help of Christians, and was now the representative of Cardinal Basil Hume, one of the trustees. Taking advantage of the recommendations in the Charities Act, which had received the Royal Assent in 1993, he proposed a necessary alteration to the Centre's constitution. The purpose was to provide a more transparent system and avoid dangers of misappropriation and corruption. This followed the scandals which surfaced after the death of Robert Maxwell.

It was proposed that the Centre should become a limited company, with directors as trustees, effectively what the new Charities legislation demanded. The Act laid down precise rules for trustees, and Denis Cormican set about recruiting replacements for the series of bishops who had been in the largely nominal position of patron-cum-trustee since its inception.

It was also proposed that all the bar and catering services should be separated from the limited company, so removing from the director and the social committee the endless problems that they seemed to cause. Any profit, perhaps a rare occurrence, could be covenanted to the welfare and advice service. On paper this seemed a good idea, but in practice it was to present different sorts of problems.

In due course the first two trustees, Lord Farnham of the Benevolent Society of St Patrick and Peter Fitzpatrick, a building contractor, were appointed. Tragically, Peter Fitzpatrick had died at an early age but was replaced by his brother Philip. This process of reorganisation was concluded after Jerry Kivlehan had arrived in 1994.

They had a worrying period of scrutiny. In 1992, the committee had carefully assessed the situation and concluded that unless the Centre could trade its way out of debt, it would indeed have to close and apply for liquidation.[11] Despite obvious good business, there was something seriously wrong when on a turnover of £71,000 the bars and catering made a profit of only £2,603. In December they became so alarmed at the disappearance of stock that they introduced spot checks.

Enter Saxon Inns

Having looked at the options, it was decided to franchise the bar and catering services to an outside company with experience in the trade. This was just as well, because as a director of the new limited company, Jim Myers was *"shivering with apprehension."* He was now aware that the Centre had been trading illegally. Maeve Heath, who had been working behind the bars for many years, has said, *"If we hadn't franchised out the bars we would have closed."*[12] However, Joe Davis believed that to use the bar to subsidise the welfare service was wrong. He said that the decision had been *"signed, sealed and delivered"* before anyone knew about it. *"We wouldn't have accepted it"*, he said.[13] On the other hand, it was described by Jim Myers*"as a life-line"*.

The company which was appointed was Saxon Inns, on a five-year contract from 13 January 1993 at the low price of £25,000 a year. Unfortunately, only limited searches had been done on the company, and its accounts had been unavailable for examination.[14] Denis Cormican told the administrative committee how sad he was so say farewell to Jimmy McCluskey who could have been re-employed by this company.

There was another farewell. Paddy Keegan retired from his work as a voluntary accountant in 1991, but assisted as a staff accountant on a part-time basis with

Irish Centre Hostels, at Conway House. Jim Reynolds later took over as accountant at the Centre in February 1991 from Touche Ross.

After Tommy Dunne died, he was replaced by Donie Egan, who obviously enjoyed chairing meetings, but the mood became much more sombre. A Vice-Chair at the time was Jim Myers and while Tommy Dunne was ill, he took an AGM as Chair. It was not a pleasant experience, because there were unhelpful factions at loggerheads within the committee, and he felt that a conspiracy led by some of the county associations was conspiring against him. He was also acutely aware of the debt, and the liability that he was under. He felt that others did not share this responsibility with due seriousness.

Prior to the full committee meeting Jim Myers says that there often would be a pre-meeting of a small group which agreed everything beforehand. Many of them were fiercely opposed to the views of Denis Cormican. The administrative committee then tended to rubber stamp the decisions of this group, although individuals were allowed to express their views. They did so more often to jump onto their hobby horses or to hear the sound of their own opinions than contribute in a constructive manner.

At times the director was under siege. He was often insulted, and was accused by Sean Bourke, a member of the committee, who said that *"You can never get a straight answer from Denis."*[15] It was clear that their hearts ruled their heads, and their judgement suffered.

Extricating the Centre from the persistent and increasing debt of the hall was just one of the more serious problems that Denis Cormican and the committee faced. External circumstances did not improve matters. The grant from the Dion Committee had been reduced during the previous two years, but he was heard to say that he was "not going to be a fool and ride around Ireland on a bike". CamdenCouncil also cut the level of its grant.

The routine reports on the welfare service revealed that figures for callers had dropped by around 30% in the years between July '92 and '93, from 485 total interviews in the first year to 370 in the second. In view of budget difficulties, as a result of the cut in the Dion grant, numbers were reduced to three Social Advice Workers, but this was also a result of the falling off of arrivals at the Centre needing assistance. In September 1992, Paul Murphy, who had run the welfare service as co-ordinator, resigned to take up a position at the Hammersmith Irish Centre. The post was covered by the overstretched Denis Cormican, but finally filled by Geoff Holland.

Throughout this time there were those members of the committee who appeared somewhat destructive, whether they realised it or not, and the atmosphere of meetings was thick with tension.

The Kennedy fire

As if this was bad enough, a fire broke out in the Kennedy Hall. One Saturday night, a wedding reception was taking place in the McNamara when a fire began in the passageway on the ground floor leading to the Kennedy Hall, which had just been redecorated. The Hall itself was not in use that night, and its fire doors were closed. Peggy Campbell, who was working in the kitchen near to hall, said that a young man came past her saying he wanted to have 'a kip'. She said that the Kennedy was closed, but he replied that he needed to lie down somewhere. He was carrying a lit cigarette.

Soon after, he came running out, shouting to Peggy Campbell that there was a fire in there. The flames spread quickly

207

to the top of the wall and into the passage-way, damaging the ceiling and the electrical wiring. It began to attack the top rafters and break through to the Douglas Hyde Lounge upstairs by the time the Fire Brigade arrived, who swiftly extinguished the flames. One man was taken to hospital with breathing difficulties, but nobody had been injured.[16]

Although the Kennedy was not in use, a dance was taking place at the Douglas Hyde upstairs and there was the wedding reception in the McNamara. The coincidence, however, was that this celebrated a marriage between a fire-fighter and his bride. Maeve Heath, who was in charge of the bar, said that when the Fire Brigade arrived the bride and groom at first could not believe that this was not a prank from his colleagues at the station. Very soon the wedding party, along with everyone else, realised the truth. They evacuated the premises, but as they did so they ensured that they carried outside the food and much of the drink from their reception. This was carefully laid out along the garden walls of Camden Square and the party continued alfresco, with plates perched along the walls, until the early hours.

Before the bride and groom departed for their honeymoon, their uniformed colleagues, who had earlier been fighting the fire in the Kennedy Hall, ceremonially raised their hatchets to create an arch under which they could proceed to their waiting car.[17]

The fire was a considerable blow. First, repair costs of some £30,000 had to be raised, because the insurers would only pay for the minimum. Second, new fire–resistant materials had to be used in the refurbishment. And third, the Hall would have to be closed for letting for a number of weeks or months.

The following day Denis Cormican said that the Centre would use the money raised from its car raffle at the London Irish Festival on 2 July to repair the damage. This took time, but the Kennedy Hall was finally redecorated in an American theme, with US flags painted on the walls.

An effort to restore control

The opening good fortune of Denis Cormican's era had certainly disappeared. The fire added another considerable sum to the debt. Examination of the desperate financial situation by an outside consultant revealed how astonishing it was that a busy bar and catering service should still run at a loss. The consultant noted that the manager, Pat O'Dwyer, simply could not cope with the pressure. He had been interviewed for the job a couple of years before by Tom Scully and Tommy Dunne, and Paddy Keegan remembers that in those days staff were hired with no references. He remembers when there was a vacant post for a welfare worker, Denis Cormican had maintained that *"All they need is commonsense. Any complications would involve referrals"*.[18]

There is a story that as guests left after a St Patrick's Dinner, Pat O'Dwyer, who was dressed in a green cummerbund and green dickie bow tie "like a little leprechaun", stood in the foyer thanking everyone for coming and presenting them each with a bottle of champagne. When he noticed what was happening, Denis Cormican had to intervene.

The new trustees took a little time to assert their authority. Meanwhile there were committee members who resented the fact that their own decision-making powers had been appropriated.

Previously, the bar and catering policies had been decided by a social committee with little experience. It is said that it set its prices too low. Some members also believed that, as members, they were entitled to special favours. Others insisted on particular guests having complimentary or cheaper meals. As one director said, "county associations who might be willing to pay £30 per head for a dinner at another venue expected to pay only a fiver at the Irish Centre". The associations who raised considerable funds for the Centre also believed that they should hold their events here at a discount, or that at least free bottles of wine should be provided at their dinners.

In order to try to bring some controls to the catering accounts, an expensive and unsuccessful attempt was made to computerise the system. On Monday mornings, as if there really was little expectation of proper business practice, it was Mary Kenny who took the takings by car to the Bank of Ireland in the Holloway Road. This was perhaps a vulnerable arrangement.

A mistrust of Saxon Inns

The contract with Saxon Inns, began to unravel. The catering service slipped into decline, which led to unpaid bills and payments being withheld. The company started to owe the Centre a considerable sum. What made matters worse was that there was little accountability. There was also a turn-over of managers. The first manager, Eamon Dowling did not stay. A successor, described as "a proper gentleman", Malcolm Jones, was poached by the Irish Club. He was popular with some, but disliked by others of the committee because he was not Irish. Hilary Collis lasted two years. The chefs she engaged also did not remain for long.

Standards deteriorated. Traditional Irish cooking was forgotten in favour of more cosmopolitan menus. There were complaints by key members of the county associations of poor quality and, on one occasion from Clare, "not enough potatoes". These comments even dominated debates within the committee. Many of the associations voted with their feet and took their dinners and dances to other venues.

Saxon Inns were later severly criticised. The company defaulted some months later on its payments to the Centre, and there then began a long chase for arrears. Saxon Inns understood the running of pubs, but an institution like the London Irish Centre, with its different functions demanding different approaches, proved too unpredictable and awkward for it to operate. Influential people such as Bridie Shaw proposed that the company should be sacked. She wished to return to the previous arrangement, of a manager directly employed by the committee. Others had been convinced that the franchising decision had been the correct one for the circumstances, but most unfortunately the company selected was seen to have been a mistake.

Meanwhile the Centre continued with its other activities. The welfare service, now grandly called the Community Service Department, was now being co-ordinated by Christine Mohan. Cultural activities were popular. The Centre's reputation as an advocate for the Irish in Britain had increased its media profile. Its position on miscarriages of justice was clear. Its willingness to explore the underlying reasons for the conflict in northern Ireland and the need to find solutions meant that it was taken seriously. Of course, at the same time it was desperately keen to keep some of its internal difficulties confidential.

A Camden Irish Forum

Two or three years beforehand an important conference was held. This was strongly supported by sections of the Centre and by the Federation of Irish Societies. On 21 April 1990 over two hundred people attended and participated in 'The Voice of the Irish in Camden', at Camden Town Hall. The driving force behind this initiative was Councillor Angie Birtill, who had been closely involved in the Irish 'repatriation' controversy. This conference gave a voice to the concerns of a broad cross section of Irish groups and organisations in the borough. "The purpose of this event is to provide our community with an opportunity to identify our needs, and to develop a series of proposals for consideration by the council", its programme explains. Often, what was happening in Camden gave a lead for other authorities to follow.

It had been felt for a long time that not only was Camden unaware, but also central government, of how many Irish there were resident in the borough beyond rough estimates. As a result local councils and the government did not properly target its services towards these invisible communities. The 1991 census provided figures of 11,027 or 6.5% of Camden's population as having been born in Ireland. However identification standards were extremely haphazard, and this figure was probably an underestimate. There was also no mention of the second or third generation Irish, but it was estimated that 15% of the borough's population were Irish through their parents or grand-parents. There is no wonder that a campaign developed to persuade a government in 2001 to include a separate Irish category in the National Census of that year.

Irish centres across Britain believed that if the statistics were ever to become accurate, then there would be a greater case for arguing for adequate funding to meet the needs of the more unfortunate Irish emigrants.

It was also recognised from a GLC publication in 1985[19], long before the important report, *Discrimination and the Irish Community in Britain*, by Dr Mary Hickman and Dr Bronwen Walter, published by the Commission for Racial Equality in 1997, that Irish people experience particular disadvantage and discrimination in housing and employment markets, and do not enjoy equal access to statutory services.

During the day, there was a series of workshops. Paul Murphy of the Community Services Department spoke on the work of the Centre which demonstrated the kind of self-help that the Irish community had been engaged in for nearly four decades. Alluding to the repatriation controversy of a few years before, he said that *"It is imperative that the work done by the Association of London Authorities on the homelessness policy of Camden be carried forward"*. He also added that *"What we want for the Irish in the borough is a 'five star' service – not luxury – but an adequate comprehensive service that combats the homelessness that bedevils this inner London borough."*[20]

It was resolved that Camden should recognise the Irish as an ethnic minority in common with the more visible ethnic minorities, and undertake ethnic monitoring of its workforce to determine the numbers of Irish employees and their positions in the council. Other recommendations of the conference argued for a better practice of equal opportunities for the Irish ethnic minority, a training programme in Irish awareness and the advertising of council positions in the Irish press, and a clear recognition of the status of travellers.

It was a successful event, obviously filling for the first time a need felt by many Irish organisations in the borough. From it grew the Irish Consultative Forum, which later became known as the Camden Irish Forum. Described as an independent, and non-party political body, often meeting in the Centre, this took forward the recommendations of the conference and tried to monitor their progress.

This initiative by Cllr Angie Birtill was repeated about six years later by a new group of councillors, some of whom were elected in 1994, and who identified themselves as Irish. There still remains a caucus of Irish councillors, from the north and the south, on Camden Council. In spite of other pressures on their time they can be relied upon to work together on specific Irish issues.

The Camden Irish Forum was behind a number of local campaigns. It lobbied Camden's Housing Department to improve council policies in relation to homeless applicants, Irish housing associations and victims of harassment and tenant mobility. It was clear in its opposition to the anti-traveller Criminal Justice Act, and urged Camden to make more provision for travellers. It lent its backing to the 'Repeal the PTA' campaign.

It also supported Sinn Fein's desire to rent accommodation in the borough of Camden, pointing out that this was a legitimate political party. The council's leadership had refused Sinn Fein an office. It justified its stand on the grounds that if the peace process broke down, members of the public could be exposed to the threat from anti-Irish groups. In this somewhat extraordinary argument, the Leader, Cllr Richard Arthur was supported by the two Camden MPs, Frank Dobson, who had been Leader of Camden himself from 1973 to 1975 and entered the House of Commons in 1979, and Glenda Jackson, who had been elected in 1992. The Irish in Britain Representation Group issued a statement, *"Dobson will soon come begging for Irish votes, and he will get his come uppance"*.[21] It did not seem relevant when pointed out to the council that the African National Congress had used an office in Camden Town for many years.

New Activities

The forum also campaigned against the impending closure of the Four Provinces bookshop, an outlet since the late 1960s for the Connolly Association in Gray's Inn Road, and of the Green Ink bookshop in Archway, north London. The Four Provinces shop never closed, but unfortunately the Green Ink shop did.

The Green Ink Irish Bookfairs had their origins in the bookshop. Selling everything from serious books on Irish political history, through fiction, to CDs and tee-shirts, it began to develop dramatically with fairs at local venues. Irish writing was not as popular then as it is now. The first fair was in March 1985 and held at the Camden Centre behind Camden Town Hall. Pat Reynolds of the IBRG was listed as one of the organisers. This suggests that the fair had an overtly political stance, but one assumes that the poems of W B Yeats were on sale as well as *Prison Poems* by Bobby Sands.

During this period, the potential of the McNamara Hall as an earner of revenue was ingeniously explored. It was available to all-comers. During Claude Malone's time it had also become a venue for theatre, with Shane Connaughton, an actor and writer from Co. Cavan, bringing in productions. It had also been a regular venue for Karate and for boxing tournaments. Another potential was spotted in using it as a venue for Greek wedding receptions. This was a useful arrangement, because all the Centre was providing were the premises. A negotiation took place with a 'Michael', an elder in the Greek Orthodox Church in Peckham, South London. He arranged the events, hired the Greek caterers and the entertainers. Not only did they bring their own chefs, they also brought their own refreshments, with numerous bottles of whisky, vodka, gin and brandy placed on each table. These were huge affairs, with between 300 and 400 guests at a time, including a large number of children. The cleaners remember that they usually made a terrible mess. Nevertheless, they were excellent money earners, bringing in at least £1,000 cash on each occasion with very little effort on the part of the Centre, apart from that of the long-suffering cleaners.

In spite of the new variety of activities, the core social business continued. Bacon and cabbage suppers were less popular, particularly since the arrival of Saxon Inns, but the majority of county associations still held their dinners and dances in the McNamara. The Kennedy Hall was a smaller venue, but used for the same purpose. The Douglas Hyde Lounge was busy as a more informal venue and also the domain of the social club. They were all from time to time hired out for special functions.

As something of an experiment, on one night the McNamara was let out for a 'rave'. Once the reality of what was happening had sunk in, the latest bar manager for Saxon Inns, Martin, realised that although not much alcohol was being consumed there was a clamour for bottled water. He quickly increased the price of a bottle from 90p to £2.50p and when the empty bottles were collected he simply filled them with tap water and re-sold them over the counter. No one seemed to notice. The evening unfortunately turned nasty later on when there was a fight in the corridor which resulted in a stabbing. Police and an ambulance were called. A few drugs were found but no weapon.

This was the first and last rave. One reason was that the neighbours were once again angry at the noise and behaviour from such events that spilled down the steps and out into the street.

More problems with the neighbours

From time to time travellers' caravans were parked in Camden Square, creating a nuisance for residents. Their wedding receptions were still a problem. They were sometimes booked by a man in a suit whose appearance would not reveal his interest, although again the prospect of useful revenue was welcomed by those who also suspected that he might be a part of the travelling community. Because they were a useful source of revenue, they were at times kept secret from the administrative committee, which would have cancelled them. They paid top rates, on one occasion £4,500, in advance and in cash. Almost as a measure of their success, the police approached the Centre to ask whether they could observe from an upstairs window those who were arriving, but this request was refused.[22]

Travellers were separately alleged to be causing disruption locally, breaking into garages in St Augustine's Road and Agar Grove, and the Centre received some of the blame. However, when they came to the Centre for a drink, they were tolerated if they behaved, because a lot of money crossed the bar. Once or twice there were so many of them inside the building, however, that members of the Centre itself found that they had no room for themselves and made complaints.

On the whole the wedding receptions were reasonably quiet affairs, but occasionally there was trouble, including fights in the street outside. At a well-attended AGM in November 1991 of the Camden Square Neighbourhood Association at which Denis Cormican was present, David Grace reported that there was a group of drunken 'youths' persistently gathering in the Square near the Centre, who harassed and frightened local residents. They apparently came from other parts of Camden, such as Somers Town and the

Regent's Park estate, but it was thought that they had been thieving from the Centre. The police were regarded as completely ineffective in dealing with them. Members of the Association decided that they should write to their local ward councillors to see what they could do.[23]

On one occasion these young people were caught stealing cases of wine from the kitchen. Denis Cormican locked them in a room while the police were called, but they were finally allowed to go because of their youth. Fortunately, as Maeve Heath says, there was no more trouble.[24]

Radical options

The various crises that befell the Centre were crowned by the scale of its debt. The individual debt to the Oblate Fathers which had first been negotiated by Tom Scully was £300,000. There was trouble with the banks once again. Drastic measures were envisaged, including the sale of the building. This was not the first time that it had been suggested. It was estimated that it would now raise £900,000 on the open market, although a potential purchaser might be a housing association. This figure, however, was thought to be well under its market value. The McNamara Hall was even considered for offices. Another option was that it should relocate to the Van Zeit Centre in Arlington Road, which was a part of the church of Our Lady of Hal. One advantage, which was pointed out by the adherents of this plan was that this relocation would put it in the heart of Camden Town, closer to public transport links, and the relative compactness of the building would be sufficient for the core activities of the Centre and its welfare service.

Needless to say, there were some local residents in the Camden Square area who might have been hugely grateful to see the departure of the Centre.

The new constitution, first conceived by Father George Stack and coinciding with the change in legislation, had clarified the true ownership of the building, which many had thought was owned by the Diocese of Westminster. It was made clear that the London Irish Centre is owned by the Irish community of London, through its trustees as representatives, and the various committees that still surrounded it.

The Presidential visit

President Mary Robinson visited the Centre in May 1993, which was an opportunity to restore pride. In her honour Bridie Shaw pestered Denis Cormican to fly the Irish tricolour above the main entrance, and he had agreed to do so. She was extremely annoyed therefore when she arrived to help with the preparations for the visit to see that nothing had been done about it. Fortunately there was enough time for her to race home to collect her own tricolour, which with the help of a couple of ladders she had borrowed from the neighbours, she herself attached to the window above the entrance. She was only just in time because just ahead of the Presidential party arrived a photographer from the *Irish World*, who snapped her still up the ladder.[25]

As the Irish National Anthem was played on the flute by two young girls, the President of Ireland and the Ambassador, Joseph Small, were welcomed at Camden Square. Denis Cormican formally greeted her as the first president to visit Irish care agencies in Britain, and described the meeting as *"a great source of encouragement."* President Robinson, who had specifically asked to meet representatives from Irish welfare organisations, praised these groups for "reaching out" to every member of the Irish community in Britain. *"It is very central to my sense of being the President of Ireland that I communicate to you just*

Bridie Shaw raises the tricolour outside the London Irish Centre for the presidential visit, 1995.

President Mary Robinson.

how much you are valued and appreciated in Ireland."[26] There must have been some present who remembered the refusals of various Irish governments to acknowledge the debt they owed to the work that such Centres had done for their emigrants, not to mention the amount of remittances that had been sent home over many years.

The visit of the president marked a change in the fortunes of the Centre and of its director, Denis Cormican. He had laboured for over three years with a committee that had sometimes made his life very difficult, and he had felt trapped in administrative duties and dealing with the debt, rather than with the pastoral care that he preferred. Her visit to the Centre, however, implicitly marked the belated thanks of the Irish nation for what had

been achieved for its emigrants. Denis Cormican's efforts in changing the structure of the organisation to bring it into line with new charities legislation was some achievement.

The need for change

The Oblate provincial in the mid-1990s, Fr Tony Quinlan, later put it, *"The old model was of the priest-in-charge. These people were effective but they operated on a highly personalised basis. They operated with committees that existed in name but not in reality. The people on the committees were not strong, and they did not seek out professionals. Decisions could not be taken when he was absent. None were trained in management, but they took important decisions about building and then moved on, resigned or retired or left their successors to sort out. Decisions were taken single-handedly and not on a collaborative basis. Nowadays you have to operate collaboratively and facilitate others. You can't order people around any more. Young people tolerate authority rather than respect it now – the old type of operation is gone."* There were of course exceptions to this, at the London Irish Centre and elsewhere, but his remarks were well-timed. *"Oblates should work on the welfare side, not running bacon and cabbage dinners in a mausoleum built in the 1950s"*, he added.

However, at the end of Denis Cormican's assignment he was seen as "disillusioned and very tired". As Jim Myers has said, *"to live alone as a priest when things are going wrong must encourage depression if not the drink."*[27] It was indeed a very lonely period for the director and he finally left Camden Square "a broken man", and in need of a rest.

Before he left, a special cash collection was taken to buy him a present. This followed the precedent, for which special dispensation had to be sought from the provincial, of the gift for Paddy Sheridan. Oblates were normally not permitted to accept such favours. For Denis Cormican's leaving reception, members of his family crossed over from Co. Antrim to see him presented with three Waterford clocks.

It has been said that *"the trouble with priests is that they are too trusting."* Denis Cormican famously announced that he had been ordained to say Mass and hear confessions, and not to run a bar. During his time as director the Centre was regarded as being slackly managed but also well-intentioned. It desperately needed to be more focussed and businesslike. The changes that were made by the interventions of George Stack, its incoming trustees and accountants such as Paddy Keegan, all demanded by legislation and later sharpened by the arrival of Father Jerry Kivlehan, helped slowly to drag the London Irish Centre out of its long years of debt.

[1] *Cruel Fate* by Hugh Callaghan and Sally Mulready, published by Poolbeg, 1993.
[2] *Guardian*, 15 March 1991.
[3] Interview Sally Mulready, May 2004.
[4] Interview Maeve Heath, May 2004.
[5] Correspondence with Sally Mulready, July 2004.
[6] LIC minutes, 9 December 1986.
[7] Interview Jim Myers, May 2004.
[8] Interview Maeve Heath, April 2004
[9] Interview Bridie Shaw, May 2004.
[10] Interview Joe Davis, May 2004.
[11] Directors' minutes, 11 February 1992.
[12] Interview Maeve Heath, February 2004.
[13] Interview Joe Davis, May 2004
[14] LIC Council minutes, 4 June 1992.
[15] Administrative Committee minutes, 9 February 1993.
[16] Interview Peggy Campbell, March 2004.
[17] Interview Maeve Heath, January 2004.
[18] Interview Paddy Keegan, July 2004.
[19] Greater London House Conditions Survey 1985, Census Tabulation 1981, published by the GLC.
[20] 'The Voice of the Irish in Camden', Conference Report, August 1990.
[21] Issued by the Irish in Britain Representation Group in January 1996.
[22] Interview with Paddy Keegan, July 2004.
[23] CSNA minutes, 1991.
[24] Interview Maeve Heath, March 2004.
[25] Interview Bridie Shaw, May 2004.
[26] *Irish Times*, 28 May 1993.
[27] Interview Jim Myers, 2004.

CHAPTER TWELVE

A lot of different thinking

Father Jerry Kivlehan

After it was decided that Denis Cormican was leaving the Centre, Father Jerry Kivlehan was assigned by the provincial, Father Tony Quinlan, to be his successor. He was aware that Denis Cormican was looking forward to another assignment, and on his own arrival Jerry Kivlehan immediately informed the trustees and the advisory committee that he was not putting up with the sort of treatment that Denis Cormican had received. Jim Myers, who had been on the administrative committee as its Chair, said *"Jerry was a Godsend to this place."*[1]

As soon as Jerry Kivlehan arrived, he could see that changes were necessary in the way that the building was being managed. He noticed that there was a large amount of space committed to bar and catering, but there was clearly not

Fr Jerry Kivlehan

enough trade to deserve it. A number of people he met there had remarked that the crowds who once enjoyed the Centre for social and other functions were no longer coming. Many of them had moved away from Camden, and there were now other distractions. Even the county associations did not have the same attraction of companionship and identification that they once offered. Above all, as people were growing older they were less willing to come out for a social evening. *"I could see that a lot of different thinking was necessary"*, Jerry Kivlehan has said.[2] He realised that these patterns of change already had an effect on the viability of the building, and it could no longer be same kind of place. It had to adapt.

Questions about a future direction for the Centre and the role of its priests had been posed by Claude Malone twenty years earlier. More recently Fr Tony Quinlan had seen a way forward. The need for an appraisal had surfaced during Denis Cormican's time as a result of the new charities legislation, but it was unfortunate that he had to face a powerful reaction from some vocal members of the administrative committee who expected the Centre somehow to continue as it always had. Unfortunately he was also preoccupied by the huge debt, so his energies were more directed towards reducing that rather than in accommodating the social, demographic and perhaps even religious changes among the Irish community.

As the previous provincial, Paul Byrne has said that *"My frustration particularly in the case of Denis Cormican was we felt Oblate directors were always over-worked and they were always underpaid. He was the bar manager, he was the debt manager, he ran the cultural side of things, he ran the whole welfare side, which was becoming increasingly difficult to fund, and increasingly unswerable to the bureaucracy. He*

would be managing the grants, managing the staff and on top of that had a huge debt, and what he had was not always a great a management committee because it was elected by the council at the AGM. There was the frustration that we were not the managers. One of the very great things that Jerry Kivlehan did was to turn the constitution upside down." This final point was not entirely accurate, because some of the changes had been provoked by the new legislation and were already being implemented.

A change in the constitution

Established forty years before, under Tom McNamara, the council and the administrative committee had been designed to spread power by including a wide range of Irish organisations from the Irish Club to the GAA, to corporations like Aer Lingus and to all thirty-two county associations. Protecting the building was one intention. *"They realised then that they had a valuable physical asset"*, said Paul Byrne. *"There was always a danger in Irish circles that some thief would take it over. On top of that there were the trustees, who initially were the church authorities, the Archbishop of Westminster, the Bishop of Southwark and the Bishop of Brentwood. They were recognised in name only. They were there as troubleshooters to pull the thing out of the fire if necessary".[3]*

Jerry Kivlehan could recognise a challenge when he saw one. His arrival brought a new, strategic sense to the Centre.

He is a Sligo man, from Strandhill, and it was there that he was later ordained. He completed his secondary education at Summerhill College in 1966, and at eighteen continued in Dublin at Milltown Park Jesuit College where he studied Theology. He had six months left at the end of his theology studies and spent this at the Irish School of Ecumenics, a part of University

College, Dublin, where he examined the work of other denominations in Ireland. As a field study he undertook the influence of Methodism, and did a project on the sermons in Ireland of John Wesley. A well-travelled man, Wesley visited Ireland forty-two times between 1747 and 1789, so there must have been many sermons.

When Jerry Kivlehan later arrived in England, this work had gone before him, and he found that he was invited to speak at a number of Methodist churches. Wesley's pastoral missions amongst the poor must have been something of an inspiration for the young man wishing to becoming a priest, for as he says, *"The thing that motivated me more that anything else was that the order I belonged to, the Oblates, was dedicated to working among the poor and marginalised, but also all of my life I had wanted to work in areas where I would make a difference to people's lives, and try to improve the quality of life for people."*[4] He has added that he feels that at the London Irish Centre he has been able to do that.

Before he came to Camden Square, Jerry Kivlehan spent six years from 1973 at St Anne's in Rockferry in Birkenhead as a parish priest. Here the two major employers, Cammel Laird and North Western Ship Repairers, were entering a serious period of decline, with thousands of workers being made redundant. Younger people also obviously suffered. He decided to get involved with different agencies to find ways of creating training schemes and other employment opportunities, not an easy task in the debilitating context of Merseyside at that time. He trained as a youth and community worker and also became a tutor training youth workers for the local authority. Since then his work has always been focussed on welfare and community development.

A spell at Belmont College followed, after which he returned to the same part of England to develop a Retreat and Conference Centre near Nantwich in Cheshire. Here, as director, he ran self-development and community leadership courses. Remaining in that area he was then assigned to another parish, St Teresa's in Norris Green in Liverpool. This was located in a large housing estate just outside the City centre, and had particular problems of deprivation and the social issues that often stem from it.

With a background in diverse community work, it is clear why the provincial, Tony Quinlan, had picked him. Soon after he arrived, Jerry Kivlehan said, *"There are so many different aspects to the job here. We have based in this building a number of different projects which address the needs of the Irish community, not just in Camden but across London. We also have a range of cultural programmes, and our role is very much about trying to present a positive image of Ireland and its people."* He added, *"The recent IRA bombings make the job harder in a context of increased prejudice against the Irish. The Centre is often called upon by the media to be the voice of the Irish in London, and we let them know that our community desperately wants peace in Ireland and wants to make an effective contribution to that."*

Interestingly, Jerry Kivlehan has since mentioned that the Oblates were at this stage considering that perhaps the order's ministry at the Centre might have come to an end, and after the departure of Denis Cormican it might have been appropriate to make a change. *"I think the Oblates had a view and a strategy that eventually we would endeavour to resolve the problems that existed around the Centre, and having done so we would take it to a point where it was in a good condition, the building, the management structure and the finances, and then it would be an appropriate time to move away from Camden Square".*[5] However, this plan was not implemented, at least at this time, and he arrived at the front door in September 1994.

Like his predecessor, Jerry Kivlehan was on his own, living in the house in Murray Street. He had no support from chaplains, because there was no appropriate person available among the Oblates.

The need for new catering arrangements

A start had been made by Denis Cormican on the new constitution. Jerry Kivlehan realised that this could only be continued with immense tact and persuasion, but first he should try to resolve the disastrous impacts around the catering arrangements. These had serious effects on the debt, the sort of use of the Centre and its wider reputation among the politicians in Dublin and Camden, the clergy and lay people. He privately felt that there was too much emphasis on bars and catering, which really distracted the centre from its primary function of providing support and care for the Irish community. Many younger Irish people, the people who might have used the bars, had now moved away to bars elsewhere, leaving behind the first and second generations. It was these older people who now also needed support from the Community Services Department of the Centre and other voluntary agencies.

At the time of the decision, it had been sensible and some would say unavoidable to franchise out the bars and the catering, and the choice of Saxon Inns was later regretted. The company had not performed well, and relations were poor if not disastrous. As well, there were there issues of security and stock. Despite promises by the company to supervise the behaviour of customers leaving the building at night the neighbours were sometimes disturbed. The exit from the McNamara Hall into Murray Mews had been a particular concern.

Saxon Inns had been in charge of the catering and bars for two years before Jerry Kivlehan arrived. Somewhat predictably, because its performance elsewhere was not much better, it was then taken into receivership and placed into the hands of the administrators Ernst and Young in February 1996, to be broken up.

Mercury Management, a bar management company which was based in Staffordshire, bought the assets of Saxon Inns which included its franchise at Camden Square. It then negotiated for a reduced contract in the region of £30,000 a year. However, this appeared to be a jump from the frying-pan into the fire. The company is immodestly described on its website as "one of the largest specialist licensing consultancy service providers", but in spite of this claim there was little improvement in performance. It appointed five different managers at the Centre within fifteen months, and it was still unable to control the noise and supervise customers. Within a year the company realised that it was not making a profit. In time, Mercury Management terminated its agreement, but it then sued the Centre for breach of contract.

Rather than renegotiate its terms of contract, the company chose to put a case against Jerry Kivlehan personally through the Crown Court in Manchester. The charge was one of 'fraudulent inducement'. The accusation was that he had misled them. It alleged that when it had been considering its contract with the Centre he had informed it that the business had potential. He does not deny this, but he also had been unable to see the trading accounts in the books of Saxon Inns, and so this was speculation. However Mercury Management, when it took over Saxon Inns' business, did ensure that the former company's accounts had been available to its own accountants.

Mercury Management eventually dropped its case.

The company decided to take direct action. One morning soon after the hearing, Jerry Kivlehan was astonished to come across four Transit vans, driven down from Staffordshire, parked outside the building. The intention was to remove all the stock and the bar fittings. Mercury Management owed the Centre about £12,000, and there was a similar value to their stock on the premises. Fortunately he managed to prevent the drivers from entering and they returned up the motorway empty-handed.

With help from one of the new trustees, he immediately changed all the locks on the bars and other doors. There was a wedding reception booked for that afternoon, for which it might have been a problem if there had been nothing in the bar.

When the contract from Mercury Management was terminated, the control of the bars reverted to the Centre itself. This was a temporary arrangement, so a manager had to be directly employed. Two catering firms were engaged to provide the dinners in the McNamara and other halls for the county association dances, wedding receptions and other functions. It was a hands-on time for Jerry Kivlehan. Its value was that gradually during this period the Centre ran the catering and bar management itself, and was able to put good systems of management in place. It was also a time for the new director to look around and take stock. Things got back on track. In due course Terry McEneaney, a Waterford man with a long history in the licensed trade, was appointed to take charge in 2002.

The control of disturbance

The troubled relationship with local residents, which had recurred sporadically over the years, had been exacerbated by the poor supervision by both Saxon Inns and Mercury Management. Jerry Kivlehan has said, "*When I came here there was a lot of difficulty with the neighbours. The reason being that Irish people were not using the Centre as much as before, so Saxon Inns and Mercury had to market to a broader community. As a result, people leaving the Centre just didn't care, it was another venue*".[6] To reach a broader community, Saxon Inns had even experimented with a gala dinner, followed by the culturally insensitive Bernard Manning as cabaret, for its customers. Jerry Kivlehan was very aware that he was not the first director to experience difficulties of this sort.

In November 1995, Camden's Licensing Committee reduced the hours of a late Public Entertainment Licence because of "excessive noise, brawls and lewd behaviour". A deputation to the meeting said that the Centre had become a problem in recent years. "*Saxon Inns had been contracted to boost the number of private functions. There was a consistent lack of supervision by door staff. The worst disruption had come during three travellers' weddings, after which there were fights in the street. At one point it was so bad that there were thirty-five police cars lining the streets in case of trouble*", said a neighbour, Bob Buchanan, who at the meeting read from a statement prepared by the objectors.

Jerry Kivlehan maintained that the London Irish Centre was being victimised by local residents and by Camden Council because it also held functions for travellers. "*The hearing was grossly unfair because it concentrated on three functions for travellers, which is not our main business. We feel we are being victimised because of the sensitivity we show towards minority groups.*"[7] He added that residents had "*grossly exaggerated*" the true situation. "*We try to be sensitive to minority people but were disappointed with what had hap-*

pened". Asked why the travellers were allowed back, he said that sometimes they got someone else to make the booking for them.[8]

In the past the bar staff had also tended to encourage the guests to keep drinking for as long as possible, because then they would be quiet. If there were fights, they were usually provoked by the women or the children. Sometimes the party would last until the early hours.

There is a lighter side to the travellers' nuptials. At one reception the bride, having climbed out of a be-ribboned Rolls Royce in her bridal dress, "fell up" the steps to the building. After she had changed in the ladies' toilet, the elaborate and expensive dress was stuffed into a black bin bag. By chance it was required for another bride at a wedding in Newcastle a few days later. Unfortunately the black bag was forgotten, but it was later placed outside with others for the council rubbish collection. When the travelling family realised that they had no bridal dress for the next wedding they threatened to return. Perhaps reading the nature of the threat correctly, Maeve Heath and Hilary Collis, the manager from Saxon Inns, chased after the dust-cart to the dump but were unable to locate the black bag which contained the dress. The cost had to be reimbursed.[9]

In April 1996 the Centre appealed against the reduction in the licensed hours. The council enlisted the support of local residents, who had been amusingly if inaccurately described as "claret heads", to the hearing. In the face of this anticipated opposition the Centre withdrew. Jerry Kivlehan has since admitted that Saxon Inns had been brought in to manage functions three years before, *"Because the Centre was having difficulties finding revenue to subsidise its own charitable activities. Following complaints, it had already spent*

£1,900 to quieten the air conditioning and had appointed an acoustic expert to advise on changes to reduce noise."[10] A number of residents had been earlier invited to meet Hilary Collis to discuss their concerns, but no changes were made as a result.

At one point the Camden Square Neighbourhood Association arranged a protest meeting. It invited Frank Dobson, the local MP. It was unfortunate that he arrived late, but he also had to leave early to return to the House of Commons. Those in the know suspected that he was in a dilemma between his conscience regarding minority groups and the political need to placate some vocal constituents.

Now that the travelling community in Camden is relatively settled, with two or three fixed sites in the borough, the conflict between it and residents of Camden Square seems to have subsided. The changes in the use of the Centre, largely the result of evolving demographics and patterns of behaviour, have undoubtedly helped. The disappearance of cabarets, youth clubs, discos and other noisier events has made a difference. One presumes that the new manager, Terry McEneaney, would think twice about permitting events which might reopen such a risk. What have also helped are the Bengali or Somali wedding receptions at which alcohol is never an issue.

"I think that there have always been a number who were uncomfortable with the Centre for a variety of reasons", Jerry Kivlehan has since reflected. *"I assume that the greatest reason was that some disturbance would take place as people were leaving the Centre at night. But having said that, even when complaints were coming from some neighbours we would also receive a lot of encouragement and support from others. It was always the case that those who were more for the Centre remained silent and those who were not in favour of the Centre*

spoke the loudest."[11] There is no doubt that relationships between the Centre and local residents have improved.

The Beerel Report

Changing the constitution was a formidable task. It was to become not so much a change to follow the law, but a more fundamental review of structures which would revitalise the organisation of the Centre and the services it provided. Jerry Kivlehan says,*"The administrative committee probably saw me coming. I had a reasonable knowledge of charity management at various levels because of my involvement in charities over the years in north-west England. However a lot of people who had been here for a good number of years felt that this fellow was going to turn the place upside down. The tendency was to react to this change."*[12] He requested support from Niall Gallagher of the Allied Irish Bank to enable the Centre to carry out an evaluation of the services provided, and to enable it to employ a business consultant. Niall Gallagher introduced him to Annabel Beerel. She was commissioned and her report was delivered in April 1996.

This made some pertinent observations. She noted that the age group using the Centre the least was the middle aged, the forty to fifty-year-olds who were in the prime of their life, approaching the height of their earning powers and often in decision-making positions; the building itself was in a poor state of repair, and what used to be a *"vibrant thriving centre is now an erratically used sombre place"*; the Centre placed *"a greater emphasis on the social side than the welfare and cultural aspects."*[13]

Various options were discussed. A complete overhaul of the constitution was the first, but this was already in progress. The scope for clearing the debt created by a sale of no. 52 Camden Square, which Irish Centre Housing under Patsy Carolan was possibly considering for purchase, was another. If this took place, the welfare section would remain at no. 50 Camden Square, with a relocation of the Centre's social activities to the Van Zeit Centre in Arlington Road, in the centre of Camden Town. There were other permutations on this arrangement, which was not altogether a new idea. On the administrative committee many supported these proposals, but some including Bridie Shaw and Donie Egan disagreed. The disposal of no. 12 Murray Street was a certainty. After this, Jerry Kivlehan would have to move to the presbytery in Quex Road.

Annabel Beerel proposed the separation of the revenue streams which were coming through the bars and catering and hire of rooms, from the grants or charitable funds which were funding the welfare service. The cultural events, such as the Irish Bookfair and the musical performances, she felt should continue. Interestingly she noticed how the three different activities, the social, the welfare and the cultural, rarely overlapped in terms of users. Although there were a few individual exceptions, most people visited the centre for just one of these three reasons.

Fortunately, many of her recommendations coincided with the new legislation which ended the confused role of the trustees and patrons. The Archbishop of Westminster and the Bishops of Southwark and Brentwood, who were once so committed to the establishment of the Centre forty years before, had been replaced many times. The current incumbents, who included Cardinal Basil Hume, were now relatively remote. The legislation said that trustees should take a much more direct role in the administration of the charity. Monsignor George Stack, who was Cardinal Hume's representative, wrote to the trustees who were all willing to resign.

Their replacements, some of whom had already been approached by Denis Cormican, included Lord Farnham, who had property in Co. Cavan, and Philip Fitzpatrick, who had replaced his late brother. There was also John Higgins, a businessman, and Fr Paul Byrne of the Irish Episcopal Commission for Emigrants. Paul Byrne was the only religious figure in this group, a man of great experience with an understanding of the changing needs of the Irish emigrant community. In effect, the new trustees worked as associate directors, and took over many of the decisions that had been previously handled by the committees. They were given an oversight of the accounts, took an interest in the uses for the building and dealt with any problems brought to them by the director.

Perhaps surprisingly, considering the original objectives of the Centre, the first constitution had no religious dimension, apart from the appointment of bishops as trustees. At different times, individual directors and chaplains would give this aspect of their work a greater or lesser emphasis, but the purpose of the building was also to provide a welfare service for Irish people, assist with housing, develop cultural activities and offer a place for people to meet. This was the brief that Jerry Kivlehan had assumed. He regarded the Irish community now as extremely diverse, with a variety of shades of opinion, thoughts and outlooks, and his wish was to be inclusive to all.

This was also the time that Lord Longford finally stepped down as president. Since 1956 he had held this position, a figure-head but at times a source of guidance. He was of course highly respected in Catholic circles, but at the Centre his eccentricities were beginning to be noticed. Although he lived in Chelsea and later in Chiswick, for his journey to or from Camden Square he used to ask the Centre before a meeting to pay his fares or to arrange his collection from home and return him afterwards, which Paddy Keegan maintains was partly because he wanted to catch up during the journey on the gossip of what had been happening. Lord Longford's request was declined by some because it meant they could not have a drink beforehand, but he was willingly taken by Frank Ryan who was a Pioneer. During the changing and often difficult periods, Lord Longford's presidency had provided some stability for the Centre.

A time to clear the debt

Once the constitutional issues were being tackled, for which a lawyer provided *pro bono* advice, there was the question of the debt. As Jerry Kivlehan says, *"When I came the debt here was somewhere around £400,000. It was a big burden on the Centre, particularly at a time when its services with the bar and catering area were not performing very well. The Centre also had the house across the road which had to go, so we looked at ways to clear the debt. I would think that about 1998 we had all the debt cleared, and that gave us the great opportunity to start looking at future development."*[14] The Murray Street house was valued at £180,000, but the trustees insisted that it went for auction where it raised £228,000. The debt to the Oblates was also cleared.

A business plan was designed to steer the way forward. Before this could be done the entire building and the services within it had to be professionalised, from its management right through to the role of the surviving committees and the delivery of the services themselves. A complete restructuring was carried out. This soon placed the Centre in a much more favourable position to bid for funding from the Community Fund and other bodies such as the National Lottery.

A sale of the Camden Square premises was ruled out, because it was seen easier to balance the books by other means. Grant aid from the Irish Soldiers' and Sailors' Land Trust Fund was used to refurbish the derelict rooms upstairs, which had been part of the previous hostel accommodation, so that they could be now rented to Irish organisations, some of whom had been using the premises until then at no charge.

It was also time to divest the Centre of two of its bars or halls, and return to the core business.

In the winter of 1999 the Kennedy Hall was leased to a Spanish group affiliated to the Embassy. The Centro Social de Mayores 'Miguel de Cervantes', is a social group at which Spanish elders are involved in joint activities and converse in their own language. The Douglas Hyde Lounge was leased to Camden Women's Aid, a partnership between Camden Safety Net and the council and funded by Neighbourhood Renewal. In some ways they are reminiscent of two of the original purposes of the Irish Centre, one where emigrants may meet and the other where disadvantaged people may receive advice.

The Migrant Training Company

One of the organisations with premises in the Centre was the Migrant Training Company. This had been established in 1989 to provide emigrants with IT and computing skills as well as engineering, childcare, nursing and hotel management training to compete for jobs which offered career prospects. Some £418,000 had been granted to the Migrant Training Company from the European Social Fund, which had been match-funded by companies such as Aer Lingus and Toyota, thanks to the efforts of Tommy Dunne, and nine London boroughs, including Camden, in the form of resources.

A newly equipped training area was fitted out at the Centre and operated successfully. However, soon after Jerry Kivlehan arrived it was on the move into new premises, and Camden Council was considering the withdrawal of its grant. At the same time, Irish Centre Housing had developed its own training and employment arm, to be known as Job Powerhouse, which took over this part of the building.

As a rising star of Tony Blair's Shadow Cabinet, Mo Mowlam, MP, anticipated a senior position when Labour came to power. She had looked forward to the Foreign Office as her destination.[15] She was slightly taken aback, therefore, to be offered the shadow Northern Ireland Secretary post in 1996, replacing Kevin McNamara who was greatly appreciated by the Irish community but was also regarded as too close to the nationalist persuasion.

Her first official visit with this portfolio was to Camden Square to present certificates to the latest graduates of the Migrant Training Company. Jerry Kivlehan remembers her *"treading very gingerly"* on Irish sensitivities when she entered the building with her special adviser. She made a careful speech before she handed out the certificates, which she opened by claiming it was such an honour to speak here in the McNamara Hall which had been named after her predecessor, Kevin. Her advisers could have briefed her better.

New priorities for welfare

When Jerry Kivlehan had first arrived, the welfare team at the Centre consisted of just five people. The client base had changed from former days when many callers were employable and needed housing. The 1960s had usually been an era of optimism.

Mo Mowlam's visit to the London Irish Centre, 1996. From left to right are Jerry Kivlehan, Hilda McCafferty, Chair of Migrant Training, John McDonnell MP, Cllr Dave Horan of Camden, and Dr Mohammad Sadiq, Scheme Director of Migrant Training.

Although the causes of disadvantage may have changed, the same conditions for deprivation existed. As Jerry Kivlehan told the *Irish Post*, *"That is the first thing that struck me when I took up this job ten months ago – the number of people still coming over. The popular perception is that emigration from Ireland has decreased but that is not reflected in the numbers coming to us,"* He mentioned two distinct categories of Irish emigrants. The first arrived well-prepared, highly motivated and with plans generally well laid out for work and housing.*"A significant number of them would have tried to get work in Ireland and failed"*, he observed.*"There is a still a re-*

cession on there and even these people will struggle for some time in London before getting the start they are looking for. Then there were the other kinds of emigrants who, for a variety of reasons, felt compelled to leave Ireland at short notice with little thought or preparation for what awaited them on the other side of the Irish Sea."[16]

There were now also elders who had made little or no provision for their retirement. Women were also living to a much greater age and often alone. Some of the men who had worked on the lump under false names were not receiving the full benefits to which they may have been entitled. Advice on how to access these benefits was vital to improve the quality of their lives, but the government had tightened the criteria. Jerry Kivlehan had noticed this early on. *"There are an increasing number of elderly Irish people living in London who are struggling to exist in poor quality housing and, unless these people have budgeted and planned for their retirement, there really is not enough from state benefits for them to survive on."* He illustrated this with a recent story. *"It was horrific. An elderly Irishman arrived here one Saturday night after coming out of hospital having had an eye operation and finding that all of his possessions had been dumped in a bag outside his flat, which his landlord had re-let to someone else. The poor man had been too ill to draw his pension, and could not pay his rent. His landlord could not have cared less and just wanted him out. We put him into emergency accommodation and found him somewhere more long-term. Without our help he could not have handled the situation as he had no-one else to turn to."*[17] The London Irish Elders' Forum is also based at Camden Square, giving advice to such callers.

The first grant from the Dion Committee in 1984 had been achieved largely as a result of lobbying from the London Irish Centre over very many years. From then on this became a vital, although fluctuating, source of funds. It stood at about £70,000 until more recent increases were awarded.

It was Fr Ambrose Woods from Southwark who had first approached the Irish government for resources in 1950. Almost every chaplain or director of the Centre had followed the beseeching route to Dublin. The intransigence of successive governments became notorious, particularly when Jack Lynch's Fianna Fail refused to match the National Collection of 1971. In addition to the directors of the Centre, key clerical figures in the welfare

of emigrants, from Eamonn Casey to Paul Byrne and many others, campaigned incessantly for government support for those who were once called 'exiles'.

In 1995 the Dion Committee awarded a grant to the Centre of £62,000 as a contribution to salaries and overheads for social workers. One of these, Mairead Carney, was a resettlement worker with a slightly different emphasis on her work. She was aware of a number of people visiting the Centre with specific needs related to alcohol or drug abuse, mental health problems and other factors.*"My job is here because there are now so many under 25s turning up at the Centre. About 75% of our clients are homeless or have housing problems and, of these, a growing number are young people. I would estimate that a quarter of the people on our books are between 16 and 25 years of age. The Irish Centre and other voluntary agencies are having to take the flak for government cutbacks."* On her first day in the job three college students from Kerry showed up just off the boat in need of accommodation and advice about finding summer jobs. Some clients were homeless or in unsatisfactory accommodation. Others, especially single women with young children, had problems coping emotionally in low-rent private accommodation. Some were drug users who had fled because of vigilante activity against suspected drug dealers. She added, *"Some drug users I see left Dublin because of harassment. London is the cheapest place for them to come to, and it's safe because it is so big."* Drug users received a non-judgemental service at the Centre, dealing realistically with drug abuse.[18]

The grant from the Irish Soldiers' and Sailors' Land Trust Fund was also used to expand the welfare team from three advice workers to five in order that they could now specialise. The team had also noticed that, over time, there had been an increase of callers who were not Irish.

A business plan

With this help, a five-year business plan was developed, which considered a range of needs which would reach the needs of the Irish community. *"Over the years the High and Dry Club, the Day Centre, the Outreach services, the setting up of an office in Kilburn with a volunteer project that is based there. We also developed a Healthy Living Centre here and also a service to those who are the victims of, or the survivors of, institutional life in Ireland."* [19] This project, known as LISOS, gives information and advice on redress or compensation and other claims.

These projects are funded by grants and charitable foundations. For example Camden and Islington Health Authority have funded the post of a mental health outreach worker, a sessional worker for the High and Dry Club is funded by the Health Action Zone, Camden Council has funded an alcohol assessment service, and an Oblate Trust is developing the volunteer programme. With regard to Camden, Jerry Kivlehan says, *"I appreciate the situation here because of the high number of ethnic minority groups and the council has to be sensitive to this. But we could always do better."* Camden's annual grant to the Centre, through its Voluntary Sector Unit, is currently around £44,000.

Using the refurbished offices, a variety of agencies and activities are now based at the Centre, some of which rent rooms and offices to carry out their work. Some of these such as the Federation of Irish Societies, the Irish Chaplaincy, the Camden Elderly Irish Network or Solas Anois, a domestic violence project, are relatively independent of the structures of the Centre, but others such as the Healthy Living Centre are part of the Centre's own services. The welfare team under John Twomey has now risen from five to sixteen people, and in 2000 won the *Irish Post* Millennium Award for their services to the community. To demonstrate equality of opportunity, perhaps, the centre also won an *Irish World* Community Award in 2004.

Another moment of recognition which should not be forgotten was the surprise birthday party for Mary Kenny in December 1996. After her last bingo call she walked downstairs to be surprised by one hundred and fifty people, who included the Ambassador Ted Barrington. *"It's people like Mary who keep the community together"*, said Cllr Gloria Lazenby, Camden's Mayor.[20]

An important figure in the fund-raising process is the Head of Development, Paul Murphy. The annual amount raised by the Centre, exclusively for welfare purposes, is now around £650,000 which is granted from a wide variety of sources. As Jerry Kivlehan says, *"I am a great believer that all development must be planned to allow structured development, and then when the plan is in place the project is good. We can see how it can deliver clear outcomes, and then we go looking for funding for it."*[21] In May 1997 the National Lottery provided the funding for the refurbished luncheon club and drop-in centre.

In its concern for the marginalised, the Centre has consistently identified with the welfare and rights of travellers. The issue had not entirely retreated from Camden Square with their wedding parties. The Centre was chosen as a venue to launch a report, 'Rights for Travellers', on 11 December 1995. This had been based upon the results of a London-wide survey carried out by the London Irish Women's Centre.[22] Research was collated prior to the introduction of the Criminal Justice and Public Order Act, which had repealed a previous Act that had previously made it mandatory for local authorities to provide sites for travellers.[23]

Room for meetings

At the same time the building was still available for political meetings, but not for political party meetings. For this reason Sinn Fein had at one time been banned from meeting here, but the cease-fire in Ireland meant that this could be relaxed, just as the British government had begun to recognise the potential for leadership in the Peace Process of members from this party.

The broadcasting ban on Gerry Adams was lifted in January 1994 and a visa to visit the United States was extended later in that month, despite protests from Unionists, and he went to New York. In October he visited Washington. In late October Prime Minister John Major lifted the exclusion order on him and Martin McGuinness, and they came to London.

A rally of Sinn Fein supporters which took place in the Centre on 18 November 1994 was attended by Gerry Adams. It had been arranged in the McNamara Hall to celebrate the Peace Process and the lifting of the exclusion order. Outside, the *An Phoblacht* and the inevitable *Socialist Worker* newspaper sellers were in force, and in what must have been a rare sight outside a political meeting there were also ticket touts selling the £5 entry tickets for £15.

It was clear that this was going to be a massive event. Unfortunately, the Douglas Hyde Lounge had already been booked for a dance. Additional bar staff were hastily phoned, and asked to come in. As Maeve Heath has said, *"The place was mobbed that night."*[24] The McNamara Hall, where a band performed on the stage, was packed, and the Kennedy had to be used for the overspill. The bars were described as *"selling out of everything. There was no time to pour out pints, so we were just handing out bottles."*[25] At 10.00 pm Gerry Adams himself stepped onto the stage, while the press photographers jostled for the best angles. He made a speech praising Britain's Irish community for its part in moving forward the Peace Process, and followed with a list of the reasons down the years for emigration: "Famine, repression, civil war and the Treaty". He could of course have added economic depression and an encouragement in Ireland to escape from this. He ended with the hope that people may soon one day return to a united country, and added that Unionists have as much right as anybody, "but no more", to live in Ireland. At the end of the evening he slipped out into Murray Mews.

On another occasion he came to London to launch one of his books at the House of Commons, which had been arranged through Jeremy Corbyn, MP. The Whips prevented the event in Westminster, and a new venue had to be hastily substituted. This was the London Irish Centre, which

Gerry Adams, MP, adjusting his microphone at the London Irish Centre.

provided rooms for a less massive but more serious crowd than on the previous occasion.

Jerry Kivlehan says, "There is an *aspect of life at the Centre that was probably undervalued within the Irish community. The building provided a place and space for real dialogue to take place for groups within the Irish community itself and between the Irish community and other groups within British society regarding the issues of northern Ireland. I am absolutely convinced that those meetings and discussions ultimately made a big impact on the Peace Process that later developed. I think also the fact that the centre was courageous enough to host these for a start, and secondly that it facilitated a number of key players in political life in northern Ireland to speak here, that they were able to be listened to but also challenged in their point of view."*[26] The Centre now remains open to a range of speakers of all political colours.

Because it provided an accessible and well-known venue to groups which could not afford West End charges, a number of campaigning bodies used it for their regular meetings. *"The SDLP had always been at the Bookfair, which always ended with a discussion involving speakers from here and from northern Ireland. At different times virtually all the key players were here, from John Hume and Brid Rogers of the SDLP to Mo Mowlam. Kevin McNamara also came, in fact he hosted one of the conferences we held on northern Ireland. Mitchell McLoughlin of Sinn Fein announced two Cease Fires from the London Irish Centre."*[27]

There was a conference in June 1996 called 'Options for a Lasting Peace in Ireland'. As Kate Foley, one of its organisers has written,*"It did capture a real moment of optimism. We were hoping and expecting to see a Labour government very shortly, and there was a great expectancy* that change was both possible and likely. One of the really positive things of the Agreed Ireland Forum was that it managed to win respect and trust from all sides. We therefore had Unionist and Loyalist groups as well as Republicans and Nationalists. Negotiation and compromise were required, but the process would need human rights and equalities guarantees built into it."* She adds, *"Jerry Kivlehan was always very supportive about us using the Centre. The conferences didn't make any money, but we did not have any to start with. Because of the essentially political nature of what we were doing, none of the charitable foundations would touch us. Jerry was helpful and accommodating".*[28] In spite of the non-appearance of Mo Mowlam and John Hume, who had sent letters of apology, this conference was regarded as something of a break-through.

The view of the director is that these events were important. *"While a lot of people think that all of the Peace Process was worked out at government level, the impact of organisations at the base, and concerned people, also had a part to play in creating the environment of the Peace Process to happen. I think that really needs to be acknowledged."*[29] Very much a part of this was the campaigning against such measures as the PTA and against the miscarriages of justice. As Kate Foley says, *"We carried on using the Centre for meetings and we founded (rather grandly) the Britain and Ireland Human Rights Centre. That group was instrumental in lobbying international bodies around human rights concerns. Paul May, of the Guildford Four campaign, played a big part, as did Fr Gerry McFlynn of the Irish Commission for Prisoners Overseas. We campaigned on various miscarriage of justice cases, including the period when Roisin McAliskey was held in Holloway Prison."*[30] The late Paul Foot was often in the Centre at meetings of the campaign on behalf of the Bridgewater Four.

Jerry Kivlehan never forgets that, although he wears many different hats, he is also an ordained priest. With members of the Council of Irish County Associations he travelled to Omagh in Co. Tyrone to participate in the commemorative open air Mass on 15 August 1999, one year after the devastation of the Real IRA bomb. Over two years later, he presided at the funeral Mass in February 2002 of the valiant Sister Sarah Clarke, Gerry Conlon's *"This wee Irish nun, who is a kind of mighty atom."*[31] A few months later, in August, he officiated at the funeral Mass of Paddy Maguire, husband of Annie Maguire, at the church of the Immaculate Heart of Mary in Kilburn. It was Sr Sarah Clarke's commitment to Giuseppe Conlon that had brought her into contact with the Maguire family. President Mary McAleese was represented at the Mass, as was the Ambassador. Jerry Kivlehan later said that *"The family had to endure huge injustice and trauma during one of the most regrettable times in Irish life in Britain."*[32]

Although there was a natural pre-occupation with Irish politics, the Centre was not immune from the British variety. Ken Livingstone had been to Camden Square many times as a Camden councillor and as GLC Leader. He returned as part of the hustings during the election campaign in 2000 for his first mayoral bid. With him were the other candidates. *"I think that because all the candidates turned up for the event meant that they did appreciate that the Irish community was a significant community. And that their vote could make a difference to them. I thought the most interesting thing about the evening was that they were so positive about the role played by the Irish in London life."*[33] As politicians, they would of course be saying precisely that if they wanted the important Irish vote.

The political meetings continue. The families of the Derry victims of 'Bloody Sunday' have held rallies here, and many others have made use of its facilities. The very last speaking appearance of the northern Irish lawyer, Rosemary Nelson, was held in the Douglas Hyde Lounge with residents from Garvaghy Road in Portadown, only a week before she was murdered in 1999.

These meetings have led to obvious consequences. During the Troubles the Centre had attracted the interest of the police. Even while the Peace Process was slowly moving forward, their curiosity continued.

One night in 1995 Jerry Kivlehan returned to his flat on the other side of Murray Street to discover that he had been burgled. *"Documents and a camera were taken. Money and other items of value were not touched, no, which makes me think that it wasn't petty theft. It was very clinically done, there was no indication of a break-in."* On another occasion the staff arrived at the welfare office one morning to discover somebody had broken in overnight. All the computer leads had been cut and the computers themselves removed. They were missing for two days and then returned in perfect working order, but carefully placed across the road, on the pavement outside the children's playground in Camden Square. The staff picked them up and put new leads on them and they worked once again. As Jerry Kivlehan says, *"There was nothing on them, only a lot of professional advice to welfare clients."*[34]

The Green Ink Bookfair

Irish politics, literature and the arts have been symbiotically linked for centuries. The 1994 Green Ink Bookfair was opened by Hugh Callaghan, one of the Birmingham Six, who had written his story with Sally Mulready, and Niamh Cusack, the actress. It was later joined by the authors,

Tim Pat Coogan and Robert Kee, and by Bernadette McAliskey.

At another, Tom McCartan, one of the organisers, announced, "It is a celebration of Irish culture and maybe, more importantly, a celebration of its survival, and in fact its growth in all its forms, particularly here in Britain. This is an important time for the Irish with respect to the recent ending of the ceasefire. Now, more than ever, Irish people need to gather together to discuss their political direction and to enjoy and extol their culture."[35] The last Bookfair, in 2002, featured the Fermanagh actor Adrian Dunbar and Kieran Prendiville, the television writer.

While the Bookfair has died, largely as a result of publishers preferring to mount similar events and the loss of a grant, the cultural medium has slipped gracefully from words to music.

Return to Camden Town

Overlapping it by a couple of years, the 'Return to Camden Town Festival of Traditional Irish Music, Song and Dance' has now replaced the Bookfair as the largest cultural event of the Centre's year. With a quiet beginning in October 1999, it has since grown rapidly. It now continues for ten days and reached beyond Camden Square to other venues in Camden Town, such as Camden Lock, the Shaw Theatre in Euston Road and Cecil Sharp House in Primrose Hill. Its origins are in the legacy of Tommy Maguire and the young musicians that he taught in the 1960s and 1970s. One of them, Karen Ryan, took on Tommy Maguire's inspiration to create, with Geoff Holland and the support of the Centre, the 'Return to Camden Town' festival.

Karen Ryan and her colleagues spend much of the year fund-raising from private sources and public bodies such as the *Irish World* newspaper, the Bank of Ireland, Camden Council and London Arts. As

A leaflet for the Bobby Casey Memorial Concert at the 'Return to Camden Town' festival at the London Irish Centre.

Jerry Kivlehan says, "The Festival has also reflected the change that that has taken place in traditional Irish music. At one time it was a voluntary endeavour, with musicians coming together for sessions, but now there is a very big pool of professional Irish musicians who do nothing else but travel from festival to festival, across Europe and America, and make recordings."[36]

A final festival

One festival that has survived for twenty-four years, and is thought to have been the longest-running festival in England, was the London Irish Festival in Roundwood Park organised by the Council of Irish County Associations. Throughout that period there were only two days of rain, but more importantly it had raised over £1.25 million for charitable purposes, of which at least half has been donated to the London Irish Centre. The balance went to the CICA Welfare Fund, which in turn helped to pay towards a variety of causes from St Joseph's Hospice to the Crumlin Hospital for Children in Dublin. It also bought a minibus for use by the Camden Elderly Irish Network, Aisling and other groups.

The last festival was held on 1 June 2001. It finally closed, according to Bill Aulsberry of the Waterford Association, *"Because we could no longer afford to put it on. It required over £50,000 up front, and the committee did not want to take the risk."*[37] Apart from ordinary Irish people and their families who enjoyed the festivities, the performers over the years included major figures from Irish showbusiness. Daniel O'Connell, the Indians, Dana, Big Tom, Larry Cunningham and Joe Dolan were some of those who made their way to Willesden. Up to 90,000 attended each event, and it is said that Joe Dolan attracted his own fans from among the travelling community.

The Centre had always interested visitors, particularly from Irish politics and from the world of entertainment. It even attracted some from across the Atlantic, such as Bing Crosby who came in 1968 to discuss an Albert Hall performance with Paddy Hackett.

The final London Irish Festival at Roundwood Park. (Joanne O'Brien)

Another Presidential visit

President Mary Robinson had been welcomed during Denis Cormican's period as director. A visitor to the centre in 1999 was the new President of Ireland.

President Mary McAleese was invited by the director and trustees in December to reopen those areas of the building which had been refurbished, and to view the range of work now carried out. From Belfast, she had been elected two years beforehand as the eighth President of Ireland.

With a background in the law and in the media she gave, as Jerry Kivlehan said, *"A wonderful speech"*. She described how the Centre, with its eighteen different yet complementary services, had become synonymous with the experience of the Irish in the capital. *"It is an invaluable space for the local Irish community"*, she said, *"a place of belonging, of recognition, where you can find a friend or get a helping hand, celebrate or get some advice ... it is a credit to its founders and to the generations who have sustained and developed it."*

The president also met many people who have, in one way or another, contributed to the longevity of the Centre and to the well-being of Irish emigrants in London. She also took this opportunity to present an award to Brian Duggan, former councillor, Centre committee member and mainstay of the Missing Persons' Bureau. He had already been recognised with an *Irish Post* Award in April 1995.

President McAleese concluded that the strength of the Centre was its diversity and the philosophy of *"N neart go cur le chéile"* – our strength is in working together. Like Ireland herself, the Centre has undergone a great deal of renovation and regeneration, and she hoped that it would enjoy the mood of hope-filled renewal currently being enjoyed by Ireland's improved economy, cultural

President Mary McAleese presents Brian Duggan with an award during her visit, 1999.

strengths and political developments."[38]

The better Irish economy is one reason for the reduced number of Irish emigrant organisations. Across London and the country, large and small Irish centres which had once provided a home from home for Irish emigrants have quietly closed. One which closed less quietly was the Irish Club in Eaton Square, a forerunner of the London Irish Centre itself and an institution which shared members and members of committees with the Centre, including some fine chairmen in Dominic Donnelly and Charlie Gallagher. There is, however, talk that it might reopen.

In London a number of more local Irish or Catholic social clubs and advice centres have closed, for various reasons. Rising land values, lack of grants, loss of interest and political vindictiveness are some. Aware of the sometimes perilous history of his own Centre, Jerry Kivlehan has reminded us that *"The people that built these buildings never dreamt that the people who had ownership of these Clubs would sell them on, putting the pennies of the poor into the hands of the rich."*

The future for the Centre

The future of the London Irish Centre itself has at times been uncertain. Over its fifty years its purpose has changed. Originally conceived to save the Catholic souls of those who had travelled to Britain, a land of temptation and worse, it quickly adapted to provide practical help through hostels and advice. It expanded at huge cost, almost destroying itself in the process, but has since recovered. In so doing it has learned to be flexible in its use of space and in the service it delivers.

Over the future of its chaplains or directors, at first recruited from the Westminster Diocese and since 1967 provided by the Oblates of Mary Immaculate, there hangs another question mark. Jerry Kivlehan, who has served the Centre since 1994, is the last priest to be in charge as director. He retired in August 2004, after an unusually long assignment as director, and will be followed by a chief executive.

At the Retreat of the Oblate Order in Inchicore, Dublin, many of its members are elderly. They are not necessarily serving in active ministry, in fact the likelihood is that the majority are retired. They will be the first to agree that fewer are now following them through the seminaries. Attendances in churches, and at the seminaries that feed them, have been rapidly falling. There are various reasons for this. Some suggest that allowing priests to marry, or even allowing women into the clergy, may be an answer, but this may not reverse the decline. It seems that even priest-ridden Ireland is becoming a more secular society.

Much has changed since the days when a priest in the family was an achievement and conferred some status. For some sons it was a relatively comfortable alternative. But for a variety of reasons, including the drastic effect on its self-esteem as a result of the cases of abuse which have come to light, the priesthood is no longer seen as a comforting career.

At one time the London Irish Centre had room for a chaplain or a director who was a priest, sometimes with two assistant chaplains and during the summer often a student priest. Denis Cormican and Jerry Kivlehan have managed on their own.

Although there is now a separate catering function under the capable control of Terry McEneaney and an efficient advice and welfare team lead by John Twomey, Jerry Kivlehan has said *"The number of clergy involved in welfare and community services has diminished. There are not enough doing this work, just the few like me. We need to make sure that there is no more downsizing because this affects the outreach work that we do in the community."*[39] He believes that the Catholic Church is a positive influence in Britain, particularly in the areas of education and community care. Its history has been on the side of the poor and marginalised, yet he is convinced that if priests had stronger systems of support, personal, spiritual and communal, some of the problems of the past may not have occurred.

The Centre now has a skilful Board of Trustees consisting of Mary Allen, John Higgins, Jim Quinn, Paul Byrne and Philip Fitzpatrick, with an effective Management Committee chaired by Tom McCasey. There is also now a highly motivated staff.

It remains to be seen how a Chief Executive will now take forward the tradition of the London Irish Centre into a very different and challenging world.

1   Interview Jim Myers, May 2004.
2   Interview Fr Jerry Kivlehan, June 2004.
3   Interview Fr Paul Byrne, January 2004
4   Interview Fr Jerry Kivlehan, June 2004.
5   *Ibid.*
6   *Ibid.*
7   *Irish World*, 15 December 1995.
8   *Camden New Journal*, 30 November 1995.
9   Interview Maeve Heath, January 2004.
10 *Camden New Journal*, 30 November 1995.
11 Interview Fr Jerry Kivlehan, June 2004.
12 Interview Fr Jerry Kivlehan June 2004.
13 'A Review of the London Irish Centre' by Annabel Beerel, April 1996.
14 Interview Fr Jerry Kivlehan, June 2004.
15 Interview Mo Mowlam, MP, 1996.
16 *Irish Post*, 30 September 1995.
17 *Ibid.*
18 *Irish Post*, 12 July 1997.
19 Interview Fr Jerry Kivlehan, June 2004.
20 *Irish World*, December 1996.
21 Interview Fr Jerry Kivlehan, June 2004.
22 *Irish World*, 8 December 1995.
23 Caravan Sites Act, 1968.
24 Interview Maeve Heath, May 2004.
25 Interview Peggy Campbell and Jeanette Whelan, March 2004.
26 Interview Fr Jerry Kivlehan, July 2004.
27 Interview Fr Jerry Kivlehan, July 2004.
28 Correspondence with Kate Foley, June 2004.
29 Interview Fr Jerry Kivlehan, July 2004.
30 Roisin McAliskey is the daughter of Bernadette Devlin McAliskey, the former MP for Mid-Ulster, who had been arrested and detained but never charged, following a mortar attack on a British Army barracks in Germany in 1996. In Holloway she gave birth to an under-weight baby but was released after 16 months.
32 *Proved Innocent* by Gerry Conlon, published by Hamish Hamilton, 1990.
32 *Irish World*, 30 August 2002.
33 Interview Fr Jerry Kivlehan, July 2004.
34 Interview Fr Jerry Kivlehan, July 2004.
35 *Irish Post*, 9 March 1996.
36 Interview Fr Jerry Kivlehan, June 2004.
37 Interview Bill Aulsberry, June 2004.
38 *Irish World*, 10 December 1999.
39 *Irish World*, 9 August 2002.

CHAPTER THIRTEEN

The Irish will be back

In the 1950s, on the Sunday nearest to St Patrick's Day, in affirmation of their identity as much as their faith, Irishmen and women walked slowly from Horse Guards Parade to Westminster Cathedral to celebrate Mass. In due course they organised themselves into individual county associations and they then formed the Council of Irish County Associations.

Nearly fifty years later, in 2000, the first Mayor of London arranged the first St Patrick's Day parade to Trafalgar Square. This had been an election manifesto pledge, but once elected Mayor Ken Livingstone approached the Council of Irish County Associations and transformed their quiet ceremony. Once a small unreported group it is now a public event involving tens of

The St Patrick's Day Parade, central London, 2000.

thousands, Irish and otherwise, celebrating Irishness in a display of extravagance and fun which is lapped up by the media.

Over those fifty years there have been periods of Irish pride and Irish scorn. There were times when Irishmen and women were not welcome and when some were afraid to admit their nationality. Ireland has slowly escaped from a grey country dominated by one political party and the church, lurching from crisis to crisis, towards a proud nation content with a largely secular democracy and an economy that has been buoyant for longer than anyone dared to imagine. Irish success in the arts, in sport and in commerce has brought the country out of its own dark ages.

An undated report from the London Irish Centre of the mid-1970s supplied a London perspective: *"Irish priests who had worked for years in London parishes, served ghettoes and areas with a high concentration of Irish people became acutely aware of the hardships and exploitations to which naïve labourers were exposed by landlords in squalid, over-crowded lodging houses. Lonely for the wide open spaces and the cool, clean air of home, for the easy pace of life, there was little available to the them at the end of a toilsome, dust-ridden day of construction, demolition and maintenance but the companionship and seanchai of their own kith and kin in the pub. Driven there through sheer loneliness, drink became a temporary palliative for their gaucheness and sense of inferiority and, for many, heavy drinking became a way of life, devouring their hard-earned money and destroying their family life. Girls who emigrated became resident domestics in hotels, hospitals and bars or worked in factories. Being young, lonely and vulnerable some were unwittingly initiated into the undesirable and sordid aspects of night life. Those with drive and ambition, shrewd and intelligent, if uneducated, became self-made men and women needing no supportive props to keep them in social and occupational circulation. It was the plight of the former group of immigrants, projecting the image of an ignorant, inarticulate race with a propensity for booze, belligerence and crime, especially in areas like Kilburn and Camden Town that evoked sympathy and concern and gave impetus to a small group of people, clerical and lay, to improve the lot of the Irish working man."* The language is colourful, and could well have been part of a speech by Fr Bill Cagney, but it described well the problems and solutions of that time.

On a local scale, the identifiable Irish presence in London has all but disappeared. A mini-scattering or diaspora has taken place. The Irish neighbourhoods of Camden have become diluted by the arrival of other ethnic minorities in some parts and by gentrification in others. Centres like Camden Town are now tourist attractions.

Government support

The years of lobbying by priests including Eamonn Casey, from his earliest days at Slough, to Paul Byrne of the Oblates and Bobby Gilmore of the Irish Chaplaincy to try and persuade the Irish government to put its hands in its pockets for the emigrants in Britain and elsewhere may finally have achieved major success through the Dion Committee, which in July 2004 disbursed £3.3 million to sixty-five different organisations. The London Irish Centre will receive, directly, £105,370. Intense lobbying by the Irish community in Britain followed the example of these priests, in a sometimes frustrating attempt to convince the Irish government to do more for those who were its exiles. For apart from anything else, those who emigrated enabled unemployment figures in Ireland to be lower than they might otherwise have been. The disappearance of the workless to Britain and elsewhere meant that there was less of a drain on the public exchequer, but in the weekly dispatch of a few pounds or shillings to the family back home, it can be said that it was emigrants who laid the foundations of the more prosperous Ireland that we know today. As Jerry Cowley, TD, said *"The generation of emigrants who left Ireland in the 1950s gave us far more than the EU ever gave us. These people gave up the chance of pension plans, comfortable homes and any future for themselves, to send home a pound, a fiver, a tenner sustaining the Irish economy when we didn't have one."*[1] There were also those, it is said, who took the boat before their case was due to be heard in court, or who were discharged from institutions with a suitcase and quiet advice to find their way to England. The Irish government did not then have to accommodate them, in prison or elsewhere. *"I think it is fair to say that no Irish government has ever done enough to deal with the problem of emigration"*, Foreign Minister Brian Cowen has said, almost as a response.

The Task Force
A Task Force report, published in September 2002 and described as "wildly innovative", proposed the establishment of a body called the Agency for the Irish Abroad. This would encourage and co-ordinate services for emigrant communities. It would have a substantially increased budget that would be devolved to the voluntary organisations that serve Irish communities abroad. This new body had the backing of the Irish Episcopal Commission for Emigrants. Its director at the time, Paul Byrne, who is a trustee of the London Irish Centre, said:*"We are absolutely delighted. We have been looking for this for long enough. We have battled for this for years."* He continued, *"A key thread running through this report has been a conviction that the Irish abroad are an integral part of the Irish nation and must be recognised and treated as such. As the Constitution recognises, nationality is essentially about identity, not territory."* Article 2 of the Irish Constitution states: *"It is the entitlement and birthright of every person born in the island of Ireland, which includes its islands and seas, to be part of the Irish nation. That is also the entitlement of all persons otherwise qualified in accordance with the law to be citizens of Ireland. Furthermore, the Irish nation cherishes its special affinity with people of Irish ancestry living abroad who share its cultural identity and heritage."* This last sentence is critical.

In terms of emigration, the Task Force has called for travel rights that were enjoyed by Irish pensioners to be extended to elderly emigrants visiting Ireland on holiday. This issue has been the subject of a long campaign, most recently led by the London Irish Elders Forum. As well as at emigrants returning home, Task Force also looked at those who might be considering leaving the country. It argues that much more information and advice should be made available to prospective emigrants, something that John Dore and Eamonn Casey tried to pioneer in the 1960s. The Marian Employment Agency was one expression of this. This information need not be seen as encouraging emigration, in fact it might deter many.

After considering the evidence, and in spite of the cautions that have followed from them, the report also offers a more cheerful analysis of some other emigrants. *"There is an emerging Irish business and professional class who are fully integrated into British life while retaining their Irish identity."* It continues: *"There is a growing confidence among the Irish in Britain in expressing that identity, as evidenced by the unprecedented numbers who took part in the St Patrick's Day parades in London, Birmingham and other cities in March 2002."*

The need remains

This is of course true, but the experience of the London Irish Centre in recent years has been that there has been no reduction in the numbers of Irish people using its culturally sensitive and supportive facilities. The welfare department still provides a valuable service, but the nature of the enquiries has changed, and the client base has shifted slightly towards other ethnic minority groups. However, once there was a chapel and three Masses on a Sunday, only one Mass is now said occasionally, in the drop-in Centre. The Centre still has its bars, but instead of the four or five in its heyday there are now only two. The Council of Irish County Associations still has its annual dinners and dances, but instead of a possible thirty-two tables there are far fewer.

There are all sorts of reasons for this. The Ryanair generation has replaced the *Irish Mail* from Dun Laoghaire to Holyhead and onwards to Euston. Emigrants now arrive at airports. And in recent years there has been net immigration to Ireland, with people who wish to take advantage of the vibrant economy of the country, or the 'Celtic Tiger' as it has been oddly called. But perhaps the most obvious reason is that prosperity has reached much of the Irish community, which has spread out from Islington, Camden and Brent and the other boroughs with a significant Irish population towards the leafier suburbs of Wembley or Harrow or the newer towns outside London such as Harlow and Luton.

The Centre is adapting to this. The stringent measures adopted by Jerry Kivlehan and others to give it stability have meant that it is almost unrecognisable from just ten years before. With the arrival of a chief executive there are a number of projects now based in the Centre which it is hoped will continue to flourish.

Three Projects

One is the Aisling 'Return to Ireland' Project. Aisling is the Irish word for vision or dream, and this is a joint initiative between the Centre and Arlington House. The intention is to bring back some of the most vulnerable of the emigrant community to Ireland for a rehabilitative break. Its first venture in 1994 brought thirty men and women to Ballybunion in Co. Kerry for a week.

For the next year, 1995, the destination was Bundoran in Co. Donegal. Many of the holidaymakers are over 60 years of age and for some this will be the first glimpse of their homeland for 25 years. One woman who had not been home for many years was about to board the bus in Murray Street. *"She was about to get on the coach"*, it is reported, *"but she could not make that initial step, because the memories were just too much for her. Even though she had not been home for 45 years, she still could not make it. Her childhood memories were just too powerful to make that return journey."*[2]

The Aisling Project is going from strength to strength, taking groups to different parts of Ireland, from Mayo to Wexford, and throughout its life has been superbly aided by Ardal O'Hanlon, the stand-up comedian and actor who plays Fr Dougal McGuire in *Father Ted*, as its patron. Its co-ordinator is Alex McDonnell.

Another project which has worked closely with the Irish Centre is ICAP, Immigrant Counselling and Psychotherapy, a pioneer in the provision of culturally sensitive psychotherapy to people of Irish origin. Today ICAP is a national service, with its head office in north London, an office in the Camden Irish Centre and a regional office in Birmingham, with plans to extend to five other regions with a high Irish population. When Teresa Gallagher established ICAP in 1996, she was met with resistance from some Church sectors who felt it should be under the auspices of the Irish Chaplaincy. Teresa Gallagher was very definite that this would not be the case and that the very nature of the project meant it had to be independent and non-sectarian. Jerry Kivlehan saw the wisdom and the need for the service and came on board as one of the Trustees.

Funding was also a problem. *"During this period counselling was not considered a priority by the funding bodies either in Ireland or England"*, Teresa Gallagher adds. *"It was an uphill battle all the way."* Counselling was among the list of exclusions for Dion grants. She lobbied the Irish government to support counselling and psychotherapy, and it was taken off their exclusion list. Today, ICAP relies on Dion for some of its funding.

Research shows that the mental health needs of the Irish are the highest of all the minority groups in the UK. ICAP now can contact 200 highly qualified psychotherapists throughout the UK. And this number continues to grow. ICAP is currently negotiating for new premises in north London, and the struggle to acquire the necessary funds is on-going.

Meanwhile, the Irish have indicated by their use of the service that they are willing to engage with professional psychological help when required. The professionalism and confidentiality enables people to use ICAP rather than not knowing where to turn.

When speaking of the role of Jerry Kivlehan in the work with the Irish, Teresa Gallagher says *"The fact that ICAP has been such a success is in no small way due to his guiding wisdom."*

Downstairs from ICAP is LISOS, or London Irish Survivors' Outreach Service. On 11 May 1999, the Taoiseach, Bertie Ahern, set up a Commission to Inquire into Childhood Abuse in Industrial Schools and other children's institutions in the Republic of Ireland. This followed the breaking waves of scandal that shook the Irish community here and in other communities abroad. He had noted the "collective failure" of Irish society to hear their cry or respond to their plight.

The office based at the Centre welcomes clients who wish to discuss their histories. One arrived, not sure why he was there, but saying he had been in an institution. It was emotionally difficult for this man to expose his memories after so many years. He had made his way from the institution in Ireland and travelled to England. He could not read or write, had no self-confidence, was emotionally disturbed, but the fact that he had escaped from the abuse was a comfort. Unfortunately, the horrific incidents of his childhood led him to depression and this caused marital problems. His partner finally left him, and he found his way to LISOS.

In 2002 the Irish government passed the Redress Act. This enables survivors to seek fair and reasonable awards for sexual, physical or emotional abuse or serious neglect. LISOS was the first outreach service in Britain, and one of its aims is to inform all survivors of such abuse of the Redress Board. It also encourages hits clients, the victims, to come to terms with the tragedy through free legal representation, counselling and psychotherapy.

The wider service
These three services are in addtion to the ongoing range which the Centre provides, such as the Befriending Service, the Outreach work with elders in Camden Town and Kilburn, the youth resettlement work, the High and Dry Club for rehabilitating alcoholics, the Irish Healthy Living Centre, the Day Centre, the Missing Persons work, and the frontline advice

A notice board in the Community Services Department of the London Irish Centre.

for those who arrive at the door.

It is through projects such as these that the London Irish Centre will itself survive under its chief executive. The constitution, which Denis Cormican and Jerry Kivlehan have introduced with patience, courage and a vision, should not affect its future management.

A different Camden Town

However, in the fifty years of its life the landscape of Camden Town, and the people who once populated it, have certainly changed. The London Irish Centre survives, but the founding Fathers would not recognise its hinterland. An example of this is the transformation that over the years took place with the venue that was once so familiar as the Buffalo. Earlier this has been described as a venue where Irish men and women, once part of "the scattering", used to enjoy themselves on Sunday afternoons or in the evenings after the

pubs had closed.

Fifty years later, it is still there, with its entrance, once in Kentish Town Road, now in Camden High Street. However, few Irishmen and women would recognise it as a place for them. It now welcomes a totally different clientele, under a new name, the Electric Ballroom. Surprisingly, its management remains the same. In 1978, the founder, Bill Fuller, got together with Frank Murray, a former tour manager of the Irish band Thin Lizzy, and realised that his majestic old ballroom, with two-levels, three bars, an upstairs restaurant and viewing areas, would make a great rock venue. With this in mind, the Buffalo turned from the Carousel into the Electric Ballroom and reopened on July 28, 1978.

However, it was forced to close nine months later, after objections to noise levels from local residents. It was given new sound-proofing and reopened once again

241

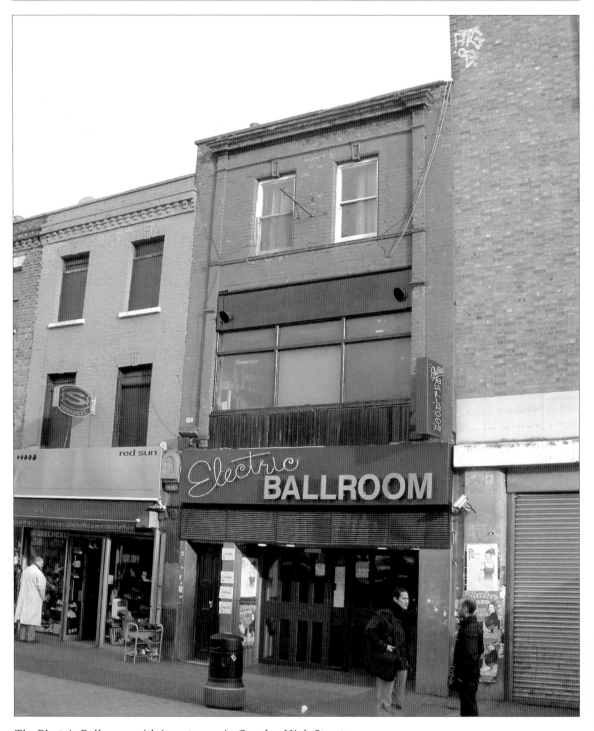

The Electric Ballroom, with its entrance in Camden High Street.

in July 1979, under another manager, Terry O'Neill, who had previously run McGonagles, one of Bill Fuller's clubs in Dublin. In 1980, Brian Wheeler became the new manager and has run it ever since.*"This place was an eye-opener because it was always jam-packed and seemed like a complete madhouse to me,"* says Wheeler. *"Most concerts that I'd been involved with were fairly well organised but, in this particular venue, it was always total mayhem and that was part of its appeal. It was laidback and seemed fairly indestructible so people could do what they wanted, within reason."*[3]

At one time, hundreds of Irish men and women on a weekend evening were navigating their way past the bouncers on the doors of the Buffalo, hiring ties to wear if necessary, to enjoy each other's company, make contact with home and perhaps fall in love to the music of Irish bands. Now, the customers of the Electric Ballroom arrive at all hours. There are still bouncers, more threatening in appearance and equipped with walkie-talkies rather than fast thinking and the gift of Irish wit, but the intentions remain the same. The music has changed. Tattoos, piercing and jeans have replaced the shiny clean faces, the white shirts, flared trousers and taffeta skirts.

The centre of Camden Town is considered ripe for redevelopment. The key is the reconstruction of the decrepit Camden Town Underground Station. This can only be financed by property development above ground, which has been costed at £130 million, for a major retail and office expansion in the surrounding block. Within and beneath this block is the Electric Ballroom.

The irony is that whatever sort of redevelopment does take place here, the Irish will be back. Not as customers of the Electric Ballroom this time, but once again they will be in the seats of the bulldozers and cranes of demolition, construction and reconstruction. It is also likely that there will be a few shovels to hand.

And at the end of a day's work the local pubs may notice an infusion of Irish accents once again.

[1]   *Irish World*, 6 September 2002.
[2]   *Donegal Democrat*, 31 August 1995.
[3]   From *The Rock'n' Roll Guide to Camden* by Ann Scanlon, published by Tristia. Reproduced by 'Keep it Camden' with the kind permission of Ann Scanlon and Tristia.

Index

An asterisk denotes an illustration or caption.